ELECTRIC LANGUAGE

ELECTRIC LANGUAGE:

A PHILOSOPHICAL STUDY OF WORD PROCESSING

MICHAEL HEIM

Second Edition, with a Foreword by David Gelernter

Yale University Press: New Haven & London

Designed by Sally Harris and set in Melior Roman.
Printed in the United States.

Library of Congress Cataloging-in-Publication Data

Heim, Michael, 1944–
    Electric language : a philosophical study of word processing / Michael
  Heim ; with a foreword by David Gelernter. — 2nd ed.
        p. cm.
    Includes bibliographical refernces and index.
    ISBN 0–300–07746–7 (alk. paper)

    1. Word processing—Philosophy. 2. Language and languages—
  Philosophy. I. Title.
  Z52.4.H44 1999
  652.5'01—dc21   98–7716

A catalogue record for this book is available from the British Library.

The paper in this book meets the guidelines for permanence and durability of
the Committee on Production Guidelines for Book Longevity of the Council on
Library Resources.

10   9   8   7   6   5   4   3   2   1

For Joanna

The relation of the new to the old, before
the assimilation is performed, is wonder.

—William James

Contents

Foreword to the Second Edition

The written word used to exist in two basic states: in the mind or on paper. Words traveled from the author's mind onto the page, from the page into the reader's mind. Nowadays there are three basic word-states: mental, written, or suspended like tomatoes in aspic in the electronic cybergel that surrounds us. But not *exactly* like tomatoes in aspic. Electronic words have strange properties that make them seem halfway between physical and mental. They can be revised and rearranged easily and endlessly; they never wear out. They can be reduced to paper at any time but don't need to be, ever. They can be shipped near-instantaneously around the world, and copied exactly as often as you choose.

Writing is civilization's most important technology. Does it matter if the logistics of writing change dramatically? How could it not matter? But exactly *how* it matters is not clear.

For example, is the coming of electronic language good or bad news for prose? Will people write better or worse? You could argue either way.

Electronic language could be the best thing that ever happened to prose for several reasons. Word processors make revising simpler and less time-consuming than ever before. Electronic publishing has made it cheaper and easier to deliver printed words to the public. Websites and network bulletin boards offer new ways to publish. Email and fax machines restore the place of the written word in everyday communication, which was almost lost entirely during the 1970s and early 1980s. As late as the early 1960s, Americans communicated mainly by writing letters, when they weren't chatting with local friends on the phone. Many towns had two regular mail deliveries a day, plus "special deliveries" on demand. Some large cities moved intraurban traffic pneumatically; E. B. White comments on New York in 1948: "When a young man in Manhattan writes a letter to his girl in Brooklyn, the love message gets blown to her through a pneumatic tube—*pfft*— just like that." But in time nearly everyone got a phone, and long distance calls became (relatively) cheap, and the mails lapsed into seediness. The personal letter seemed on the verge of disappearing. Today, writing is back in a big way; once again you can send a love message to your girl in Brooklyn—*pfft*— just like that—over the Internet. Surely the Golden Age of Prose is at hand.

Then again, maybe not. Electronic words seem more casual and transient than written words, and we're tempted to take less time arranging them. When I write email, ease-of-revision turns me into a compulsive reviser, and my email is more polished than my occasional handwritten letters. I'm a writer by profession (a computer scientist on the side); I know other writers who revise as much as I do. But for some people, email is so easy to generate and so evanescent that it isn't worth bothering about. The Web turns everyone into an editor and publisher. Editing in general is a dying art; electronic language isn't the only culprit (TV, not computers, ushered in the postliterate age), but it is certainly a co-conspirator. The decline of editing is a catastrophe for prose.

How does it all add up? I don't know, but I do know that such questions are important. I've approached them here in a rough-and-ready way; I'm no philosopher. Michael Heim is, and he gives such issues the serious attention they deserve. I don't buy all his conclusions, but it's impossible to read his book and not learn something and be moved to think. The discussion ranges from Plato's definition of *psyche* through the technology of computer encryption, with lots of interesting, concrete information about software thrown in along the way.

One thing is certain: the right time for this book is now. As Heim points out, electronic writing is ubiquitous, but most of us still remember when it wasn't. Before we who remember typewriters and linotype machines get old, lose our memories, and die, we ought to take stock of the big changes we have lived through and helped along. Hence this book, which is a fascinating step in the right direction.

DAVID GELERNTER

Electric Language was the first book to track the shift from print to digital text. It was written during the years 1983–86 when the computer was becoming a personal writing tool for me and many others who were using computers for the first time. The 1987 introduction to *Electric Language* suggests that the impact of word processing might appear more clearly after some historical distance comes between us and the first word processors. In the 1980s, computer hardware and software systems were changing rapidly, and back then it seemed that ten years would show a clearer picture of how digital text affects culture. Today, ten years later, we can indeed see a few things more clearly, but the horizon still hides many surprises as we see systems changing unabated. Still, so much has become manifest that we are encouraged to pay close attention and sift through what has already shown itself.

What stands out today with great clarity is the "linkage" inherent in digital text. *Electric Language* analyzed three intrinsic features of digital text: linkage, automated manipulation, and information-based formulation. Linkage has emerged in the 1990s in ways that were implicit but still obscure in the 1980s.

The full meaning of linkage had to await an increase in personal computing power. The hardware of the early 1980s showed little sign of how far the microchip could extend writing. After all, the laptop on which I wrote the first chapters of *Electric Language* limped along with eight kilobytes of active memory, and a later 32K upgrade allowed half a chapter to reside in the computer while I uploaded portions to and from storage on audiocassettes. (I shiver to recall the screeching tone of the tape recorders that preserved—not very reliably— the data.) My workhorse Radio Shack Model 100 now occupies a place of honor on the dusty garage shelves, and the Tandy Model 1000, with its 360K floppy disk drives, only vaguely resembles today's Pentium workstation or Apple PowerPC. Back then, I could not have imagined writing on a multitasking machine with two gigabytes of storage, a one-megabyte removable disk drive, and Internet connectivity.

The hardware limitations of the 1980s could not support the full linkage of electronic text. Advances in storage capability, transmission, and computing power have now made linkage manifest. What was there in principle now exists in fact and with cultural repercussions. The intrinsic linkage of digital text has become embodied in the operating systems that undergird the personal computer. My current Windows NT workstation, for example, functions not merely as a stand-alone personal computer but also as a networked computer. The operating system mirrors the client server technology that makes the Internet possible. The Internet in turn increasingly alters the way personal computers are used. People now routinely communicate on nationwide and worldwide networks. The Internet's World Wide Web highlights what *Electric Language* calls "linkage in the psychic framework of word processing." Every hot spot on a Web page reveals linkage to be an intrinsic element of digital text. The Hypertext Transfer Protocol (http) is included with the operating system of the most widely used computers today.

Growth in hardware power and sophisticated operating systems leads to practical implications for reading and writing. It means that my desktop interface is no longer an isolated desk in the metaphor taken from physical furniture. My workstation hosts seminars that I conduct completely online, as well as book chapters that connect to other books on the Internet. (Chapter 5 of *Electric Language* exists digitally on the

World Wide Web, with the blessings of its author and publisher.) Electronic text has everywhere become a hypertext with reference links in all directions.

The linkage made possible by current hardware and software precipitates a cultural transformation, what many critics since 1987 have called a digital revolution. A third of American homes now have computers, and 80 percent of written English passes through bits and bytes. The widespread use of electronic mail was barely noticed in the 1980s, but today's businesses could not function without email. Over 12 million people have access to the World Wide Web, and the website address is ubiquitous in commercial culture. Some fifteen-year-olds now spend more time in front of computers than television sets.

The cultural transformation marks a change in attitude toward the computer. In the 1980s, the microcomputer was not widely perceived as a personal tool. People still thought of computers as massive electrical brains that threaten to overtake the human mind through artificial intelligence. Computers still shared the mystique of the famous ENIAC machine that occupied an entire room. Philosophers debated hotly whether the mainframe machines could think, whether they could compete with the human mind. Today, we work with machines far more powerful than ENIAC, and we daily incorporate the computer as an information aid to our memories and to our communication activities.

The same linkage that extends digital text spatially like a web across culture also brings a new emphasis on interaction. The temporal aspect of linkage is interactivity. Every link is a point of personal decision and action. What this means for literacy is a greater sense of nonlinear temporal jumps and leaps into multiple sensory media. What *Electric Language* saw as the contemplative character of traditional reading is mutating into an active sampling of multiple media. The multimedia reader chooses a hyperlink to follow, clicks on video animation, a graphics file, or an audio clip, and then clicks again to find more text. The interactive text can flash messages or brief narratives or it can become a gateway to photo images; it can attach narrative passages to audio or video. Interactive linkage means that file folders contain pieces of graphic art, photo illustrations, and videos clipped from online conferences. Articles now incorporate chunks of audio, voice, and email communication. Animation files support written words. Processes can be explained by movies and the structures of text highlighted by colorful icons. The multi-media reader discusses ideas or stories via newsgroups or mail servers. Participation beckons at every corner.

Once accustomed to the mode of interactive reading, people begin looking again at the quiet pleasure of the alphabet printed on paper. While hypertext sometimes pulls people from book culture, a second look at linear text seems a welcome vacation from hectic hypertext. A month in hyper-space can scatter the brain. Traditional books offer readers respite from hyperactivity. The book's definitive, closed, linear argument lets mind and sensibility enjoy moments of inner harmony. Linear text offers the kind of contemplative thinking that goes beneath the surface. Plain-text argument fosters a nonsensory, conceptual focus, and the book reader can bring a thought to a fulfilling conclusion. Both hypertext and traditional modes of reading each have their strengths and areas of application. Reading skills are expanding today to include these different and often opposite modes. We need to use these various modes in ways that are complementary and not one-sided.

If full linkage has become clarified by the reader's browsing through hypermedia on the Web, then the writer's side of the equation has yet to be clarified. We are still exploring what it means to write hypertext, to build hypermedia and virtual worlds. It is one thing to scan print texts into the computer, and it is another thing altogether to create texts that fit appropriately into online interactive media.

One area we are about to see emerge, I think, is the expanded visual responsibilities of writers. The software mentioned in the original acknowledgments of *Electric Language* cannot hold a candle to present-day software like Microsoft Word. Earlier word-processing software could be easily distinguished from layout software or desktop publishing. Today, the distinction no longer holds. You used to write in one program, an editor, then do layout, or print preview, in another. Today's software offers nearly perfect what-you-see-is-what-you-get. Word processors allow sophisticated display and layout options. Top designers might still prefer the two-dimensional graphic layout programs like Quark XPress or Adobe Pagemaker, but you can achieve nearly all the same effects with a standard word processor like Word. If, as *Electric Language* argues, the line between composing and editing has become blurred, so now has the line between editing and layout. Writing and text design skills are gradually merging. The word processor is as much about linking images and visually structuring text as it is about words. The division between the word artist and the graphic artist may weaken as has the division between the business executive with laptop computer and the amanuensis who formerly was "the typist."

The contemporary word processor brings new responsibilities. Because the look of the page, the fonts, and the graphic design now belong to software, the writer more easily controls the elements that formerly stood outside text creation. The work of layout artists, typographers, and even graphic designers now falls under the control of anyone using a standard word processor. While the trained eye may abhor the crude results often produced by desktop publishing, the evolution of culture would seem to merge or at least cross-fertilize text and design elements.

We may see such skills increase throughout the population.

Writing will no longer be understood as producing text. Even electronic mail now comes with many of the formatting options of the contemporary word processor. The definition of writing is about to widen. Where in the past it was the exceptional William Blake who illustrated his writings, in the future we may see an enormous creativity blossom. The word will consort again with the image. Writers and readers will learn to control fonts, frames, and graphics on screen, and this educational process will evolve over time as what was once the exclusive and arcane province of the typographer and printer becomes available to everyone. We will have to develop the taste and the ability as well as the visual literacy to make distinctions that we have not made before. Our visualizing capacity will rise with our text competence. Widespread development of visual design skills may take decades, just as the earlier literacy took generations to assimilate. And the sophistication works both ways, for the readers as well as the writers of text.

For readers, visual literacy no longer falls under the passive spell of television, video, and movies. What has powered the Internet's World Wide Web was the introduction in 1993 of the graphical browser. The Mosaic browser, developed at the Center for Supercomputing at the University of Illinois, spread the Internet's appeal by juxtaposing text with graphics so the total "page" could become a mosaic. The resulting multimedia is a rich brew made from ingredients of various information types. Strands of video, images, and audio return text to its original sensory meaning of "texture" or woven cloth. Simple text may never look the same. Computer graphics enhance text with hyperlinks graced by interactive illustrations. Digital text has liquid properties that invite movement and animation. Photos and videos can illuminate the written word in new ways. We see this innovative influence already in the type used on film and television screens. The dynamic mosaic extends the reach of electronic text. Reading—as most people read today—falls under active browsing rather than under the traditional reading that follows an extended linear sequence of text. While the Web's underlying HTML (HyperText Markup Language) still slants toward linear concatenation, the hypertext interface breaks with the austerity of pure alphanumeric text.

The graphic power of present-day software eliminates one of the concerns voiced in Chapter 8 of *Electric Language*. Chapter 8 revolves around the fact that word-processing software constrains writing in ways that paper and pencil never did. Text on screen tends to limit us to the monitor and keyboard. Chapter 8 describes my need to work on oversize sheets of paper to map ideas while writing *Electric Language*. The word processor could not at the time allow the writer to visually sketch ideas. The computer would not allow me to pencil in links between distant sections of an outline; computer document margins would not let me fill them with notes and diagrams. So Chapter 8 suggested that the writer use paper alongside the computer to complement the text with clustering techniques that concentrate the scattered, dissipating process of digital composition. Today's software, however, answers that earlier complaint. Graphic user interface (GUI) software now takes charge of the computer screen, and the paper clustering I recommended works better on screen now with programs like Inspiration or Visio than it does on paper. We need no longer turn to paper because the digital element simulates paper and often surpasses it with sophisticated image manipulation. The computer desktop resembles more and more the graphic textual mosaic that defines the World Wide Web.

The World Wide Web has become the major venue for digital text. A small portion of Web text appeared previously on paper, but most of it has been designed for the electronic screen. With the Web comes a basic challenge. The great energy of Web words, their interactive dynamics, contrasts sharply with words published in other media. Even though the underlying values remain tied to the same alphabet of sequential phonetics, Web text communicates in other ways as well. It uses active hypertext references; it scrambles meaning in a hyperspace where an extra dimension is added to sequential phonetic space by interactive reader choices. Much as chess played in 3-D becomes hyperchess, so too text in the interactive element becomes hypertext. The transition from traditional to hypermedia shifts reading into another dimension. The transition to hypertext feels less abrupt as the older media in turn make references to the new media and acclimatize the population. Print media, like newspapers, often appear in online versions. Today, you can see invitations to visit websites in daily newspapers, on television, and even in books.

The challenge of Web text lies not only in its novel integration of text with dynamic screens of graphics. The challenge also arises from the promise of three-dimensional environments that will soon house and display text. Here we come indeed to the edge of the horizon. There is little clarity here, but in my opinion the future belongs to three-dimensional worlds of visual and auditory immersion. While the Internet still represents the low end of immersion, the Web is rapidly developing miniature versions of virtual reality in the browsing software shaped by VRML (Virtual Reality Modeling Language). This three-dimensional interactive graphic environment becomes a powerful navigational tool for online information and it may one day replace the prevalent HTML.

Yet we do not know at this time how information, especially in its symbolic textual form, fits into the three-dimensional world of cyberspace. For centuries, the human race experimented with ways of locating text within the three-dimensional world of primary reality: inscriptions, signs, books, paper, paint on asphalt roadways ("STOP HERE"). Some text formats have proven immensely valuable throughout history.

How will two-dimensional text best fit into three-dimensional interactive environments? How will text in three-dimensional space meet the needs of users?

The answer—even the propriety of the question—is over the horizon. Experiments at the Massachusetts Institute of Technology by David Small and Muriel Cooper's students only scratch the surface by pouring older texts, like the Bible or Shakespeare's works, into a three-dimensional environment. The larger problems of how to merge readable text with 3-D remain unresolved, especially issues of how to convey a sense of location in a textual fly-through. What we can see is that all the human senses will become more fully engaged in electronic environments, including the kinesthetic sense of orientation and spatial location. Here reading will achieve levels of sensory intensity untapped by books on paper.

These are some of the areas where we have gained greater clarity and some of the areas where light only glimmers on the horizon. In 1999, the last line of *Electric Language,* about the iterative nature of text on the computer, must be read again.

Acknowledgments

"The Impact of Word Processing on the Human Thought Process: A Philosophical Investigation" was originally a paper I presented as part of the regular program of the American Philosophical Association in New York City in December 1984. I delivered an expanded version of the paper, written in German as "Die Auswirkungen der Computer-Textverarbeitung auf den Denkprozess," at the invitation of Professor Ernesto Grassi and Dr. Viktor Langen as part of the Zurich Discourses held in Switzerland in 1984. The material was then further developed for a paper given in Oakland, California, in 1985 at the Ninth Western Educational Computing Conference organized by the California Educational Computing Consortium. Discussions at these meetings provided stimulating occasions for reflection.

Walter Ong gave his time in personal conversation and on the telephone to clarify points in his work. Early on I had informative and scholarly exchanges with many philosophical individuals, including the following: John M. Anderson, Michael Scriven, Jim Karpen, Ernesto Grassi, Hugo Schmale, Jeanne Ferris, Boyd Ready, Edward Giese (Acroatix Software), John Seely-Brown (Xerox Palo Alto Research Laboratory), Gary Cole (Summa Technologies), Mike Pincus (Clarity Software), Reiner Schürmann, Ryogi Okochi, Shizuteru Ueda, Bin Kimura, Mark Rectanus, and Eugen Baer. Jim Mehl shared a lively interest in Johannes Trithemius; Sally Radmacher offered helpful suggestions concerning the social psychology of stress; and Gary Shapiro joined me in studying the tombstones in the Roman museum in Cologne. Librarians Susan Bushhammer, Lynne Kupchinski, and Jonathan Birnbaum provided frequent assistance in gathering otherwise inaccessible reference materials. My thanks to all.

I wrote this book on two microcomputers, the notebook portable Tandy 100 and a desktop IBM-compatible, the Tandy 1000. The main desktop software used for the first half of the book was a combination of *Framework* and *WordPerfect 4.1*; for the second half, I used *XyWrite III* in conjunction with Borland's *Lightning*. On the Model 100, the *Ultimate ROM II* ran along with Larry Groebe's *THINK*. I also wish to acknowledge the following companies, which provided software and sometimes hardware useful for assessing the current state of computerized writing: Ashton-Tate for *Framework I* and *II*; Borland International for *Turbo Lightning* and *Superkey*; XyQuest for *XyWrite III*; Acroatix Incorporated for *TMPC*; Satellite Software International for *WordPerfect*; Dragonfly Software for *Nota Bene*; Micropro for the *WordStar Professional Plus*; Pro Tem Software for *Notebook II*; Ideaware for the *Idea Processor*; Leading Edge for the *Leading Edge Word Processor*; SoftWorks Development for *PC-Outline*; Newstar Software for *Newword*; PowerSoft Products for *Super Utility*; Hayes Microcomputer for a 1200 baud modem; O'Neill Software for *Elektra-Find*; Living Videotext for the *Ready!* outliner; Knowledge Engineering for *Zen Word*; Productivity Software International for *PRD+*; Central Point Software for *PC Tools*; Clarity Software for *Logic-Line 1*; Channelmark Corporation for *One-Key DOS*; United Software Industries for *Einstein Writer*; SDA Associates for *FilePath*; North American Business Systems for *Memory Shift*; Emerging Technology for *The Professional Writer's Package*; College Software for the *Edward Editor*; Writing Consultants for *Word Finder*; Select Information Systems for *Freestyle*; Portable Computer Support Group for *Super Rom* and *Write Rom* for the Model 100; Bellsoft for *Pop-Up DeskSet*; Polytron for *PolyWindows*; Traveling Software for *Ultimate Rom II* and *Idea!* outliner; Lifetree Software for *Volkswriter Deluxe*; Oasis Systems for *The Word Plus* and *Punctuation and Style*; Decisionware for *Rightwriter*; Airus for *AI-Typist*; Sigea Systems for *Telecommuter Plus*;

Awesome Technology for *Multiple Choice;* Symantec Corporation for *Q&A;* and Peter Norton for the *Norton Utilities* and *Commander.*

The litany of commercial firms and institutions should not cover the fact that my deepest acknowledgments remain personal, as is indicated by the dedication to this book.

Introduction

The word-processor is erasing literature.
—Gore Vidal

With a book tucked in one hand, and a computer shoved under my
elbow, I will march, not sidle, shudder or quake, into the twenty-first
century.
—Ray Bradbury, as cited in *Digital Deli*

What impact will computerized word processing have on the
process of human thought? People who write letters, memos, or
books quickly become converts to word-processing technology.
Even those who use dictation in the composition process can
experience the greater flexibility and rapidity that digital writing
gives to the written word. Whereas formerly the digital aspect of
writing (*type*writing) was relegated to the clerical procedures of
the professional typist, the new computer technology has put
keyboards into the hands of professionals of all kinds. The text
processor is transforming the way philosophy, poetry, literature,
social science, history, and the classics are done as much as
computerized calculation has transformed the physical sciences
based on mathematics. The word processor is the calculator of the
humanist. Wherever knowledge must be accessed, selected, stored,
and modified, the practice of writing on a computer is becoming the
standard operation for information workers; word processing is no
longer restricted to the narrow domain of office automation. It
would seem that not only the speed of intellectual work is being
affected, but the quality of the work itself.

A feverish enthusiasm usually descends upon the person first
learning the convenience and power of computer-enhanced writing. Language can be edited, stored, manipulated, and rearranged in

1

ways that make typewriters obsolete. Extensive sources of knowledge can be accessed electronically and incorporated into the planning and drafting of ideas. This new text management system amplifies the craft of writing in novel ways. But could Bradbury's language of marching into the twenty-first century, besides conveying a confident bravado, imply mindless regimentation? Does the conversion of twentieth-century culture to a new writing technology portend anything like the revolutionary changes brought about by the invention of the printing press and the widespread development of literacy? If so, what are we to make of the changes?

Voices can be heard affirming a revolution in the way we communicate and store thoughts. Among the affirmative voices are those of rhapsodic futurists whose prognostications are propelled by the hope of all revolutionaries. For them, the technology brings us closer to the perfectibility of the human species. Jonathan Kamin, for instance, writes, "Children who grow up using *Think-Tank*, or a program like it, may develop the capacity to handle large amounts of information, and to structure it at an early age. Thus, they may be able to solve problems more effectively than their elders."[1] To someone beginning to use the powerful word-processing programs, or "idea processors," as they are called, this sort of statement does not seem to be the raving of crystal ball gazers. Even someone using text processing through the mediation of clerical help senses that something is happening to us, something more than a mere increase in the ability to edit writing conveniently and efficiently. But does this warrant optimistic projections for future problem solving? For perfecting the human mind?

There are less extravagant affirmations by those involved in composing texts and in teaching composition and English language. "Neither writing nor literacy is threatened by the computer.... The clear prospect is that word processing will enhance the craft of writing," says Andrew Fluegelman.[2] The Modern Language Association and other teaching organizations have embraced computerization without any apparent reservations. Educators seem to accept implicitly the epistemological evolution proposed by the developers of word processing: The "augmentation of the human mind" begins with thinking as an ability to deal with patterns of thought-percepts, then the symbolization of writing exteriorizes thought, first through manual, external manipulation of phonetic symbols (writing), then through mechanical symbol manipulation (printing and typewriting), and finally through a superior kind of automated manipulation on computers. Each step, presumably, makes writing easier and therefore better because more control can be exercised over the manipulation of thought as it becomes externalized, especially as it becomes available in the electronic element.[3]

But other voices are filled with anxiety about a supposed threat to the skills developed by the earlier literacy and by mastery of the printed, predigital word. With the advent of digital writing and digital text reproduction, will literature—and the culture based on respectful care for the word—be eroded? Or if the print culture is preserved will printed books possess the same exotic value that poetry recitals and fifty-foot scrolls in museums have today? The anxiety is heard in the words of Gore Vidal, the American novelist:

> As human society abandoned the oral tradition for the written text, the written culture is giving way to an audio-visual one. This is a radical change, to say the least; and none of us knows quite how to respond. Obviously the change cannot be all bad. On the other hand, what is to become of that written language which was for two millennia wisdom's only mold? What is to become of the priests of literature, as their temples are abandoned?[4]

The sense of historical drift, from oral to literate to telecommunications culture, has become a familiar topic among our writers. A complex philosophical-historical thesis about the connection between expression and the development of writing technology has become a commonplace explanation of our sense of drift. The explanatory power of the thesis vaguely covers but does not yet disclose extensive transformations in our pedagogy, epistemology, and theology.

Another anxious voice is that of an editor at a university press who sent me the following clipping from the New York Times News Service containing a journalist's opinion:

> There is no denying that even a limited word-processing program makes writing easier than a typewriter ever did. The almost instantaneous acceptance of the technology by forward-looking writers soon established it as a standard occupational tool. Then a curious thing began to happen. Much of what was being written became unintelligible. The neatly printed words could well, in McLuhan fashion, become the message. I wouldn't say word processing has no saving graces. For some people, it's an aid to leaping over writing blocks—for most, a reasonably painless way to handle revisions. Still, I think we may be heading toward a future in which word processing cranks out fast-food prose, generating millions of copies of contentless words assembled for appearance's sake.[5]

But such anecdotes and bons mots from either side do not help us grasp the full scope of the issue. If one wishes to further evaluate both affirmative and cautionary voices, one must find the central source from which both emanate. To focus on it clearly, that source must be perceived in its philosophical principles and not merely as possible ways of looking at technological change. The philosophical principles behind the sense of transformation itself must be laid bare and evaluated. Only then can we achieve a critical evaluation of word-processing technology.

The central source from which both sides of the issue emanate is the phenomenon itself, namely, word processing, also known as text processing. What could be easier than spotting this phenomenon? Word processing is computer-assisted document preparation, which includes writing, editing, storing, proofing, printing, and electronically transmitting documents written in one of the natural languages. But is it, in fact, so simple a matter to *grasp* a phenomenon of our time *in its essential nature*, with all its far-reaching force? When we speak of word processing, we are speaking of a true phenomenon of our time, in the sense of something appearing with a certain historical uniqueness. But while such eventful things are phenomenal or striking in their appearance, the *essential nature* of such a phenomenon may not thrust itself upon us as easily as the recognition of it as an unprecedented appearance. If phenomena disclosed themselves immediately in their truth to those who experience them arising in history, then the source we are seeking would be conspicuously simple. We could sketch the historical phenomenon in terms like the following:

International Business Machines coined the term *word processing* in 1964 to describe a certain capability of a brand of typewriter. The IBM Selectric with word processing capability, then known as the MTST (Magnetic Tape "Selectric" Typewriter), used magnetic tapes to store pages of text. Electronic memory retrieval added to the procedures of mechanical text processing was a leap forward in writing technology. Another leap occurred when the electronic retrieval of text was implemented on the digital computer during the 1970s. Memory storage was enhanced by the ability to manipulate language electronically, controlling and editing the encoded language through direct interaction on a keyboard. As the microcomputer became cost-effective and as software programmers began to exploit the text transparency of the inexpensive video display CRT, the leap in writing technology became a quantum leap. The advantages of computerized digital writing over the earlier writing technologies became so compelling that late twentieth-century culture was destined to adopt it as surely as earlier it was compelled to embrace other forms of automation, such as that of transportation in the form of the automobile. Word processing is no longer a brand name but the name of a cultural phenomenon.[6]

While the above is indeed the story of word processing, such an account does not grasp the phenomenon in its essential nature, that is, it does not reflectively come to grips with the phenomenon in the process of experiencing historical change. In other words, our immersion in cultural phenomena makes us both part of as well as reflectively responsible for the phenomena. It would be easier to judge or evaluate the phenomenon of word processing after some historical distance from it has been established, once detached, historical accounts of the computer revolution became available. Even a five-year distance in time would afford a clearer picture of the computer hardware which is developing so rapidly now and which promises ever greater changes in the technology of written communication. To investigate the transformation of writing now might seem premature or hasty.

Yet it is precisely this point in time that causes us to become philosophical. For it is at the moment of such transitions that the past becomes clear as a past, as obsolescent, and the future becomes clear as a destiny, a challenge of the unknown. A philosophical study of digital writing made five or ten years from now would be better than one written now in the sense of being more comprehensive, more fully certain in its grasp of the new writing. At the same time, however, the felt contrast with the older writing technology would have become faded by the gradually increasing distance from typewritten and mechanical writing. Like our involvement with the automobile, that with processing texts will grow in transparency—until it becomes a condition of our daily life, taken for granted.

But what is granted to us in each epoch was at one time a beginning, a start, a change that was startling. Though the conditions of daily living do become transparent, they still draw upon our energies and upon the time of our lives; they soon become necessary conditions and come to structure our lives. It is incumbent on us then to grow philosophical while we can still be startled, for philosophy, if Aristotle can be trusted, begins in wonder, and, as Heraclitus suggests, "One should not act or speak as if asleep."

By itself, the wish to become philosophical does not guarantee we shall find ourselves philosophizing about word processing. There is a widespread tendency in academic philosophy to lose the cultural phenomena in one way or another. Sometimes the pursuit of rational discourse leads to elaborate analyses that have gone completely adrift from their moorings in everyday life. While adrift, discourse preens itself by defending a distance from popular culture. But, in achieving ever-greater distance, philosophy loses its power of illumination and becomes verbal mathematics or an elegant system of thought without connecting roots in human concerns. Such divine detachment is purchased at the price of human intelligibility; mere mortals can only stand back and admire the angelic intelligence of philosophers who speak transcendental tongues.

Against such rationalist-scholastic excesses arose the protest of Pragmatism, in the golden age of American philosophy. But while Pragmatism, in the works of James, Dewey, and Peirce, promulgated vigorous criticisms of a culturally isolated rationality, it concealed within itself an affinity for Positivism, for the conviction that how we think is, in the end, part of the continuum of scientific rationality. As a result, Pragmatism lost the cultural phenomena by siding with a particular—and eventually polarized—dimension of culture. Where once it was necessary to see the continuity of scientific thought with everyday needs and practices, today we are instead concerned with examining and evaluating the impact that scientific work has on practical life and on the surrounding environment. Nevertheless, the memory of Pragmatism and its diatribe against "the genteel tradition in philosophy" (Santayana) is a healthy antidote to the pseudo-Platonic tendency to identify reason with mathematical abstraction. It is easier to raise charges of "nihilism" and attack any detailed immersion in current experience as historicism than it is to articulate in all detail and accuracy what it is that intuition actually sees. Reason, even and especially when defeating nihilism verbally, is all too often reason bereft of concrete cultural phenomena, a naked reason without experiential content or what Ortega called "razón vital."

Too often the studies that find modern philosophy nihilistic do themselves no favor by remaining exclusively historical in content, confining themselves to previous reconstructions of phenomena. Where such studies proclaim a restoration of classical philosophy, they usually do so without a fresh elucidation of contemporary phenomena. As a result, they either leave the student of philosophy lost in the abstractions of an academic dialect or they drive the student away from reflecting on the continuity of classical thought and contemporary phenomena. Where such continuity is explored, there must be a more thorough investigation of experiential phenomena than the dry assertion of an unchanging human nature. Too often what is known as the linguistic approach to philosophical problems has meant trying to stand outside language to examine it rather than struggling within it to see what is happening to language as we write and speak; language philosophy that does not perceive the transformations happening in language has missed its phenomenon entirely. To *find* the phenomenon today means to find ourselves where we spend our lives, at the interface with the machine.

Sometimes too efforts to grasp cultural phenomena philosophically reach far beyond, or beneath, speculative reflection—as in the current attempts to cultivate an oxymoronic applied philosophy. By taking over pregiven problems, an illusion is created that cultural phenomena are understood philosophically, while in fact certain narrow conventional assumptions are made about what the problem is and what alternate solutions to it might be. Philosophy is then confused with policy, and the illumination of phenomena is exchanged for argumentation and debate. But both Pragmatism and the more recent applied philosophy reflect the need to reclaim cultural phenomena for philosophical reflection. Reclaiming the phenomena for philosophy today means not assuming that a phenomenon has been perceived philosophically unless it has first been transformed thoroughly by reflection; we cannot presume to perceive a phenomenon philosophically if it is merely taken up ready-made as the subject of public debate. We must first transform it thoroughly by a reflection that is remote from partisan political debate and from the controlled rhetoric of electronic media. Nor can we assume we have grasped a phenomenon by merely locating its relationship to our everyday scientific mastery of the world. The impact of cultural phenomena must be taken up and reshaped by speculative theory.

When turning to speculate on cultural phenomena, we may be faced with false choices in academic philosophy. There is pressure to choose further specialization. Does the question about word processing belong to the area of the philosophy of technology or to the philosophy of language or should it perhaps be relegated to empirical psychology? We are asked to pick a card so that we can observe some skillfully prepared routine, as though thinking in detail meant thinking through specialized techniques of analysis. To accept the label philosophy of word processing or even philosophy of technology is already to have confined reflection too narrowly. When philosophy is conceived of as belonging essentially to any particular area or topic, then it has shrunk beyond recognition, for philosophy is an open inquiry in which we can be touched by a sense of the wholeness of things. This is not to say that philosophy can ever grasp itself as a whole, as a systematic and all-inclusive endeavor. The living sense of wholeness that only philosophizing can convey is either an impulse or a by-product of thinking and never the explicit achievement of thinking by itself; where wholeness seems to grasp itself intellectually as a system, the living impulse of wholeness is already in danger of being relegated to the oblivion brought on by anxious closure. Helpful as techniques may be, we must forego such categories if we are to philosophize or even think directly about a completely new phenomenon. Appeals to any pregiven specialty are sure to sidetrack us from reflecting on our own experience of the phenomenon. The anxiety of losing a hold on professional integrity and sinking into popular culture must be restrained for the sake of thinking out a phenomenon we are now living through and in which we are participating. This is admittedly a risk, as thinking always is.

If there is to be any philosophical reflection in our culture, the present may be something of a privileged position from which to begin. The present moment is a felt transition. From the existential perspective of the future world meeting and clashing with the past, some critically important visions of the nature of thought and its connections with language and technology may emerge. We can, at least, begin to formulate the problem, explore interpretations, find explicit connections with the past of Western theoretical philosophy. The fragmentary or dynamic approach to thinking and writing fostered by word processing is now upon us, and its advent may make increasingly difficult the task of determining the connections that make for a continuous tradition. Transitions are privileged locations for philosophical reflection. By examining ourselves as we experience the computer revolution, we may be able to pass along to the inhabitants of the unknown future some fleeting glimpses into our common human destiny.

Certain assumptions must be made, though, about the future of computer technology if we are to engage in philosophical speculation. Two assumptions about the future are not at all extravagant but rather are already upon us: Writing will increasingly be freed from the constraints of paper-print technology; texts will be stored electronically, and vast amounts of information, including further texts, will be accessible immediately below the electronic surface of a piece of writing. The electronically expanding text will no longer be constrained by paper as the telephone and the microcomputer become more intimately conjoined and even begin to merge. The optical character reader will scan and digitize hard-copy printed texts; the entire tradition of books will be converted into information on disk files that can be accessed instantly by computers. By connecting a small computer to a phone, a professional will be able to read "books" whose footnotes can be expanded into further "books" which in turn open out onto a vast sea of data bases systemizing all of human cognition. The networking of written language will erode the line between private and public writings.

But the reach into the future should not cause us to lose the balance of reflection. Empedocles fell into the volcano and Marshall McLuhan fell into the random, fragmentary world he was describing. My study is not part of the genre of futurism, which celebrates with euphoria wondrous gadgets that may come to exist as technology develops. Nor does it examine philosophically the question of whether or not the computer can be said to think or, conversely, whether in fact human thought is based on sequences of formal operations, much like programmable algorithms. Nor is the inquiry into whether or not the human spirit is threatened by its interaction with artificial intelligence. All these views which postulate an exterior and reified intelligence, as well as the attempts to compare a pregiven human nature with its externally created facsimile, should not distract us from the phenomenon happening most intimately to ourselves.

Characteristically, Western thought attempts to understand thinking by externalizing the thought process and then looking distractedly at the externalized model for the mechanisms of thought. By contrast, ancient Chinese civilization failed to develop a technological system precisely because Taoist belief held that Ch'i, the essence of nature, was an all-encompassing, participatory occasion. Such an occasion, here and now, could not possibly be externalized in any serious way; any externalization could be but an absurd parody of the overpowering oneness that suffuses "the ten thousand things" of Taoist belief. A mechanical-technical device, to the ancient Chinese mind, represented a dead and grotesque effigy of actually living occasions. Western civilization has, so far, taken a divergent road. In the quest to exteriorize every process so it can be controlled and reproduced at will, we have come to assume, philosophically, that the best way to come to understand human thinking is by first seeing how and to what extent we can create an artificially intelligent device. This is the basis for the heat generated today in philosophical circles discussing so-called AI. The assumptions underlying the discussion of artificial intelligence seem to hold as beyond consideration the possibility that human thought, inasmuch as it is sustained by the inviolable life of the psyche, cannot be truly externalized. To enter into this argument properly is to enter into the long-standing philosophical—not merely cultural or economic—gap between East and West. The task and scope of this book permit a sole aspect of this debate to unfold, especially in later chapters. My principal effort here is to present, in Western terms, a positive philosophical delineation of that side of technology which belongs to the inviolable psyche.

We denizens of the late twentieth century are seldom aware of our being embedded in systematic mechanisms of survival. The instruments providing us with technological power seldom appear directly as we carry out the personal tasks of daily life. Quotidian survival brings us not so much to fear autonomous technological systems as to feel a need to acquire and use them. During most of our lives our tools are not problematic—save that we might at a particular point feel need for or lack of a particular technical solution to solve a specific human problem. Having become part of our daily needs, technological systems seem transparent, opening up a world where we can do more, see more, achieve more.

Yet on occasion we do transcend this immersion in the technical systems of daily life. When a technological system threatens our physical life or threatens the conditions of planetary life, we then turn to regard the potential agents of harm or hazard. We begin to sense that the mechanisms which previously provided, innocently as it were, the conditions of survival are in fact quasi-autonomous mechanisms possessing their own agency, an agency that can drift from its provenance in human meanings and intentions. Otherwise, for the most part, we do not positively and consciously celebrate the technology that is woven into our system of needs. We use it, learn to demand it, and distrust it only when it threatens to turn against the system of needs with which we ourselves have come to identify.

When we do rise above the movement of technical systems in which we are for the most part enmeshed, we do so with a feeling of ambivalence: We at once resent our dependency on the mere props for maintaining the conditions of life, and we simultaneously reawaken to the hardly imagined potential there is to invent and transform the world around us. In a position above the present, we glimpse hopefully into the future and glance longingly at the past. We see how the world has been transformed by our creative inventions, sensing—more suspecting than certain—that it is we who are changed by the things we make. The ambivalence is resolved when we revert to one or another of two simplistic attitudes: enthusiastic depiction of technological progress or wholesale distress about the effects of a mythical technology.

The computer has catapulted this generation out of the daily system of needs and into the free space of determining a new response to the conditions under which we live. This book is a part of that response, but it chooses to sidestep the reassurances of enterprising futurists as well as the easy global reaction of gloom. It is a philosophical book. There is irony in writing a book concerning the specific technology of word processing on a computer. For such a book is both written on a word processor and written about word processors. There is irony in reflecting on digital writing in a publishing medium that is still committed, though less so every day, to the preservation and maintenance of writing in printed books in a culture where books are still a major source for the exchange of information and ideas. But irony has never crushed philosophical investigation. In fact, if we are to believe Plato's portrayal of Socrates, irony should be the best invitation to the philosophizing spirit. Writing about writing is not unusual for an endeavor that began with the imperative of Delphic self-reflection: Know thyself. Strange command, this. Yet no merely formal repudiation of the philosophic search as chasing one's own tail can diminish the need humans have to perform this intellectual activity, which makes the human being stand out as peculiarly human.

Electric Language: A Philosophical Study of Word Processing is an introductory study of the philosophical significance of the phenomenon of word processing. My investigation, even in its conclusions, remains an introduction to word processing as a whole—not, of course, introductory in the same sense that the growing volume of instruction manuals, on-line tutorials, and handbooks are ancillary to the practical implementation of word-processing technology. This is a *philosophical* introduction to the phenomenon. As the impact of word processing becomes more evident in the next decades, the conclusions reached in this book will no doubt seem prefatory and provisional. We are all just being introduced to the phenomenon. At the same time, however, there is another meaning to *introduction*. Introductions have philosophical import insofar as they first bring us into an articulation of a phenomenon, offering some basic terms by which to understand it. Introductions, then, also originate the questions against which the phenomenon can appear more sharply, and what originates sets the terms for understanding the phenomenon. At the same time, this book is deliberately set in traditional terms because the author has been educated in the tradition of scholarship and learning based on the printed book, with the attitudes fostered by that tradition.

In order to establish a philosophical distance from which the phenomenon of word processing may be properly seen, several chapters are necessary to prepare the concepts and terms within which it can be articulated. Our relationship to technological innovations tends to be so close that we either identify totally with the new extensions of ourselves—and then remain without the concepts and terms for noticing what we risk in our adaptation to a technology—or we react so suspiciously toward the technology that we are later engulfed by the changes without having developed critical countermeasures by which to compensate for the subsequent losses in the life of the psyche. Part 1 consists of three chapters designed to gain some distance.

Chapter 1 recalls the traditional question about the connection between thought, language, and reality. It invokes, panoramically, the status of language as a transcendental or ontologically relevant dimension of human existence, a dimension of the whole world we inhabit. The treatment in the first chapter is historical but not doxographical. A commemorative survey of traditional views prepares us to see more clearly the significance of the phenomenon of word processing, though historical recollection cannot perform the critical evaluation for us. Such a treatment of historical tradition can only be synoptic, but there is need to establish a sense of the broad context in which the change in language technologies has significance.

The second chapter begins the explicit treatment of the theory that claims there is an intimate relationship between writing technologies and reality apprehensions, though that theory of transformation is couched in terms of social communication rather than in terms of ontological-psychic structures. Chapter 2 is an exposition of the outlines of a major and widely held theory of the thought-transforming powers of writing technology. It treats the epistemological and historical assumptions operative in the works of Walter Ong and Eric Havelock.

Chapter 3 is a critique of Ong's theory of transformative technology by way of explaining one twentieth-century philosophy of cultural finitude, a finitude emphasized in the existential analysis of Martin Heidegger. Through an exposition of Heidegger's theory of epochal transformation, and through a treatment of his critique of the suppression of finitude through technological thinking, chapter 3 develops the concepts of *historical drift* and of *cultural trade-offs,* or gains and losses in reality apprehension. Some keys to the phenomenon of word processing are found in Heidegger's analysis of temporality and in the primordial function of language as creative (metaphorical) speech.

The fourth chapter, which begins part 2, develops the first articulation of the phenomenon of word processing by finding the terms in which to address the phenomenon. The notion of different *symbolic elements* and of the *psychic frameworks* of symbolic elements is worked out by criticizing the terms of the transformation theory as they were found in the previous chapters. I also turn here to the Platonic notion of psychic motion as developed in the *Dialogues* and as carried out in the tradition of Platonic philosophy.

Chapter 5 describes the psychic framework of word processing. The three aspects of the psychic framework are described in turn: manipulation, formulation, and linkage. Software aids to writing, such as idea processors and outline generators, are described as metaphoric attempts to alter the thought process through a new symbolic element. The theoretical-practical origin of word processing is traced to research having the express purpose of furthering certain kinds of thought formulation. The chapter deals with the transformation of the text as a closed product or book into a vast open center for electronically accessible variations on a theme.

With description behind, part 3 begins with chapter 6, which prepares a contrast of the new digital writing with the classical model of psychic activity. Traditional writing skills and traditional books constitute a different symbolic element than the electronic. As a result, the traditional cultivation of reading and of the book fosters a different psychic framework. The psychic framework of the book was based on the mental vision of ideas, on a model of contemplative intelligence. The manipulation, formulation, and linkage of this ancient element offers, consequently, a contrast with word processing.

Chapter 7 sharpens the contrast by critically evaluating word processing from the standpoint of the psychic framework of the book. It summarizes the arguments that support a negative evaluation of the impact of word processing. These arguments are organized according to the three aspects of the psychic framework of word processing: manipulation as automation, formulation under stress, and linkage in the total text of human symbols.

The concluding chapter 8 absorbs some of the negative assessment of the impact of word processing by suggesting compensatory disciplines for countering the inevitable shifts in awareness brought about by the new technology. The trade-offs of finitude discussed in chapter 3 are now applied to the cultural changes brought about by word processing. The counterdisciplines are based on the automated practice of blockbusting, on manual clustering, and on the therapeutic practice of *releasing*, or the use of modified meditation.

Throughout the book, the emphasis on linear order and on the interdependence of terms, as well as the symmetrical structure of the chapters, is deliberate. The reasons for this will be obvious to the reader who understands the book.

PART ONE

APPROACHING THE PHENOMENON

Chapter One

Thought, Word, and Reality

Stone-cutters fighting time with marble, you foredefeated
Challengers of oblivion
Eat cynical earnings, knowing rock splits, records fall down,
The square-limbed Roman letters
Scale in the thaws, wear in the rain.
—Robinson Jeffers, "To the Stone-Cutters"

Athens, the Acropolis

On a sunny spring day, seated on the ancient stones of the Acropolis, I am putting these words into a portable notebook computer. The words question the meaning of place and the place of words in time.

The ancient Greeks were the first to teach a geometry and a mathematics and a philosophy designed to describe the features of every and all places. By describing space as such, quantity as such, reality as such, the human mind could strive for placelessness as well as timelessness—or at least the mind could model itself on a vision to which time and place are irrelevant. Ancient Greek philosophers attributed such a state of mind to the immortals, the divinities whose happiness was designated by the word *makarios*, meaning "blissfully carefree." The triangles and circles of Euclid, the numerical proportions of Pythagoras, and the essences of Plato were not immediately pertinent to any specific task or any given problematic situation. To know was to transcend the confines of particular places and to transcend the restrictions of particular times and peoples. To think was a "displacement" attained through the pursuit of pure theory.[1] Contemporary life, by applying a combination of logical theory with electronic engineering, has

21

made displacement a practical achievement. These words, even as visual symbols, are electrical impulses.

Human thought was once supported by books copied by hand. Learning proceeded primarily through memorization and through arguments based on fixed and socially stable topics, *topos* being Greek for "place." Destabilizing these fixed places for discourse, modern culture obviated the slow pace of memory-intensive learning by overcoming, through the printing press, the place-bound, restrictive nature of rare handwritten and hand-embellished texts. With another recent change, the sense of place is even further attenuated by the virtually instantaneous transmission and alteration of digital writing; words now enter into computers to become electronic data. Journalists tote four-pound plastic "word calculators" into phone booths in Athens and Beirut and in minutes transmit written materials to transatlantic destinations, conveying their copy without the problems caused by mail services or differences in time zones.

For electronic writing, place is even less relevant than for the printed book with its light and transportable materials. Even more than the book, digital writing offers written symbols a share in the "everywhere and nowhere" that has long been the prerogative of electronically accessible sounds and images. Yet it is the fixity and stability of the written symbol which is now destabilized and electrified. Even though the words I write, according to the distribution and economy of the print culture, are presently found printed in a book for the reader's convenience, the way in which these words are shaped is quite independent of the traditional book.

Written words, as symbols within a culture, exist under varying conditions and in different elements. Symbols carry meaning under concrete conditions. The significance of symbols, their meaning in diverse cultural contexts, is affected by the concrete conditions in which they appear. Yet *appear* puts it too mildly, for symbols have their actual existence in their appearing and being recognized by someone. And this means that concrete conditions are intrinsic to the appearance of verbal symbols. The meaning of symbols is affected by the horizon of significance in which they appear. This horizon, or set of conditions, constitutes what I will call the *element* of writing, which I will later distinguish from the *medium* of written symbols.

If it is true that old signs change, then they do so not merely in the absolute sense of the truism according to which everything changes in the passage of geological or astronomical time. Rather, under a different set of conditions, say, in the element of electronic codification, the significance of written words is affected. It is not that we pay more attention to the medium in which things are said. Instead, what is said comes to be said under different conditions, in a new element. The point is not that the medium is the message. It is that language can come to be taken for a set of messages. There are elemental conditions that situate cultural symbols.

Like an architectural beacon, the Parthenon symbolizes the Western world's orientation on a longing for placeless and timeless form. The exhilaration of the heights of the ancient fortress still speaks and constitutes a public language. The formal symmetry of the columns speaks of the millennial traditions of intellect and organization. Here is a symbol of the birth of Western planning, of intellectual organization, of what I will later call the *logos-tradition.*

Literacy has been long regarded as the stabilizing pillar of culture and of intelligence. Yet the stability of literacy is like the stability of the Parthenon: there has been not one but a plurality of meanings for *literacy.* As I shall explore in chapter 6, literacy serves not only as a functional skill or as a criterion for a certain stage of operational behavior; it is also a model for certain psychic attitudes, for certain dispositions of the mind. Because of its connection with mental skills, literacy, in the sense of alphabetic literacy, has meant the ability of the individual to rise above particular circumstances and enter a shared world of intelligibility. This shared world of intellect is believed to disclose a superior reality which encompasses and masters the commonsense and mostly inarticulate grasp we have on things we deal with intuitively. Literacy, the skills of reading and writing, have come to symbolize a higher understanding of reality.

A philosophy of word processing begins by noticing the connection we make between human skill with symbols and the reality we aspire to or admire. We attribute to the literate mind a higher ground, a more informed grasp of reality, a greater contact with the world at large. Literate understanding serves as a model for understanding in general, for getting a hold on reality as such. In other words, the skill of cultivating fixed symbolic forms traditionally guides our notion of intelligence. Though this general notion of literacy includes mathematical intelligence, especially the communication of mathematical ideas, a traditional bias holds that intelligence is best articulated in natural language rather than in the stipulated constructs of numerical symbols.

But are not all symbols arbitrary or stipulated? Or are symbols merely a part of the equipment of thought instead of belonging to the essence of thought? Is not natural language itself a tool of the mind instead of an essential component of thinking? How could word-processing technology affect thinking since word processing deals merely with the symbols of thought and not with the substance of thought itself? If language is no more than a condition of thought—maybe even a necessary condition—any tool we might use for the manipulation of symbols would seem to be far from affecting everything we think about. Does thought itself change if the mind works with symbols under different conditions, using different signs? And if old signs do change, does this have anything to do with the changes we make in our manipulation of the signs and in the skills we develop in manipulating the signs?

To begin answering some of these questions we must return to Greece. The return to Greek thinking is done not out of cultural piety for the historical origins of the philosophy of mind and of language—though, of course, our *alphabet* does echo the *alpha* and the *beta*, the first two letters of Greek phonetic symbols. We return to commemorate early Greek thought not merely out of historical piety or in search of genealogical reassurance. Philosophy begins with the Greeks because the effort to philosophize freshly about phenomena requires returning to a certain simplicity and intensity which can only be fostered by stripping away accretions of the nonessential. To gain a broad overview, we must first ascend to a narrower terrain where confusion is less and where complexity can unfold from a unified vantage point without distractions. To enable us to attain such a lookout, the Greeks are indispensable.

Another reason to commemorate ancient Greek thought is that it serves as antidote to the information technology in which our thinking increasingly transpires. As we shall see in chapter 7, one major criticism of word-processing technology is that, through the more and more effective standardization of the writing process, the etymological roots and the subtle network of historical echoes will fade even further from the living awareness of our language. Dead languages—or more properly, the languages no longer spoken—will cease to provide fertile root connectives that preserve, on the level of subconscious imagination, some of primeval human experience. By commemorating Greek thought, we can at least make explicit an effort to hear some of the complex linguistic cognates still active in English. We recall through such an exercise that words are not merely labels denoting something in propositional terms, that words do not simply point to things before us in an effort to describe their features. The word is also a cultural record, or more properly, the remainder of experiences undergone by a community of speakers who have encountered the thing named by the word and placed in the name their experiences of the thing. The experiences engraved in words run parallel, cross one another, bifurcate. Etymological resonance, as a recall of experience, articulates this development. Embedded in symbols is memory, however faded, and the memories contained in ancient languages are symbols standing like ancient ruins in a new element.

Through its efforts to rise above the conditions of particularity, ancient civilization paved the way for us to master the general conditions under which we live. In a sense, then, our historical heritage is itself a condition under which technological mastery continues. Yet, though Greek thought inaugurated the increasing placelessness of Western civilization, we can still experience localized symbols bound by their significant element to distances of place and time. The ancient origins themselves are not merely one condition among others, not just another condition over which we can gain further control and mastery. The ancient origins themselves we can never master. They are more like an inheritance upon which we draw. They still stand as ciphers, never fully transparent, but always providing the unseen "leading impulse"—a phrase which will serve to translate the Greek word *archē,* also rendered by "principle" or "origin" or "cause." Thinking about word processing, then, begins with a recollection akin to *archeology.* It may be the highest achievement of a civilization to recall what it could once afford to forget.

Cultural memory aids us in avoiding two misunderstandings about the philosophical question of word processing, both of which we must be on guard against early on. One of these rests on the assumption that it is essentially the computer we are talking about when we pose the question. The computer becomes central to philosophical inquiry as a form of artificial intelligence. Even when negative answers are given to the question "Can computers think?" there is still the assumption of a fundamental square-off between the computer and human intelligence—as if the latter were of itself something fixed, unquestionable, and given. The assumption creates a more specialized question and thereby leaves unquestioned the intimate connection between written word and human thought. When that connection is established, then the question about the computer becomes less of a special question about our relationship to something we have been able to produce; instead, the question becomes one about the changes occurring in ourselves.

A second possible misunderstanding is to try to comprehend the phenomenon of word processing by looking directly at the writing activity as it transpires in the individual mind. Here the mind empirically observes its own activity in writing on a computer and evaluates the phenomenon accordingly. The word processor appears to be a mere tool, something subordinate to human purposes; its effects must then be no more than necessary by-products insofar as the computer gets the job done and does so with less effort and greater control. We will try to prevent each misunderstanding in turn by recalling the philosophical impulses of two ancient Greek thinkers, Anaximander and Heraclitus, respectively.

The Transcendental Intimacy of Thought, Word, and Reality: Anaximander and Heraclitus

It is tempting to regard the question about the influence of word processing on our thinking as continuous with the question about the way the computer—understood vaguely as a general automated intelligence—affects human self-awareness. Such an approach examines the way humans come to perceive their own thought processes when exposed to continuous interaction with automated intelligence. After all, much of our thinking about internal matters we find generally obscure is aided by metaphors, pictures, and ideas drawn from our interaction with tools. We can think of the neurological system as a switchboard; we can imagine the internal workings of our body in terms of a complex set of hydraulic operations. The operations of the mind, or the mind's relation to the body, or the way the contents of the mind are stored in the brain—any of these might also be conceptualized by drawing upon operations with which we are already familiar because of our direct access to processes outside ourselves. Many of these operations are a result of our knowledge and skill in making things.

Yet such an approach would effectively bar us from disclosing an ontological relevance to the impact of writing technology. By *ontological relevance* I mean the mode in which realities come to be conceived as publicly identifiable and intelligible. In other words, such an approach to word processing could not suggest the ways in which word processing, because of its intimate connection with our language skills, might affect the way we think about anything and everything, including robotics and computer-assisted design. The question of ontological relevance is not the same as sociological or psychosocial or anthropological questions about the way a specific group of empirically given persons have come to experience themselves and have come to think about themselves as they become accustomed to using a middle-class, electrical appliance.[2] The philosophical question is instead the question about the way all contemporary contact with reality—including the *-ologies* of sociology, psychology, and anthropology—is affected by the new writing technology.

We reclaim for a philosophy of word processing the ontological dimension of writing technologies by recalling the *archē*, or first principle, of the philosophy of Anaximander, whom many regard as the first philosopher.[3] His conception of the foundation of reality helps us recall the intimacy of thought and word as well as the consequent import of language for the apprehension of reality.

Anaximander's discoveries, in all their simple profundity, are nearly beyond the ken of our mental sophistication. He was reported to have been the first to fashion a globe of the world from a sphere. In the fifth century B.C., Anaximander was the first to make maps of the known world as it was explored by Ionian sailors. He also invented a clock in the form of a sundial. He is said to have been the first to write philosophy in prose instead of in the traditional literary style of metrical verse. Considering the implications of cosmic symbols, such as the clock, the globe, and the map, we can only be astounded at the intense vision it took to discover these simple but sublime devices, all symbols based on the possibility of a proportionate reduction of the universe, a daring simplification of cosmic vastness.

But the basic principle of Anaximander's philosophy, his guiding genius, is far more startling than the incredible devices he put forth as emblems of his philosophy. His is a "start-ling" genius which has all the discomfort and astonishment of origins. Most Greek thinkers regarded Anaximander with a certain amount of horror, with the archaic horror of the infinite. The ancient Greeks had devised many images of their *horror infiniti*: Tantalus, Sisyphus, and Prometheus. All these suggest life as infinite, life without finality or purpose, life as repetition without novelty or redeeming insight. Tantalus is in agony as he bends to drink the waters of an ever-receding river or reaches to grasp the dangling fruit from a tree which springs up instantly to take them beyond his reach. Sisyphus too pushes toward an ever-frustrated accomplishment, toward goal-completion paradoxically never completed but each time begun again *ab initio*. The innards of the daring Prometheus are continually restored only to be gnawed away again by the Zeus-sent avenger, who punishes his proud and cunning search for human power and comfort—a never-ending task and a self-consuming agony.[4]

Even later, in the classical period, Greek philosophers retained a similar horror of the infinite by transferring the infinitude of Tantalus, Sisyphus, and Prometheus from the religious-poetic sphere to the realm of conceptual argument. Aristotle, not to mention Zeno of Elea, frequently offers indirect proofs for the absurdity of a rival theoretical account by showing that it implies an "infinite regress."[5] This horror of the infinite may well explain why Plato never mentions Anaximander; Aristotle mentions him only briefly and then with caution.[6] The reason for the general shunning of Anaximander may be the nature of his first principle: the basic principle of the philosophy of Anaximander is the infinite as origin of all stable identities.

The main fragment of Anaximander goes as follows: "The

originating source of things is infinity."[7] The "originating source," or *archē*, does not refer here to some remote abstraction or historically removed source, but rather to origin as *leading impulse*. The leading impulse from which things emerge is the boundless, the limitless open. Infinity is here positive nonclosure, an openness without territorial divisions or demarcations (the Latin: *in-fines*). Infinity first releases things so that they can become identified and then defined. Anaximander's first principle is the archaic realization of unboundedness.

For Anaximander, the world we think about is one which has been necessarily reduced to identities through the process of naming realities in language. The newborn infant, not possessing language, has no way of compacting or organizing the infinite number of details in what it sees and experiences. What it sees could only be an infinitely various, constantly shifting kaleidoscopic field. The baby has not yet separated itself from the world by naming and identifying things. The adult's cultivated understanding of things is based on the constant effort to define the boundaries of things through language. Language, then, does not describe a pregiven, fixed world. Language instead is a world, a limited order out of total chaos. The world is continually emergent in words; reality is the world we bespeak. We see the entities we can identify with words originating out of the confrontation with boundless experience. What enables humans to see definite realities at the same time holds infinity at bay. For Anaximander, language, or *logos*, is the emergence of identity out of the chaos of an infinite matrix of possibilities.

The first thing we recall, then, from early Greek philosophy is that there is an intimacy between words and thoughts by which a differentiated reality is identified. In later Latin philosophy, during the medieval period, language was said to have a transcendental character, by which it was meant that language cannot itself be regarded as something *within* reality or one reality among others; language is not merely one thing or human capacity among others.

Language transcends things and capacities by constituting the conditions under which things or capacities can be identified in the first place. A philosophy of word processing, then, encompasses more than the work habits we can identify and restrict to certain times, circumstances, and people. Language, as Anaximander's principle suggests, is fundamentally a response to the infinite and as such manifests the human encounter with the openness in which realities first obtain presence and identity.

The inquiry into word processing touches an ontological dimension, which is to say that the effects of word processing are not so much traceable to the computer as to the transcendental intimacy of language and reality. In this sense the question about word processing is more fundamental than the question of whether machines can think or whether circuits can be said to be intelligent. So too, this question is more basic than the question of whether we distort the human self by learning to apply to ourselves models taken from computerized inventions.

The second misunderstanding is to confuse the philosophical question about the phenomenon of word processing with the question about how we think here and now when we use word processors. In misunderstanding the question in this way, the phenomenon is approached empirically, with personal awareness serving as the final arbiter.

Empirically, and seen from the viewpoint of the individual I, we can observe and evaluate writing with a word processor directly and with no further ado. Writing this way is unequivocally far superior to writing with a typewriter or with pen and pencil. The reasons for this are obvious and manifold: as I write, text can be kept tentative and captured in a fluid state while the right word can be found and easily inserted later; I can edit and rewrite at the same time; the printed word no longer seems sacred or complete as soon as it is typed—improvements are always possible; I can write more, revise more easily and effectively, eliminate unnecessary words, sentences, paragraphs, perhaps save fragments which might be used later somewhere else, maybe even transmit manuscripts or letters over telephone lines to publishing houses or to other computers. To the individual self, word processing is little more than an increase in efficiency, hardly anything to which one ought to give much thought.

On the private level of personal experience, the impact of the word processor on the mind seems eminently positive because word processing facilitates the recording of thoughts on paper. The word processor is just another, more advanced tool. Like any tool, we can put it down when we are finished without having undergone any basic changes in the way we go on to experience the world. From this point of view, to ask whether our thought process is affected by word processing is like asking whether using lead pencils will make my letters heavy and morose or whether blue ink will make my thoughts blue. Just as *blue* can be used equivocally to stretch fallaciously over two distinct spheres of meaning, so would it be equally fallacious reasoning to expect anything so neutral as a tool to affect a wholly different domain such as the spirit or mind with its nonmaterial thoughts.

The first inclination is to apply to word-processing technology the same structure of analysis applicable to a tool. Tools fit nicely into the structure of means and ends set by the human will. Tool analysis permits a simple and direct approach to evaluating a phenomenon according to a utilitarian scale of personally felt satisfaction or socially evident efficiency. Evaluation based on individual observations is, to be sure, a commonsense criterion for evaluating technological devices in our day. We judge a tool by how well it gets the job done. It is we, the humans, who determine what constitutes the purposes or jobs that need to be done.

When we call something a tool, the assumption about it usually is that we can put it down or pick it up at will. The tool serves one dimension of ourselves, the dimension in which we alter the environment for our purposes. The tool serves an ulterior will; it achieves an effect in altering something in the world. Though the tool may alter the conditions under which we live, it does not itself become a condition under which we live, as does, for instance, the network of highways we traverse with automobiles. The highway system is more than a mere tool for transportation, or even a coordinated network of tools—especially when we include in the highway system the economic structure required to produce more automobiles to keep the system operative as a means of transportation. The highway system possesses a certain autonomy as a mode of transportation; we must comply with it as a system to move rapidly between destinations which are themselves in part defined by the highway system with its systematic necessities. The highway system has its own structure, and transportation from point A to point B becomes defined by the highway system; transportation makes certain demands on our will vis-à-vis the automobile. The automobile is not a simple implement of the human will, but it imposes various levels of necessity which create compliance with the transportation system. To define, in the contemporary United States, the automobile as a human tool may pass for a truth; it is, however, a gross understatement and fails to touch what is essential in the existing interface between human and machine.

Language too has a structure and a destiny independent of individual will and intention. We could try to apply to word-processing technology the analysis applicable to a set of means and ends. We could understand word-processing technology as a tool, or means for accomplishing the same end as several other means. Papyrus scrolls, chisels, the printing press, pencils, all can be regarded as nearly equivalent tools or as means conducive to one and the same end, namely, putting words down. It is true that, in their use, such tools can be experienced as extensions of ourselves in the sense that our force and our intentions can directly affect the environment with immediacy and without a feeling of sequential causation. The tool discloses a new set of possibilities in our will to create immediate effects on the environment, but those possibilities are in the service of conscious intentions. Tools, in the usual sense, can be put down or picked up at will.

Do we grasp the phenomenon securely on its own terms when we describe it by way of a tool analysis, when we describe it as a tool which is essentially applicable to human ends? Might not such an analysis lead us away from asking about what is happening with us and to us? As with the automobile, a mechanism can become culturally decisive, and no reassuring scheme of means and end, of subservient tools and conscious human goals will adequately explain it. If language is a system which we do not privately and individually create and manipulate for our own immediate ends, then might not the instruments by which thought is put into language, and is then composed, entered, stored, and exchanged, be in some sense essential to an understanding of ourselves?

To even begin to think about the phenomenon in any other terms, to find any other measures than those found in the self-determined ends of tool-using animals, we need to recall another impulse in archaic Greek philosophy. For the tool analysis has limitations, and, as we shall see in the following chapter, it may not be adequate for describing the transformations in cultural history brought about by what seem to be the merely useful and subservient tools of thought.

"It is necessary to go along with what is shared. Although the *logos* is shared, most men live as though their thinking were a private possession all their own," says Heraclitus.[8] The ancient aphorisms of Heraclitus center on the meaning of *logos*, the ancestor of our English word *logic* and of the suffix contained in the -*logy* compounds, from *aetiology* and *misology* to *sexology* and *zoology*. *Logos* is translatable by any or all of the following: language, word, speech, reason, intellect, explanation, proportion, necessary structure. It is not merely the archaic nature of the word that gives it such a wide range of meanings in Heraclitus. Heraclitus produced the first reflections on language, which are, strictly speaking, not so much reflections on language as aphorisms that play on and with language.[9] Heraclitus uses words, especially his central word, *logos*, in an explicitly ambiguous way. In other words, Heraclitus speaks of language by allowing the term *language* itself to remain inherently multidimensional, ambiguous, or "plurisignificant."[10]

But Heraclitus, being adequate to the demands of his own philosophy, does not so much reflect on the ambiguity of language as present ambiguous and highly fluid sayings. He thereby demonstrates his philosophy of language. By showing the ambiguities in language as he thinks in and through it, Heraclitus refrains from assuming a theoretical distance from language, for theorizing inevitably stipulates terms defined in a univocal way, as if to grasp privately and with finality whatever subject is under consideration. But what if the subject is language, and what if the theory sees the power of language primarily in the adaptability language has for diverse applications in ever-changing situations and for individually variant usages?

The use of symbols to intend a meaning is a procedure of definition and of the fixing of intention. Linguistic symbols are always found to have been already there with some definiteness, with some shared content. Yet, because each situation has in it something of the unique occasion, some pointing to the situation, something of deliberately creative intent, language must have in itself an essential indefiniteness. That is to say, language contains systematic ambiguity—not accidentally, but essentially. We use that inherent systematic ambiguity whenever we use a word so as to allow the context to determine what it is we mean—that is, whenever we are really saying something. The word *language* can mean, for instance, either spoken or written words, natural or artificial symbols, etc. When someone says "Watch your language" as in "Mind your tongue," the word *language* is given a definite meaning through a shared context inhabited by both the speaker and the one addressed.

Systematic ambiguity, sometimes called productive ambiguity, is different from the arbitrary ambiguity we find in the language of puns and in fallacious reasoning. Systematic ambiguity allows the same words to be used appropriately in new and different situations with creative consistency and fresh precision. Systematic ambiguity differs from arbitrary ambiguity in that the latter does not produce meaning in a given context but confuses or confounds the context, whether playfully, consciously, or sloppily. Heraclitus, whose sobriquet was the Obscure One, could not in his aphorisms produce a fixed and total philosophy of language. But, by presenting language in its systematic ambiguity, Heraclitus articulates a philosophy of language by circumventing a philosophy of language.

We usually expect a philosophy of something to be a fundamental explanation, in words, of whatever it is about. To philosophize about language would seem to require words about words. But thinking of words about words is an endeavor both tricky and notoriously suspect, for we can either seek to avoid contamination of the subject matter by creating a separate and distinct language beyond the language we are thinking about, or we can allow some transparency in our philosophizing by which our philosophy takes on the quality of a demonstration or instance of what it is talking about. In the latter approach, we cannot distinguish what is to be clarified, the explanandum, from the proof or argument. This would seem to be logically untenable—if we take the philosophy of language to be like every other normal enterprise which stands under the laws of logic, and also if by *logic* we mean something not intrinsically connected with the question of language. In the former approach, where a separate and distinct language is constructed, the intelligibility of natural language itself is threatened since we postulate ourselves as possessors of a clearer, more intelligible language of explanation—a language intended to explain what is not fully intelligible by and of itself, namely, the language we learn and speak naturally in everyday life. These two approaches constitute the fundamental dilemma of any philosophy of language.

Heraclitus circumvents the dilemma by not raising the possibility of a philosophy of language in the usual sense. Seen historically, of course, the dilemma has not yet been made explicit. But Heraclitus's philosophy is one which precludes the potential split between thought and language and does not take up the usual distance assumed to obtain between reflection and language. Instead, the thought-in-language of Heraclitus exhibits the way in which thinking moves from one thing to another while always preserving continuities through homonyms and polarities. Heraclitus bespeaks his philosophy of language, and, most appropriately, his language is ambiguous in systematic ways. More specifically, it is the systematic ambiguity inherent in thinking and speaking that characterizes Heraclitean *dicta*. He leads us toward a renewed sense of participation as we reflect on language. Contrary to the usual assumptions about thinking, Heraclitus suggests that language deepens thought in its operation; it does not remove the thinker from what is being said. Far from being a tool of thought, language, or logos, is the element of thought. Heraclitus insists: What we think about language is implicated in how we think in language; and, alternatively, the manner in which we think in and through language entails a certain stage or degree in our understanding of language.

The intimacy of thought and language is seen in the first philosophy of language articulated by Heraclitus, or, maybe we should say instead, the intimacy of thought and word are remarkably brought to word in the sayings of the Obscure One. His sayings suggest that any effort to remove thought from living, changing language into a realm apart is inimical to the nature of thought and language. The sayings point to the fluidity of logos; they insist simultaneously that the logos rules everything as universal law. The unity that persists does so essentially through strife and invariably through conflicts—including the degeneration of confusion. *Ambiguity* is itself ambiguous. There is an ambiguity indiscernible from ignorance and confusion as there is an ambiguity inextricable from truth. The identities that are wrung with great difficulty from chaos can persist in their vivacity and presence only as they remain fluid and ambiguous in the application of thought to diverse and shifting contexts.

Like flickering fire, language stays alive to shed the light of intelligibility on all our activities so long as it remains volatile and supple. Ambiguity is connected essentially with the vivacity of truth. When language is made rigid by being removed from contexts of address, then the mind loses contact with reality. But even the inevitable rigidity of language, which results from the all-too-human trivialization of the truth *about* language, is another instance of the truth of the fluctuation of mind, as Heraclitus suggests:

> Though the *logos* is always present, yet humans are never fully conscious of it—not only before hearing it, but even after they have heard it. For, though everything comes to pass according to this *logos*, humans are like people who have had no experience of it—at least if judged in the light of such words and deeds as I set forth here. When I distinguish the nature of each thing and articulate its characteristic behavior, the rest of mankind in its activity is unaware of what they are doing when awake, just as they forget what they did when they go to sleep.[11]

Far from being a tool for the expression of the individual mind, logos, as thought through and uttered by Heraclitus, is the articulated element of public existence we hold in common—that is, before public existence gets severed from private thought. The participatory conception of language peculiar to the genius of archaic Greek thought depends on the notion of a unity of the individual mind and the construction of the public world shaped by language. By recalling this conception, we can withhold a hasty, reflex judgment on word-processing technology in which the personal satisfaction of getting the job done supplants an awareness of what is happening to the language we hold in common and of which we are, in varying degrees, aware. We need to see that the personal experience of working on a word processor involves more than our own private mind with its empirical observations at one particular moment.

"By changing, it remains itself," says Heraclitus about the logos we share and in whose construction we participate; by paying attention to our private needs and by using the language for our own ends, we are often not ready for the "lightning that guides the world," the rapid shifts in language that become the "destiny of the psyche." "For the waking there is one world, and it is the shared world; but when they sleep, humans turn aside, each into a private world." But "even the sleepers are workers and collaborators in what goes on in the universe." Despite the elusiveness of what is dynamically shared in the unity of thought and language, we can make some efforts to reflect on it as the logos is immersed in the power of electronic technology. Though "Dogs bark at a person whom they do not know," we may instead be in the difficult position of having to say something about the lightning bolt that strikes us.[12]

By realizing the intimacy of thought and words, together with the independent power of language, we gain an important clue for our investigation and we avoid one possible misunderstanding of the phenomenon of word processing, but in no way do such hints à la Heraclitus encourage glibness about the phenomenon. We can only mention here most briefly some of the highlights of the actual historical reality of what can be called the logos tradition as it developed from ancient Greek thought, through the Latin Christian tradition, into modernity. To really study the logos tradition in all its complexity is to study the history of Western philosophy.

Logos still sounds in its variants in modern Greek. Not far from the Acropolis, kiosks display magazines about *hypologistē* and *mikrohypologistē*, or computers and microcomputers. The ancient symbols appear in new forms, nested among rows of photographic postcards of Mount Delphi. The historical stream connecting the logos of Heraclitus and logic systems in the circuitry of the computer is a long one. For a shorthand expression I use the term *logos tradition* to denote that stream of Western thought built upon "unifying articulation," yet another translation of *logos*.[13]

By contrast, Eastern philosophy is notable for its reliance on the unspeakable matrix, the *wu-ming*, or "nameless."[14] As the West has poured its energies into the articulation of the world, including the world of the spirit, the East has sought immersion in the silent origin from which proceeds anything defined in words. Silent, intuitive action demonstrates Eastern wisdom, while the wise men in the West, on the other hand, cultivate their sayings. The West is driven to articulate a whole into consistent parts possessing intelligible, predictable relationships. We rationalize not only natural physical and biological processes but also our religion, our sports, and now too leisure time management. Western thought needs typically to spell things out.

We can see this Western emphasis on logos in the history of Judaeo-Christian religion. It is at the word and call of the Hebrew God by which the dawn of illumination and then the whole world of living things comes into existence. In its earliest prophetic sense, the Hebrew word (*dabar* or *davar*) is the word of spoken utterance directly addressed to someone. But it was not long before an alphabetic basis was inserted under the word of Western religion. There was first the inscription of the Law and the reverence for the teachings passed along through writing.[15] By way of creative overlays from the Greek philosophical tradition, early Jewish doctrine learned to express itself in Greek terms, especially under the influence of thinkers of the Hellenistic period, such as Philo of Alexandria. Christianity also cultivated the Greek predilection for identifying reality with the logos: the highest revelation of divinity in the Christ or Messiah is designated the logos of God, that is, the underlying meaning of the world as it is articulated for human life.

So thoroughly does Western religion identify with the logos tradition of archaic Greek thought that it is difficult for us to perceive freshly the peculiar assumptions and implications of a religion based exclusively on the Word of God and on God as Word. Another way to notice this is to observe that Judaeo-Christian religion reveals a thoroughly biblical world, where *biblical* is taken in its strict etymological root from *biblia*, or "books": the world as book of God, that is, articulated by God and to be read as the articulation of God.

So too with Western science, logos is the underlying carrier of the scientific enterprise, though the nature of the scientific logos has been interpreted differently. According to one interpretation of science, logos exhibits the aspect of "logic," or methodology. Logos as logic dominates as the laying out or articulation of physical or social phenomena into what are consistent, deducible, orderly components and factors. This view stresses apodictic validation for the truth claims of scientific thinking. It ignores or plays down the historical background of scientific truth claims. This interpretation of the positive knowledge of science, so-called positivism, considers the distinctive object of science to be lawlike deductions about the empirical world perceptible by the senses. What counts as scientific is that which is deducible from the general theories framed in mathematical axioms and then instantiated in empirical experiments. The positivistic type of reflection on science no longer predominates over the historical consideration of how a given scientific truth gains credibility. Today, with the emphasis on how paradigms for inquiry develop in scientific communities, the nature of science is understood less emphatically as logic and increasingly as the logos of argument, persuasion, and communication. The logos of science is understood to reside as much in continuous discussions among scientists as it does in the logical schematics of "the" scientific method. The rigor of exclusive method is not emphasized as much as the collaborative discussion. Both reflections on science, however, are carried by the logos tradition as unifying articulation: one approach emphasizes the articulation, the other brings out the ongoing process of unification.

There is then a stream common to Western religion and science which has roots in the Greek logos tradition. And the logos tradition can be characterized as a development of the transcendental intimacy of thought, words, and reality. The term *transcendental* indicates the fundamental, all-pervasive nature of language in addressing the truth of things. It first arose in Latin translations of Greek philosophy and came to be used to describe the nature of God, the divine being who is the source of illumination; God, the Transcendent, sheds light on everything; the language of God's Word preserves the order of a common language. But the precise ways in which divine illumination is transmitted mark different interpretations of transcendence. The various interpretations of transcendence are different ways in which the illuminating word can be realized in symbolic form. The trade shield or emblematic logo of the venerable Oxford University Press is an open book on whose pages is stamped *Dominus Illuminatio Mea* ("The Lord is my Light" or "The Lord is my Illumination"). Concomitant with the entrance of the printing press into Western history, a new interpretation of the transcendence of the logos arose. Answers to the question of precisely how the Word becomes incarnate constitute the history of Western religion.

Language in the Electric Element:
The Faustian Illumination of Words

We saw at the beginning of this chapter how the significance of old signs shifts under the changing conditions of history. This horizon or background, which is not identical with the meaning of the symbols themselves, may be called the element in which symbols have their meaning. An element is not to be confused with a medium. Medium, or media, appears or exists as essentially transparent to something else, namely, to information. Transparency, at least, is the aim of the media. Media present themselves as means for the communication and exchange of ideas; media are either primarily audio or visual; some media bring communication through images and some through sound; media are based on communication, on the exchange between humans of some pre-given material.

Media are, however, only one level of the phenomenon of symbolization. There is also the element in which symbols survive or persist. The element in which the Parthenon persists does not directly pertain to the way the Parthenon communicates. It would be a superficial judgment on an artwork if it were considered solely for its message. Language too has a dimension not reducible to the process of communication. It continues to exist as written symbols in different elements: the scroll, the manuscript, the book, the computer. The element affects meaning by engaging one or another mode of the mind that interprets. In chapter 2 I examine one contemporary theory of how historical change in the technologies of media is accompanied by transformations in the human thought process. But, once I have shown the limits of the theory of media transformation, I shall of necessity return in later chapters to the element of language.

The element of language is the concretely historical way in which symbolized thought achieves placelessness, or, alternatively, in which thought achieves, through the transcendental nature of language, different modes of inhabiting place. The electronic element belongs distinctively to the twentieth century, but the emphasis put on dynamism and on the manipulable power wielded by the human will was anticipated by the modern poet Goethe. In his surpassingly strange *Faust* poem, Goethe dramatizes in a lyrical way a certain type of human being who prefigures the modern human will and its relationship to language. The anticipation of the electric element of language occurs in an early passage of part 1 of *Faust*. There, the legendary Dr. Faust, completely exasperated by the limitations of daily life, feverishly explores alchemical and magical means for going beyond the common world he disdains to accept. Faust begins his restless striving with the invocation of diverse symbols from esoteric lore. He uses symbols and incantations as therapeutic formulas to transform his psyche.

And then, as Faust reaches for the ancient biblical genesis of all things, come the famous lines:

> I've had my share of frustration.
> But this lack in me I can relieve:
> We can turn to the supernatural,
> We long for revelation,
> Which nowhere shines with nobler illumination
> Than here in the New Testament.
> I feel compelled to read the original text,
> To translate the sacred words
> Into my beloved German language.
>
> (Opening the volume, he begins.)
>
> It says: "In the beginning was the *Word*."
> Already I am stuck. I cannot go on.
> I really cannot rate the *Word* so terribly high.
> I have to translate it another way.
> It says, if I am rightly inspired: "In the beginning was *Meaning*."
> But consider that first line again;
> Watch out for the overhasty pen.
> Is it the *Intellect* that achieves and creates?
> What it should say is: "In the beginning was *Power*."
> Yet even as I write this down
> Something tells me that I cannot stick with it.
> Now the spirit helps. Suddenly I see the light:
> Assured I write: "In the beginning was *Activity*."[16]

Faust, as the modern man, turns for direction to invoke the word as part of the logos tradition. He must put that word, however, even its symbols, into his own terms, into the language and substance of dynamic action. The terms he chooses are the terms of dynamism that illuminates and of a restless power largely unknown to the ancient traditions. Only Prometheus, the Titan of archaic myth, is comparable to Faust; after all, Prometheus the Light-Bringer, besides learning to manage fire for the benefit of humankind, also invented writing.[17] With Faust, language is even more closely identified with active control, achievement, and power. The illuminating potency of the symbols becomes interpreted as an electrical, explosive energy. Meaning and symbol are united by the striving of the human will. In this poetic birth of modern humanity, we have a precursor of the glowing, electrified cursor of the word processor. The words on the computer screen are illuminated, charged phosphorescently, and glow from within. The word obtains a new kind of power in the electric element. The image of Faust shows the word transformed from the contemplative word to electrified deed.

We return then abruptly from timeless reflections on the old stones of the Acropolis to the blinking cursor of the computer screen. Here, on the steps of the great symbols of the logos tradition, are new letters: vivid, electrified symbols, connected in an electric element and invested with surprising powers. I have recalled the traditional philosophical connection between thought, words, and reality. Now, instead of reflecting on two distinct things already there before us in the world, that is, the human mind and the computer, we can begin to see in the phenomenon of word processing the operation of our own will as it extends the destiny of the logos tradition in the interface with computer technology. We are back in our current element and return to the question about the price of that new power.

Chapter Two

The Theory of Transformative Technologies

The history of what was originally the spoken word cannot be considered merely as a chain of events, a series of phenomena strung out in a neutral field of time, but rather must be taken as a succession of difficult, and often traumatic, reorientations of the human psyche.
—Walter Ong, *The Presence of the Word*

Were the word processor nothing more than yet another hubristic gimmick of Faustian civilization, there would still be a single instant of surprise during the transition to new techniques. Surprise is akin to the wonder with which philosophy, as Aristotle has it, begins. We may be startled into a philosophical reflection on the history of written symbols. The abrupt appearance of electronic writing raises questions about the concrete conditions in which symbols prevail. With the emergence of the phenomenon, the element of symbols stands out—even though digital writing strives for transparency and will doubtlessly soon achieve it. As we have seen in the previous chapter, the element in which thought defines reality through symbols touches upon an ontological dimension. This dimension, where reality is identified with symbols, was suggested by recollecting the written fragments of ancient philosophers. Eroded by time and change, the archaic sayings nevertheless recall the ontological import of language, a dimension of language deeper than the subservient and toollike aspects of writing technologies.

Suppose we do entertain the possibility that certain ways of manipulating symbols develop in us distinctive modes of referring to and perceiving realities. What sort of shift in thinking could be projected for word processing? Where would we begin to find a handle for grasping the shift in experience?

In the last forty years, following the advent of electronic media, scholars have tried to assess the historical shifts connected with the media as such. Previously philosophers used the term *media* to refer to the mental concepts or ideas by which we conceptualize realities. *Medium* meant conceptual awareness in conjunction with the five senses through which we come to understand things present before us in the environment. This natural sense of media was gradually dissipated during the modern period by man-made extensions and enhancements of the human senses. Instruments, gauges, and devices of all kinds were introduced into daily life to enhance perception and to extend and intensify the acuity of inborn human faculties. Living closely with artificial devices has come to be identified with being modern or with modernity in general.

Electronic media give new meaning to the term. We not only perceive directly with five senses aided by concepts and enhanced by instrumentation, but also are surrounded by a panorama of man-made images and symbols far more complex than can be assimilated directly through the senses and thought processes. Media in the electronic sense of acoustic-optic technology— phones, television, radio, audio and visual recording—appear to do more than augment innate human sensory capacities: the electronic media become themselves complex problems; they become facts of life we must take into account as we live; they become, in short, the media. Argument once turned on the special status of a certain set of symbols—the sacred symbols of the holy book or those of the more literal symbols of scientific methodology. Now argument moves from the selection of one or another of a particular store of symbols to the symbolic element itself.

Two shifts in the symbolization procedures of Western civilization have attracted careful study in recent decades. One shift is the changeover from a primarily oral-aural society to one based on written transmission; the other is the study of the historical changes made possible by the invention of the printing press. Studies of both changes have concentrated on the historical achievement of literacy, and both studies have been fueled by the continual need of our culture to nurture literacy as a means of preserving social memory in order to perpetuate civilized identity. Because of the concern with historical ramifications, both kinds of studies have only touched on, and then usually only by implication, the ontological dimension. Most studies have been anthropological, historical, or sociological in nature.

Once we assume an ontological import for verbal symbols— what contemporary philosophers call the semanticity of human thought processes—we take the first step in approaching the phenomenon of word processing. But the ontological dimension, though distinct from the others, is not isolated or removed from the sociological and anthropological dimensions. The latter, however, as -*ologies*, fall under the sway of reality apprehensions. We must look next into the intimate connection between the thought system of language and the ways in which symbols support cultural life. What sort of connections have been found between writing technologies and the way thinking is fostered in a given culture?

To answer the question I will draw on the work of two American scholars advocating the theory of the transformative power of writing technologies. We will then be equipped with some of the terms needed for describing the ontological dimension and for evaluating the phenomenon itself.

Both Eric Havelock and Walter J. Ong have used historical, anthropological, and sociological findings to point out the effects different communication systems have had on the human thought process. Havelock, coming from the discipline of classics, presents historical and philological evidence to show the importance information technologies have for any effort to understand the cultural activities of ancient civilization; he has applied his theory with particular cogency to the writings of the philosopher Plato. Walter Ong, with a Jesuit's background in the historical conflict between stability and cultural change, brings humanistic erudition to bear on the transformations of logic and rhetoric brought about by changes in the communications media. These contributors to the transformation theory have many points in common, and there is much continuity between them.

For our purposes, both of these influential studies of media technology will be considered as facets of a single theoretical position—what I will call the transformation theory of language technology or the theory of transformative writing technologies. Subsuming both Havelock and Ong under so streamlined a designation neglects the rich detail and manifold insights found in their work. Both are, however, exponents of the transformation theory inasmuch as each uses an analysis of the historical changes in media technology to illuminate changes in the way cultural forms are conceived and carried out. The power of the transformation theory lies in its ability to interpret and shed light on cultural forms such as education, politics, and religion by indicating inner cultural functions that connect these forms with each other. The fact that the transformation theory has been fruitful in concrete studies provides all the more reason for examining the theoretical notions it uses in formulating thought transformations. My discussion of Havelock and Ong makes no claim, however, to critical completeness; a completely adequate investigation of the work of Ong and Havelock would take this study far afield and distract us from the phenomenon of word processing.

The notions and terms found in the transformation theory serve to create the right kind of initial distance from the phenomenon of word processing. At the same time, however, I will need to make my own observations about the transformation theory. If we are to entertain a critical perception of word processing, it will be necessary to expose those aspects of the theory which might impede critical perception. We shall find, in fact, that the transformation theory harbors certain epistemological assumptions that subvert the critical assessment of word-processing technology. Because the transformation theory in its prevalent form rules out a critique of a given writing technology, certain basic notions used by the theory will need to be rejected or broadened. These include mental habits, the noetic field, information storage and retrieval, communication skills, and progressive cultural development. Such terms will have to be replaced by other notions relevant to the historically finite element of symbols and to the psychic framework developed in that element; the historical transformations will have to be understood as finite expressions of different experiences of the temporality of symbols rather than as the progressive accumulation of layered human skills. In chapter 4, when beginning to describe the phenomenon directly, I will have to criticize, reject, and modify the terms used by the transformation theory. The resulting terminology will be based on a perception of the theory's inherent limitations.

Havelock on Plato and the Dangers of Poetry

Before Eric Havelock's *Preface to Plato* it was not customary for philosophers to consider Plato's *Dialogues* against the foil of Greek culture. The history of Greece is, of course, often invoked to appreciate nuances in Socrates' encounter with the Athenians, but even then Plato's work is usually taken to be a fountainhead of pure theory. The *Dialogues* are regarded as a source book for metaphysics, political philosophy, ethics, even aesthetics. But the way many recurrent and fundamental themes in the *Dialogues* have their specific context in ancient Athens is seldom evident—unless as an instance of the blossoming of "genius" in classical Greece. Sometimes the dialogues of Socrates are regarded as purely formal models for skills in detailed logical argumentation while the content is regarded as the largely irrelevant folklore of a bygone civilization. More recently, Plato exegetes have fixed on the dramatic structure of the *Dialogues*, discovering behind the scenes some secret teachings of Plato, teachings often bearing a strong resemblance to the intuitive predilections of the interpreter. The enduring charm of the *Dialogues* seems to reside in their ability to evoke and expose the insights, limited opinions, and general shortcomings in Plato's readers.

Havelock was able to shed new light on the importance of the relationship Plato's philosophical writings have to the Greek culture in which they were written. He applied to the *Dialogues* some of the insights of Structuralism then emerging in the United States during the 1960s. Structuralism calls attention to the cultural systems in which signs function and are able to convey meaning. Language itself, regarded structurally, is a system of signs, and words can signify as carriers of meaning so long as they function within a system of mutually differentiating and mutually opposing components. Structural analysis gave Havelock a way of understanding the vast differences between the system of cultural signs as it functioned in ancient Homeric Greece (circa 800 B.C.) and the way it functioned later in the classical period of Greece during Plato's lifetime (circa 350 B.C.). Havelock applied to ancient philosophy the analysis of social structures and their functional dependence on the system of language. By noticing the different structural economies of cultural symbols, it became possible to understand with new clarity some of the themes dominating the Socratic dialogues written by Plato. Havelock located the philosophical power of Plato's writing within the context of a revolutionary transformation of the cultural system of ancient Greece.

Underscoring the essential relationship Plato's thinking has with ancient Greek culture could be mistaken for a kind of philosophical relativism. Relativism, or more precisely historicism, is usually taken to be a general premise proposing the view that a thinker can be best understood as an expression or fully determined component of a given historical or cultural situation. In this sense, relativism reduces a thinker's expressions to mere functions within the cultural context of the thinker, leaving behind nothing absolutely challenging in itself for thought as such, in subsequent periods, to come up against. Hence the term *historicism*: what has been thought relative to one definite set of circumstances is reduced to history and nothing more. This is not the sort of connection Havelock makes between Plato and classical Greek civilization. Havelock does bring out the essential relationship Plato's thinking has to ancient Greek culture but he does not reduce Plato's thought to a component of that culture. In fact, as Havelock presents it, Plato's relationship to his cultural environment was one of tension and of fundamental antagonism.[1]

Havelock's thesis about early Greek philosophy claims that the thought world of Greek civilization underwent drastic transformation as the practice of writing developed. Prior to classical civilization a "Homeric world" existed. The Homeric world is of a different cloth than the classical. The world where bards sing the fame of heroes and celebrate the actions of war is not a literate world—and the dichotomy between cultural education through heroic songs and the cultivation of civilized literacy is not accidental. Epic poems have nothing to do with poetry in the literary, or written, sense. They have everything to do with a closely knit band of people trying to preserve their spirit by passing on songs of idealized heroic action.[2] The Homeric bard captures and extols heroic characters in visually imaginative narratives, and celebrates in song the memory of those who sought and achieved glory in the hand-to-hand conflict of battle, thereby educating hearers to aspire to human greatness. But the bard celebrates in order to entertain and to instruct directly by word of mouth. The Homeric poem is the paradigm of communication in an orally based culture.

Homer embodies what Havelock calls the "ruling state of mind" in preliterate Greece.[3] In an oral culture, permanent and preserved communication has its model in the epic saga. A saga (cognate to the Germanic verb *Sagen*, "to say") is something preserved in oral form, as long as it is a living saga. Daily utterances cannot be passed along in their usual form without distortion nor can they be preserved in memory for long. The language of the saga is made memorable through an acoustic shape which includes rhythmic measures, sections linked by cross-references and repetitions, and thought orders of patterned parallels. The saga is what literate cultures refer to as poetry. In this sense, poetry is transmittable communication in the structural system of oral cultures, and in those cultures it is the primary model of significant language. Poetry is central to oral cultures not because it has some purely aesthetic value or because it engages the hearer as a work of imaginative artistry. Attractive aesthetic qualities of the saga belong to the task of perpetuating communication in an oral culture. Poetry is central to oral cultures because poetic language can endow the transmission of linguistic symbols with some degree of permanence.

In this way Havelock comes to understand the Homeric state of mind. In preliterate cultures poetry is functional in a central way. The formulaic phrases, metrical regularity, and cyclical composition patterns all operate to preserve the cultural system of signs, the preservation of ideals and of information between generations. Homeric writing shares these oral features with most ancient writing. The forms of language peculiar to the Homeric state of mind are not literary devices contrived for the gratification of an absolute aesthetic impulse or for making poetry as literate cultures understand the art form. These Homeric forms of language are, on the contrary, poetic because only in this way can words in an oral society rise above casual, ephemeral converse, which is the element of speech in daily transactions. If language is to be preserved as a fund of cultural ideals or of socially essential instruction, it must find a repeatable embodiment that makes it more or less permanent in the memories of speakers and listeners. In the state of mind of an orally based culture, significant language is memorable language, and memorable language is characterized by highly emphatic acoustic shapes, by clearly etched and simple images, by a style of (nonliterate) composition that employs music for the ear and parallels for mnemonic recall. Ancient civilization, then, was perpetuated by "oral thinkers," in Havelock's terms.

Just as the Homeric state of mind possessed its own distinct symbolic means for preserving cultural information, so too each cultural system has a paradigm of significant (preserved) speech which makes possible the "maximum of meaning to a cultural state of mind."[4] That paradigm sculpts not only certain verbal and metrical habits in the culture but also a cast of thought, a certain mental condition. The "communication technology" of poetry fosters an idiom of speaking and thinking in the culture as a whole. The "mode of consciousness," the vocabulary and syntax of oral culture, is not the same as that cultivated by a society which regards books as the paradigm of significant communication worth preserving.

Havelock illuminates the enormous tensions and ironies in Plato's work by seeing it against the background of the widespread adoption of writing by Greek civilization. He reminds us that throughout Plato's writings we find themes of education combined with suspicion and warnings about poetry. The *Republic* of Plato, ostensibly a complex treatment of political philosophy, quickly turns into a treatise on the education of youth and on the dangers of poetry for an ideal city. Plato's writings typically associate education with the dangers of poetry. The key to the seriousness with which Plato repeatedly takes up this theme lies in the fact that in Plato's time the cultural idiom of Greek culture was still predominantly Homeric and preliterate. It is not "beautiful writing" that is the target of Plato's arguments—as though literature should be banned from the Academy. When Plato attacks poetry and the poets, he is attacking the thought idiom of the Homeric tradition; he is attacking the dominance of an oral paradigm for significant communication. The thought idiom based solely on repetitive acoustic patterns and on sharp narrative images strongly reinforces an empathic, tribal emotional identification (Greek *mimesis*) with admired cultural heroes.

For philosophy to develop, it was necessary to break with immediate emotional identifications and to fashion abstract concepts capable of subsuming immediate realities under more general ideas. Abstraction is a kind of distancing, a clarity attained so as to fashion connections not altogether evident in the immediate reality. The mental vision, or idea, is an independent act of mind antithetic to the more tribal identifications of preliterate culture. Plato's argument with the poets is then an argument for philosophical thinking and against the dominant idiom of oral traditions. Havelock's thesis establishes a necessary connection between Plato as philosopher and Plato's attack on the use of poetry in education—not on account of some puritanical protest against the pleasure of aesthetic effects or because thought arrayed with fine coverings is alluringly seductive. Rather, Plato's protest against poetry was on behalf of thinking itself, in the philosophical sense, which requires a different paradigm than that offered by oral models.

"The books and the bookish tradition of a literate culture set the thought-forms of that culture, and either limit or extend them."[5] And Havelock attributes to Plato a hostility to the limitations of the preliterate, prebookish culture which residually characterized much of Greek society during the classical period. Plato sought the expansion of new, more abstract and impersonal thought forms as the Homeric paradigm was beginning to die out. Socrates relentlessly pursued the definition of single words, seeking to discover through a searching, analytical logic the absolute and abstract formal idea of such things as justice, piety, and courage. But while Socrates himself left behind no writings, the model of Socratic inquiry, with its passion for the single abstract truth, was in conflict with the oral paradigm of communication. Plato writes up the talks of Socrates to show how necessary it is to step away from the immediate identifications and repetitious cant fostered by a predominantly oral culture; Plato places Socrates into book form in order to help establish the kind of culture where a Socrates might have survived.

Where the written word is weak in a culture, the book simply preserves the information needed to carry out daily transactions and conversations as they have been carried out in previous ages. The tablets of the Assyrians and the Ugarits are no more than recorded chronicles of the daily life of the nation; it is the continuity of daily life that they serve. But as fluency in reading and writing becomes more secure and widespread, the storage procedure for conserving words turns into a place where communication can take on creative features. Criticism of the dominant talk can develop where the smooth flow of daily discourse is interrupted, where words are fixed in symbols for examination in private. At the point where the literate form of words becomes itself dominant as an academy of letters, the new paradigm comes to exert power over what is to count as significant communication in the spoken medium.

Socrates inhabits the intermediate stage, the era during which literacy is in ascendence but is still not paradigmatic for the thought idiom: Socrates' dialogues in the marketplace become the content of a book. The Socrates who criticizes the thought platitudes of oral tradition becomes the source of the philosophical tradition centered on the book. The book containing the oral exchanges of Socrates, taken seriously, becomes a force to undermine the paradigm of thought in which Socrates still moved and which proved lethal to him. If philosophy could eventually become a footnote to Plato, it was because philosophy became bookish in the first place.

The task of education in the Homeric epic tradition is to put the community in a formulaic state of mind, to enforce an overall habit pattern or common group nexus, a thought standard for individual and private expressions. In book cultures, a similar function is performed by the existing body of literature. To both cultures Havelock addresses the question "How is the apparatus of the civilization preserved?" With this question, Homer's lengthy catalogs of geographical and nautical knowledge as well as the precise how-to details of practical community activities become intelligible; they are more than inexplicable curiosities of an alien aesthetic. Mnemonic poetry, like written literature, is a structure designed for "information storage and management."[6]

This, then, is Havelock's thesis: "Between Homer and Plato, the method of storage began to alter, as the information became alphabetized, and correspondingly the eye supplanted the ear as the chief organ employed for this purpose. The complete results of literacy did not supervene in Greece until the ushering in of the Hellenistic age, when conceptual thought achieved as it were fluency and its vocabulary became more or less standardized. Plato, living in the midst of this revolution, announced it and became its prophet."[7] Havelock locates analytical thought capacities in the development of writing, and, even though literacy was for many centuries restricted to a very small portion of the population, the cultivation of a detached philosophical thought process was made possible and was supported by the practice of writing. In order for later philosophy to become a footnote to Plato, it was first necessary for Plato to make philosophy literate.

Ong's Grand Historical Vision

The many writings of Walter Ong are firmly based on the premise he holds in common with Havelock, namely, that a fundamental shift in the history of civilization occurred in the move from oral-aural "information transmission" to the paradigm of the literate mind. Ong's version of the transformation theory is more comprehensive in scope than Havelock's, and his may well be the most wide-ranging application of the transformation theory in general. By extending the theory from ancient civilizations—including present-day preliterate cultures—to the printing press and then to electronic media, Ong probes further into the transformations affecting modern thought. The visionary sweep of Ong's theory has frequently caused him to be compared with Marshall McLuhan, though this has usually been qualified by dubbing Ong the thinking man's McLuhan. McLuhan's cryptic style, however pithy, has proved to be of little help for digesting the changes brought about by microcomputers; McLuhan's words, capitulating to the non-linear mode of thought he describes, make his vision more appropriate for advertising hyperbole than for attempts to think through the computer revolution.[8] Ong's work, by contrast, shows some of the hard conceptual labor needed to sort out the problems and test the enigmas contained in the phenomenon.

Literary analysis, rhetorical theory, pedagogical practice, and even theology have profited from Ong's explorations. When he presents the oral-aural distinction, from which other versions of the transformation theory also proceed, he does so not only to explain the heritage of ancient Greek civilization. Theology, too, the proclamation of God's word in Judaeo-Christian religion, becomes for Ong a source of reflection on earlier oral cultures as civilizations dominated by an awareness of direct presence and by constant confrontations with the knowledge embodied in personal presence. Drawing on Rosenstock-Huessy and others, Ong evokes a theological principle in his presentation of the transformation theory. The ancient notion of spirit comes to have some of the connotations of modern philosophies of personal encounter, such as Martin Buber's teaching of the I-and-Thou relation (while, in turn, Buber drew on his own study of biblical and ancient linguistic sources to formulate the philosophical terms for his own work). The Trinity as a mystery of the Christian faith becomes paradigmatic for oral-aural presence where the Word of God is generated in Christ the Savior by the utterance of God the Father. There is always something of a latent religious impulse even in the secular history of Ong's version of the transformation theory. This can be overheard in the title of his central writing, *The Presence of the Word*.

The reading of secular history proposed by Ong is a history of the growing literacy of the human psyche as it comes to embody its symbolic life in elements possessing varying degrees of permanence. Cultures survive by means of the different ways they cultivate the capacities of the psyche. *Psyche* is used deliberately because the Greek word avoids the likely misconceptions accompanying more modern terms like *mind, intellect,* and *thought.* The word *psyche* does not enforce divisions between the mind and the senses and the emotions, as do some other terms, and, as I will detail in a later chapter, it connotes something like a disposition to a certain kind of awareness. The human "sensorium," another crucial term in Ong's vocabulary, is the configuration of the psyche's sensory awareness. The five senses along with kinaesthetic bodily awareness can be configured in different ways that channel the apprehension and symbolization of reality along definite lines. The habitual organization of sensory awareness results in a hierarchy of the senses. One of the senses tends to dominate or guide the others; the predominant sense serves as a paradigm for grasping reality (as the metaphorical origins of the language just used involve the paradigm of touch). Each configuration of the senses, each sensorium, fosters distinctive personality structures.[9] It follows, then, from Ong's version of the transformation theory, that each historical shift in the symbolization of reality brings with it a restructuring of the psyche—as is suggested by the epigraph to this chapter. The entire human personality is configured anew with every shift in the dominant medium for preserving thought. Persons in preliterate cultures encounter one another differently than do persons in literate cultures.

Changes in the sensorium are most evident in the contrast between oral-aural (preliterate) and print-oriented cultures. In orally based cultures, the predominant sense through which cognition is fostered is, of course, hearing. Information is passed along predominantly through direct speaking and listening. The knowledge transmitted acoustically through the presence of another human being physically envelops the attentive learner. The speaker brings the psyche's inner cognition to voice, and what is known comes to sound outside the speaker and can then pervade the acoustic space of a listener. The learner needs to actively repeat the spoken word, since there is no place where it can be looked up. By participating in the repeated vocal performance of the words, the learner endows cognition with stability. By contrast, where print culture supplants the orally based culture it is sight or vision that becomes paradigmatic for the sensorium. Knowledge transmitted visually through printed symbols fosters a spatial sensitivity to reality. The transmission of knowledge is not completely dependent on personal association with someone who knows nor is direct personal listening necessarily involved. Detachment, in the visualist hierarchy, is needed for the proper perspective on what is known. As the visual sense requires a certain amount of distance to be effective, so too the cognitive models fostered by literate cultures cast suspicion on any knowledge that does not carry the conviction of being out there, or objective.

The Kantian turn in philosophy becomes quite explicit in Ong's reading of history. No longer immersed in the participatory ambience of oral culture, with its continually reinforced stock expressions of reality and its reduction to commonplace topics, the modern man can gain the distance from social routines from which it is possible to develop an independent and critical mind. Having interiorized the spatial organization of the printed word as well as its privacy and independence, the modern man can see through the implicit filtering of reality inherent in previous forms of tribal and oral culture. What people in oral cultures learn to receive passively and to transmit repeatedly as simple and stable realties can, for the modern man, come into question and be challenged as uncritical acceptance.[10] Certainly Ong's philosophical premises are irreconcilable with naive philosophical realism, whether of Thomistic or any other provenance. Philosophical realism is the claim that fundamental metaphysical realities—realities in the first sense—are immediately evident to the senses and can be found in common sense. Philosophical realism usually assumes that natural realities are fundamental and invariant throughout history and that these realities are always more or less accessible to the mind. The mind itself, according to philosophical realism, shares in the invariance of the entities of nature.

As a modern literate man analyzing oral cultures, Ong sees the illusory nature of the claim made by organized social life that the present transmission of reality is necessarily a passive reception of what is purely and simply real. Immanuel Kant, opening the paths of modern philosophy, shows that the perception of realities in themselves is limited by the structures of intelligibility inherent in the human senses and in human reasoning about what is perceived. According to the Kantian critical philosophy, the stable realities transmitted by cultural ritual, reinforced by education, and then passively accepted are realities in appearance only, are so-called phenomenal realities—though, for Kant, many of these appearances are based on the noumenal reality of practical imperatives. Kantian and post-Kantian philosophy rejects the naive realism incapable of critically examining the media by which reality is perceived.

Ong brings out a similar point with respect to the media of communication: realities in oral cultures are preserved by metrical language with repeatable rhythmic formulas. Since cognitive form requires patterned, rhythmic speech, what is knowable in those cultures is what falls neatly into the commonplaces and formulas. What in oral cultures cannot be fitted into the topics or stable formulas must be disregarded as arbitrary, absurd, or at least of lesser significance. The new and distinctively different are regarded as forgettable, in the sense of not cognitively respectable. Oral-aural cultures in the primary sense (that is, sans electronic transmission of voice and presence) are therefore systems that in the strongest sense stabilize reality apprehensions.

Another limit of the oral phase of culture is its relative lack of analytical capability. Because it is preserved in the medium of speech, knowledge remains embedded in personal relationships (master-to-pupil) and is not easily examined in a detached manner.

By remaining closer to the sense of hearing, knowledge cannot be "eyed" carefully—in the same way that the visual sense requires distance to function well. The emphasis on presence in oral cultures accords with the assumption that real knowledge can be functional only in the actual human performance of what is known. Knowledge that cannot be performed or acted out or spoken by someone is no knowledge at all.

The same literacy revolution described by Havelock in the setting of ancient Greek philosophy is found by Ong in the general development of chirographic culture. For Ong, chirographic culture—from the Greek words for hand (*cheiros*) and writing (*graphein*)—is constituted by the alphabetic or ideographic manuscript, the ideogram being calligraphy in the traditions of the Far East. In both alphabetic and ideographic manuscripts (*manus* is Latin for "hand" and *scripta* is "something written"), writing detaches memory from speech. Memory, the storehouse of knowledge, no longer depends on repeated vocal performances. Manual writing preserves knowledge beyond ephemeral speech and beyond the lapse of memory. In chirographic cultures, the performance of language by a speaker is no longer essential.

Yet knowledge in chirographic cultures is not, as preserved information, available to many people. A select priesthood is still needed to promote the transmission of knowledge. In the Middle Ages, for instance, control of cognitive skills is retained by a scribal elite, a group with skills not shared by the nonliterate masses. The underlying broad thrust of chirographic culture is still oral; a central place is accorded public disputations and live public debates throughout the Middle Ages. To read was still to read aloud, and oral traditions were entrusted with the basic formation of culture and education.

Chirographic culture is pretypographic. But chirographic culture spearheads the dissociation of knowledge from the utterances of speakers even though knowledge continues to appear to a large extent in the vocal-oral element as disputation, rhetoric, and polemic. Despite the cultivation of hand-copied books, a general emphasis on vocal presence continues in medieval thought. The dominance of the vocal is only gradually supplanted by writing and by the literate mentality, so it is only after the Renaissance that the modern period comes into its own with the growing strength of the spatial-visualist aspects of the human psyche. The Renaissance marks the breakthrough of the spatial-visualist hierarchy in the human sensorium, manifest also in the rapid development of three-dimensional perspective in the visual arts of that period. Then, with the invention of typographical automation in the printing press, the chirographic-vocal configuration of the Middle Ages disappears behind the standardized visual symbols of modernity.

One of Ong's most striking studies concerns the connection between the ascendancy of typography and the inauguration of modern logic. Havelock's thesis on Plato posits the connection between philosophical abstraction and the growing capacity to pull back from immediate language usage in order to grasp more general and formalized meanings. Empirical studies by psychologists and sociologists like Vygotsky and Luria have also connected literacy with the capacity to objectify or think more abstractly about the things we address ourselves to in immediate spoken language. But Ong's detailed study of the teachings and influence of Peter Ramus (1515–72) provides the strongest case for the connection between typographic modes of thought and the development of modern logic.

It is true that late medieval logic in its Scholastic style increasingly turned from the intentional, substance-centered logic of Aristotle. Late Scholastic logic became to a large extent quantified, and it extended logic further into the manipulation of symbols. But the logical and educational reforms of Peter Ramus introduced the young René Descartes to a methodical, visualist-spatial logic; Descartes was to lay the foundations of modern philosophy. He learned his logic from a textbook inspired by Peter Ramus.

Ramus, as Ong shows in *Ramus, Method, and the Decay of*

Dialogue,[11] advocated logical thinking as it could be advanced through unambiguously clear visual aids. Ramus, in fact, came to identify logic, and even rhetoric, with the display of a subject on the trees and branches of visual schematics. The spatial layout of the printed page, along with the newly discovered potential for mechanically reproducing an indefinite number of textbooks, created the grounds for a whole new culture. Ramus seized this opportunity and became a reformer of the thought patterns of his society. The logic he produced is noted more for its novel format and widespread influence than for any original logical content. Ramist logic proposed the improvement of thinking through procedures for simplifying any and every subject matter; through neat diagrams, any subject could be divided into symmetrical branches and other spatial arrangements. By displaying logically the bare bones of a subject as it could be arranged and reproduced on the printed page, Ramus gave impetus to the democratization of knowledge, which later led to the proliferation of encyclopedias of knowledge. Ramist logic set the cultural foundations that displaced a narrowly based chirographic culture with a new model of the intelligent mind.

The revolutionary print media of the mid-fifteenth century had more immediate consequences, as centuries go, than did the earlier and more gradual transition from oral to literate cultures.[12] Memory in oral culture shifted to the manuscript of chirographic culture; the knowledge preserved and dignified by the skills of the scribe and by the rarity of manuscripts shifted to the printed book of typographic culture. From memory to manuscript, what is knowable is finally divorced from the speaker or performer of knowledge. Knowledge becomes identified with the content perceived with typographic fixity. Knowledge becomes something you can look up. Where personal transmission is no longer integral to knowledge, the depersonalized content can be standardized and made demonstrable equally to all. The new ideal of knowledge becomes objectivity, or cognition uncontaminated in principle by personal qualities or personal inclinations; the question Who says so? becomes irrelevant to the truth of a statement.

The transformation theory argues not that printing by itself caused the ideal of objective knowledge in seventeenth-century science in some successive, linear sense of causality. A world where the printing press offered a channel for human energy was also the world that provided the necessary conditions for the discovery and cultivation of objectivity in cognition; among those necessary conditions was the printing press and the spread of print literacy. Ong strives in each case to describe a qualitative alteration in the way the mind habitually formulates thoughts in the gradual and large-scale move from orality to literacy, and from chiro-graphic to typographic texts. He is concerned with the mode by which the mind organizes reality in its characteristic cultural formulations and how it is transformed by basic alterations in writing technology. No simple historical causality is invoked since the transformation theory seeks not so much to be a scientific explanation of specific facts of history, such as the rise of objectivity or the increase of literacy, as to illuminate connections between a number of historical changes.[13]

The transformation theory is more concerned with shedding light on writing technologies than it is with providing single-factor historical explanations or with showing unilinear causality. Or, more accurately, the transformation theory seeks to illuminate the impact of writing technologies on the human thought process. The word *impact*, much maligned by grammarians, is the precise word in this case on account of the term's more obscure, less obviously causal connotations. In an area where causal linearity has had to be abandoned, namely, in ecology, the new term *impact* has recently enjoyed widespread usage, replacing more philosophically tradi-tional terms such as cause and effect. Cause-and-effect analyses are less helpful where a holistic interaction is involved; in holistic historical worlds there is a mutual, concomitant origination of factors, not single, independent connections. But the notion of world has not been developed philosophically by the transformation theory, and I shall have to explore other sources in order to do this in the next chapter.

Limitations of the Transformation Theory

Ong's version of the transformation theory begins with an awareness of the phenomenon of modern communications technology and seeks to elucidate it.[14] Appropriately, then, the theory culminates in a study of the shift from typographic to electronic media. Since the central concern of the theory is with communications in general and not with the element of written symbols, the notion of electronic media includes television and radio broadcasting. Television and radio reintroduce, in Ong's terms, a "secondary orality." The directness of oral-aural communication is revived in the new configuration of the human senses; through electronic media, the presence of aural and visual contact is reproduced, and socially significant information is shared. To the other forms of media, that is, direct speech, handwriting, and print, a new layer is added. The older forms of communication, while no longer dominant, all support and provide necessary conditions for the communicative contact set up by the new electronic technology.

The thread uniting the changing hierarchies of the human senses is "communication systems." The transformation of cultural thought habits—what Ong sometimes calls "mentality"—is linked to "communications media." The notion of communications media, an idea gaining currency only in recent decades, provides Ong with a basis for describing changes across several historical eras. Through the common denominator of communications, Ong traces how media systems develop, are extended, then come to be imposed upon one another so as to fashion more highly developed means for the unifying end, which is communication—or, in a more ultimate and religious sense, communion. As transmitters of information (communications), each new medium builds upon and extends the previous media: literacy builds upon oral communication; typography absorbs both the voice and the skills of literacy; electronic media assimilate or depend upon the oral delivery of (usually) literacy-based texts or typographic scripts as well as upon a general public familiar with printed material available in the press, magazines, and books. The residue of earlier forms of communication persists as integral moments in the whole configuration of a culture's communication network.

The vast erudition and historical scope of Ong's thinking precludes categorizing him among narrow theorists of the electronics revolution. There is, nevertheless, a developmental culmination of the transformation theory in the study of the electronic media. Audio-visual electronics reawakens impulses of the oral culture.[15] The appearance of more direct contact alludes to the potential oneness and harmony of the orally bound tribe. The personal distance and individualism fostered by the print culture seem overcome by a further elaboration of communication technology. Ong's version of the transformation theory envisions something like a recapitulation of the communicative history of humankind. As in the thought of G. W. F. Hegel, who in the nineteenth century invented the philosophy of history, an eschatology is operative in the transformation theory. Ong is frequently compared to Teilhard de Chardin, who shares, in turn, many of the assumptions of Hegel's developmental philosophy of history. For Hegel, earlier forms of the human spirit are sublimated (sublated, or aufgehoben, is the philosophical term) into ever fuller complexity, so that, from an absolute philosophical viewpoint, they are each absorbed as parts of a single meaningful history: the story of the necessary alienation from original unity and the laborious mediations needed to regain that primal harmony. Put in Christian terms—and Hegel claimed his philosophy conceptualized the Christian religion—after the Fall, the long way of the Cross is necessary in order to bring about Redemption and achieve Paradise Regained.

Eschatology (the logos of the last things, the eschaton) implies that the way things begin is how they end; the Fall shall be healed and all shall be well (again). What appears to be total loss and Sin may one day become a "happy Fall," an alienation by which history is first propelled by painful losses which are then finally revealed ("apocalypse," or unveiling) as repaid ("redeemed," or bought back). The mythic dimension of Ong's transformation theory is the abandonment of primary orality where each individual is directly addressed and speaks in and from the common spirit (*spiritus* is the Latin for breath). The original unity of humankind is a harmony, though primitive in the sense of undeveloped and uncomplicated. To develop internal complexity, it is necessary first that the unifying harmony be broken by the individualism and distance implied by literate consciousness. Literacy makes possible an individual independence leading to greater and more intense consciousness—on the part of the individual. With electronic technology, orality brings the distance full circle.

The transformation theory hesitates at times to pass judgment on history—Ong himself refuses to identify completely the history of the secular word with the divine Word of his religion—and in hesitating the theory appears to be a form of historical determinism. That is, the transformation theory appears in some versions to be no more than a spectator's objective view of what happens when technologies are adopted by social systems. Or, in some versions, it seems to state the way it is without any potential for critical commentary. But, if we take up the Hegelian or Teilhardian leads scattered frequently throughout Ong's work, we find an optimistic judgment or even absolute affirmation of the transformations of communication technology. Of course, there are reservations about misuses of the media and so on, but there is a fundamentally positive construal of the effects of technological development in the media. As long as it remains a theory of communication, of the exchange of socially valued information, the transformation theory cannot but affirm the "progressive unfolding" of history.[16] For communications media are essentially means for information storage and exchange.

To provide the possibility of a critical evaluation of word-processing technology I will have to first look to the element in which symbols persist and to the habits of the mind fostered by that element. Rather than focus on communications alone, I will have to look to how symbols exist independently of immediate human goals and purposes, and independent of communications. The element symbols enjoy in a particular historical world cultivates a certain psychic framework with the gains and losses peculiar to that symbolic element. The gains and losses are part of the inherently finite nature of historical worlds. Instead of another layer in the cumulative development of history, electronic writing may bring with it an abrupt shift into an altogether different psychic framework for human thought. To obtain a philosophical stance from which to make such an assessment, I will first have to leave the widespread and influential transformation theory of writing technologies in order to modify it with a more existentially appropriate theory of finite historical worlds.

Chapter Three

The Finite Framework of Language

> It could also come about that history and tradition will be smoothly fitted into the information retrieval systems which will then serve as resource for the inevitable planning needs of a cybernetically organized mankind. The question is whether thinking too will be terminated in the business of information processing.
> —Martin Heidegger, *Preface to Wegmarken*

We have seen how Walter Ong and Eric Havelock trace the development of the cultural standards and models for thinking through their examination of the transformation of modes of communication, especially in the transition from orality to literacy and in the transition from chirographic to typographic cultures. The transformation theory, as we have seen, focuses on the psychic changes concomitant with historical developments in media technology. The theory neither postulates language technologies as causes of thought transformation, nor considers language technologies to be merely symptomatic of deeper cultural changes. Rather, something like a mutual concomitant origination is in play: the expression of a historical world is at the same time a shaping factor within that world—though, in the transformation theory, the notion of world has not yet become a philosophically explicit term with all its ramified significance. Only an account of the notion of world can provide a philosophical basis for a full development of the transformation theory of language technologies.

From the transformation theory, it follows that the word processor—if it be called a glorified typewriter, as some suggest—inaugurates important changes in the way truth is modeled publicly and in the way something is regarded as credible or worthy of belief. As we have seen, the typewriter itself is a step toward greater typification of language in written form, and the metaphysics of the typewriter, if indeed glorified by the word processor, is raised to a new level by electronics, to a level which calls attention to the entire development of typification. To say that the word processor is a glorified typewriter is correct—as long as we understand the typewriter to be expressive of the metaphysics of typification, and as long as we use *glorified* with its strictly historical, and even theological, connotations of holding and maintaining a model for and of human attention. Yet it is not clear from the transformation theory whether and to what extent the metaphysics of typification is peculiar to the contemporary world or how it is integral to the modern notion of truth.

Another lack of clarity in the transformation thesis is the extent to which the historical perspective of the theory rests on the assumption of a progressive layering or cumulative interlocking of human skills and capabilities. The transformation theory of technology describes the superimposition of one set of verbalizing skills upon another. Layering can be understood to be endless, or even progressive in a developmental series. The progressive layering might be additionally understood to be providential or necessary for the full unfolding of human history. The progressive amalgamation of skills was compared to Hegel's *Erinnerung*, or "cultural memory," by which history is redeemed through the constant assimilation of new skills and experience by a self-perfecting humanity.

Martin Heidegger's contribution to the study of the new writing technology may be interpreted through a brief examination of several aspects of his philosophy: the notion of existential worlds, the critique of typification or the technological "Enframing" (*Gestell*) in the postmodern world, and the existentialist conception of historical development, a conception which sees development with some continuity but also frequent losses in the process of history. These three aspects of Heidegger's philosophy fit together. The existential notion of world implies a criticism of the cumulative truth of history; the critique of cumulative history implies a self-forgetfulness and erosion of responsiveness induced by technology; and the analysis of an all-enframing technology is one which points to the reduction of the metaphorical powers of language to a single aspect of information management.

Trade-Offs in Historical Drift

Much of early twentieth-century philosophy was an attempt to dismantle the confidence in the absolute fulfillment of human history envisioned by such thinkers in the nineteenth century as Hegel and Marx. While Hegel taught that human history has become the explicit unfolding of the absolute Spirit or the divine state in which we are fully aware of "the rational freedom of what must necessarily be," Karl Marx, after Hegel, saw in a projected classless society the emergence of the final and complete human being who no longer transmits the narrowing vices of the previous economies of scarcity. These progressive and hopeful interpretations of history were based on, among other things, a sweeping study of the philosophical principles that appeared in human societies from ancient Greece to modernity. The major European thinker who in the twentieth century consciously appropriated the Hegelian scope of the philosophical development of Western society—only then to dismantle its affirmative certainties about its history—is Martin Heidegger. Heidegger's theory of reality and of the linguistic element of reality recapitulates the whole European tradition in bringing metaphysical theory to bear on a critique of modern life.

Heidegger's "history of Being" offers an account of the truth of world, and much of his writing is concerned with the extent to which the metaphysics of typification is peculiar to the Western tradition. He sees the notion of truth in Western philosophy since Plato as gradually moving toward the apotheosis of this metaphysics of typification in the mastery over the planet through technology. Furthermore, Heidegger has made critical remarks concerning the new information technologies—though he only infrequently makes direct references to writing technologies as such and did not live to see the proliferation of the microcomputer.

This study is neither doxography nor exegesis; I can do no more here than make some few connections and interpretations of Heidegger's work. The primary consideration is to bring philosophical criticism to bear on the transformation theory and to obtain thereby several concepts by which we can more clearly see and articulate the phenomenon of word processing. The suggestions made cannot even scratch the surface of Heidegger's rich analysis of human existence, an analysis which formed the basis of Existentialism in the earlier part of this century. The use of some of Heidegger's terms will require occasional modification for the sake of the investigation, but this is not to say that the interpretation of Heidegger absolves itself of any inaccuracies.

The rich terms provided by Heidegger's analysis of human existence offer both development and critique of Ong's theory of transformative technology, for Heidegger's great work *Being and Time* is a philosophy of cultural finitude. Finitude is Heidegger's theme not only in the existential analysis of the uniquely individual existent, where the personal self confronts the possibility of not existing and the irrevocableness of personal choices. Finitude is even more profoundly the finitude of Being itself, the particularity of a certain self-disclosure of reality. Finite existence apprehends reality—the term *apprehending* is precisely intended to convey an anxious projection based on abysmal or ungrounded freedom. And in this transient apprehension, the disclosure of Being, of what-is, abides as a gift. As soon as the gift is taken for granted, or given once and for all, the truth of Being is no longer authentic truth but merely "eternal truth," that is, truth for which no finite being can any longer feel responsible. In this sense, Being is finite in every reality apprehension, in every disclosure of what is.

The horizon against which Being is disclosed, or against which reality is apprehended, is temporality. Temporality should be understood as transcendental time or transcendental movement—transcendental in that it is not the movement of any particular thing, but transcendental time establishes the condition for any particular thing to move within time. Temporality is the background against which Being can make an appearance and be apprehended. So, time is intrinsic to Being and thus to everything appearing within the world inasmuch as the disclosure of truth occurs and is an event—in the transcendental sense of "the event that makes any event possible." World, then, as the appearance of Being, is the ongoing context within which things are generated, distinctions are made, and connections are established.

World is a complex of involvements, a pretheoretical, preconscious projection that is finite. World has a specific trajectory with a beginning and an end. The worldhood of the world, its continual occurrence, implies a past, or heritage, as well as a projection of a set of choices into the future. The fact that the world is historical does not mean, for Heidegger, that the background of realities is a dead set of facts, as if *history* here means solely the object of the study of historians, or some predetermined factual whole. Worlds are, rather, historical in the sense of having actual pasts and real futures that define and delimit the world as an existential matrix of possible things and possible activities.[1] World is the place where all things are shaped, including the substantivization of objects, the consciousness of subjectivity, and the coherence of thoughts and actions.

Being is intimately connected with time in that each world has its own peculiar temporalization of things, the special way in which things are gathered within the circumscription of a characteristic mood or type of disposition. This is the way in which historical worlds can differ from each other profoundly. The way things come to presence vis-à-vis time, the mode of temporality or the "tempo of life," defines a given historical world and holds its projects together in a distinctive whole, projects including politics, art, religion, work, and play. Time, in the transcendental sense, contracts in a specific way to individuate each world and to set worlds apart in epochs or in periods loosely conjoined by a common metaphysical sense or apprehension of reality.

World in the existential sense, then, admits of a plurality, a variety of ways in which transcendental time can be contracted into a determinate "presencing of beings." There are startling breaks in the history of reality apprehensions. These breaks constitute the epochal "history of Being." But, while the world-disclosures of Being are based on continuity of heritage and decisions for the future, there are also unforeseeable breaks that produce shifts in the history of reality apprehensions. No ineluctable plan by which history could be grasped overall from within becomes transparent to human knowledge. Furthermore, the finitude of reality apprehensions necessarily makes any study of past or future an act of interpretation, an interpretation that proceeds from its own heritage and that goes forward into its own future.[2] Such is the intrinsically temporal nature of human understanding.

From the existential notion of world, it follows that there are trade-offs, limitations on human awareness. There is always historical drift. Beings are disclosed through time, or time is the self-disclosive process of reality apprehensions. No world can properly incorporate the totality of reality apprehensions in a single, triumphant culmination of history. The skills called forth by the demands made in one existential world, with its special claims on human attention and concern, are not fully compatible with the demands of another existential world. At times, historical drift may even require explicit trade-offs or the obsolescence of one way of being-in-the-world for the sake of developing a wholly new approach to attending to reality.

Heidegger's theory of epochal transformation takes account of the displacement of skills and the reorganization of life energies that create upheavals in human cultures. What is philosophically radical is the connection of truth with existential world. Connecting truth with time charges reality itself with temporal élan. By connecting the truth of Being with time, a new key is provided for the analysis of diverse historical worlds. The way in which each movement of awareness has its own special pace or tempo provides a depth to the analysis of human skills as they change in the drift of history.

Like Hegel (and Ong), Heidegger takes seriously the epochal changes in cultural commitments. Changes are of fundamental significance for the philosophical understanding of things. But to this awareness of the historical commitment of human energies Heidegger adds the concepts of what I call historical drift and of cultural trade-offs, or gains and losses in reality apprehension. Rather than a developmental series of systematic improvements, epochal transformations can be understood to be sets of finite pathways which develop, lead onward, then trail off when new pathways are opened by considerably different techniques and skills. The pathways opened are finite in that human concerns project new and different directions for development while previous projects are dissolved or are taken up in ways that obscure or transform the original impulses of previous projects. Pathways are also finite in the sense that some larger ways become major thoroughfares through which alternate routes are opened and can branch out, but remain, as branches, attached and rooted to the larger highways; some choices create a new future but are dependent upon a latent set of choices made in the past.

By connecting truth essentially with the existential world, Heidegger's philosophy plants intrinsic limitation at the core of truth. While for Parmenides and the entire tradition of Aristotelian logic truth is a "fully rounded sphere" of indivisible deductive wholeness, Heidegger's notion is that Being in its finitude is never fully disclosed. The truth of things is always inherently partial since the process of revealing or disclosing things is founded upon the built-in limitations of its finite definiteness. Truth, then, is simultaneously a revealing and a concealing all at once—not that some characteristics of things remain unknown on account of human limitations. Rather, the disclosure of things as such, as truth, is concealing or self-obscuring due to the finite nature of the world, the holistic background against which any particular truth or statement is made.

Truth in this sense, however, is not restricted to a mere feature of propositions or statements. Truth in the most fundamental sense is the primordial articulation of world, of the context of involvements within which persons and objects first become definite things. As the truth of primordial articulation, the existential world is the primal language. This is why speaking is also inherent in silence:

> Man speaks. We speak when we are awake, and we speak in our dreams. We are always speaking, even when we do not utter a single word but merely listen or read, and even when we are not particularly listening or speaking but are attending to some work or taking a rest. We are continually speaking in one way or another.[3]

We bespeak the existential world even and especially by orienting ourselves in and acting upon the environment of things in the world. What then of the conventional referent of language by which we usually mean our spoken and written signs? Heidegger's thinking belongs to that long tradition, adumbrated in chapter 1, according to which language and reality are intimately connected. In a celebrated passage, Heidegger refers to language as "the house of Being." The house shelters and preserves the disclosures of the truth of existence. Against it, the winds of history blow and are held momentarily in abeyance. The meanings of one existential world become abiding dwelling places, or building sites, for the projects of another world. Whatever belongs to human life is localized somewhere in the structures of language. More than an instrument within the world, language is an overarching, limited order of nameable identities and events. The chaos of details and of possibilities becomes manifest through language as language reduces chaos by ordering things in predicable relationships.

Language, then, has power—not solely in the control over things wielded by the users of language, but also and especially in the structural power language exerts over its users.

In exercising structural power over its users, language places limitations on the way things come to presence and come to light. These limitations are the other side of the revelatory power of language. Propositions and informative statements constitute a certain kind of ("apophantic" or "illocutionary") truth about things and events in the world; and the ("perlocutionary") languages of requests, of questions, and of "performative" utterances make up diverse sorts of disclosures in the world of practical action.[4] Nevertheless, all these truths transpire on the background of a more fundamental disclosure, namely, the truth of world, the fundamental context of concerns. And the truth of world, due to its existential finitude, is a truth that conceals. So, all derived truths of discovery within the world are themselves founded upon the process of a dual opening-up that also covers over.

The full truth of language is, therefore, not exhausted by the truth of propositions or statements made within a particular language. The truth of language resides, most fundamentally, in its revealing power. This revealing-concealing power is in turn most evident in modes of speech which preserve the dual concealing-revealing at the heart of the primordial articulation of world. A dual concealing-revealing is reflected in the metaphorical dimension of human language. (Where Heidegger most frequently employs the term *saying* [*Sage*] or *primordial saying* I will take the line of interpretation and suggestion made by Ernesto Grassi and refer to saying by way of the rhetorical trope *metaphor*.[5]) Metaphorical uses of language meet the world as it moves through the shifts and transformations of historical drift.

Metaphors tell truths with a darkly illuminating ambiguity that reflects the dual nature of the fundamental truth of the existential world. Human languages have special revelatory power in their capacity to name things anew, to shape new names for what has not yet been said. *Metaphor* is the word usually employed to describe the power of language to create new meanings out of previous strands of meaning (though most often *metaphor* is still interpreted ontologically by way of the concepts of the Aristotelian philosophy of language). Where new meanings are created there the revelatory power of language is most manifest since language then both reveals or indicates something while at the same time implying the finite limitations of the naming of things as a new world begins to present itself and as a word has been found to be semantically fluid and ambiguous. Thus Heidegger's frequent citation of the lines of the poet Hölderlin: "Poetically we dwell upon the earth."

In this context it should be noted that physiological research into the intelligibility of language in general has shown that a certain degree of ambiguity in stimuli is requisite for even the accurate transmission of perceived meanings. What is true of the ambiguity requisite for direct perception seems equally true of the "genius" of natural languages in their ability to evolve an elaborate and intricate vocabulary from a number of etymons, or root words.[6] The human ability to use words in new ways, as metaphors, to imply meanings that differ from former usages, relies on an instinctive sense of ambiguity. For a programmed set of meanings, such metaphors are mistakes, for they "mis-take" one thing for another. As part of the dual concealing-revealing truth of the existential world, however, metaphor is the indication of the free response necessary for genuinely dwelling in the world, for making it one's own. It is a condition of truth or genuineness. Without the transformation of meanings there would be no history in the sense of fully human occurrences.

Ironically, it is the technological world that first makes possible Heidegger's realization of the truth of the existential world. Heidegger's existential analysis, by its own reckoning, was first made possible through the advent of planetary technology. The essential need for human responsiveness and metaphorical creativity first comes to light only after the concealing-revealing dimension of the primordial truth of world is itself threatened by forgetfulness. The concealing-revealing nature of existential truth, the essential need for metaphorical ambiguity, becomes apparent only once the nature of the world itself is threatened by extinction through rational transparency.

This rational transparency Heidegger calls "calculative thinking." Calculative thinking proceeds by typifying and systematizing what has already been grasped in principle; it is elaboration of what has been already conceptualized; it is not responsive to new situations but makes everything clear and organized on the basis of the principles of its systematizing; it attempts to situate everything before and in front of the human being so that all things are at beck and call. Through calculation, the "world" becomes in principle a set of totally manageable resource materials for the exercise of the human will. By placing everything before the human will, world ceases to be truly "world" in the existential sense of an appealing context of involvements that call the human forth into creative and responsive acts of living. Heidegger coins a name for this all-encompassing presentation of everything as manageable: "the Enframing."

The plight of language, as words are transformed by the Enframing of the technological world, is that metaphorical creativity comes to be regarded as incidental or superfluous. Which is to say that responsiveness and "poetic dwelling" are seen to reside outside of the fully manageable and calculable world. Heidegger calls this total transparency the "darkening" of the world. It is the culmination, in his reading of the history of philosophy, of the Western tradition that equates truth with lucid typification of things and world with "resources" for human consumption. Yet, at the same time, the world darkens precisely because the "world"— as a technological poem or, rather, an interpretation of things that is opaque to itself as a poem—comes into its own and becomes dominant as a world or context of involvements. The concealing aspect of all existential worlds become conspicuous through the self-concealment of the technological world as an existential world. The nature of authentic worldhood becomes conspicuous by the absence of the interplay of concealing-and-revealing, by the relegation of metaphor to a separate and privately guarded domain of the aesthetic or religious. The nature of authentic worldhood becomes conspicuous even through the very fact that this absence itself goes increasingly without notice. The "house of Being,"[7] where reality is addressed poetically or metaphorically, becomes visible as a fragile shelter only when its continued existence is put into question by the omnivorous drive to manage everything through the sharply defined geometrical structures of the Enframing.

In one of his essays, Heidegger repeats his view that the essential nature of language is increasingly distorted by the contemporary technological disposition inasmuch as language is regarded as information or the vehicle of information. There he raises his fears about the connection of machines (apparatus) with language:

> The language machine regulates and adjusts in advance the mode of our possible usage of language through mechanical energies and functions. The language machine is—and above all, is still becoming—one manner in which modern technology controls the mode and the world of language as such. Meanwhile, the impression is still maintained that man is the master of the language machine. But the truth of the matter might well be that the language machine takes language into its management, and thus masters the essence of the human being.[8]

Of course, in 1957 Heidegger knew nothing of the word processor. But he was seeking to determine the way in which the technological drive to master and facilitate every process would eventually move into the most intimate areas of thought, namely, into the expression of thought in writing. His prognosis has proven to be astute, for his critical references to the treatment of language as information have turned out to be, in fact, the historical background of what we now call word processing.

Word processing was originally developed and used by data processors who developed the first text-writing programs as handy aids to their central work of writing programs for data handling. The original text editors used by programmers in their data-handling work were programmer-oriented editors on mainframe computers. The writer-programmer uses symbological references to text rather than the direct, interactive manipulation of text on a CRT or video monitor. These text editors did not so much manipulate text as apply the reasoning of algorithmic programming to the process of writing. Such roundabout use of the computer for writing had less to do with word processing than it did with the application of information processing techniques to the construction and editing of texts. Still, the early text-editors had taken the first major step: natural language was interpreted as a standard code and then the code in its electronic form could be operated upon, edited, and transmitted so as to reappear in its natural-language form. The encoding of letters in the ASCII (American Standard Code for Information Interchange) computer code not only permitted the transmission of natural-language at electronic speed; encoding natural language on computers makes possible a new approach to language as directly manipulable in new ways. Data-handling techniques for number-crunching or for the high-speed manipulation of quantified routine information were applied to natural language communication.

Heidegger's premonitions in this matter had penetrating foresight, especially considering how recent the development of microcomputers has been. Nor was it clear when Heidegger wrote the extent to which computers could be applied to writing via programs for editing, printing, and telecommunications. Still, in places Heidegger touches upon the potential of technology for implementing a "world language" or electronic communications network through the interpretation of natural languages in mathematical-technological terms. His hunches have been connected with the claim he makes that the contemporary world is intelligible only as the extreme development of the trend toward rational typification and systematic organization pushed forward by modernity. Logic is the foundation of the systematic thinking which can become the basis for a homogeneous world language. But the logic meant here is not the traditional Aristotelian logic which organizes and evaluates inferences occurring in natural language. Rather, logic in the modern sense is a network of symbols equally applicable to electronic switching-circuitry as to assertions made in natural language; logic in the modern sense can become an underlying digital language to be used for the transmission and communication of natural language. Just as geometrical axioms are no longer bound to the domain of real circles (physical figures) but are operable with contrary postulates, so too modern logic is free of any naturally given syntax.[9]

Modern logic as a science of symbols was originally proposed by Gottfried Wilhelm Leibniz (1646–1716). Both Bertrand Russell and Alfred North Whitehead, coauthors of the epochal *Principia Mathematica* (1910–13), were indebted to him. Whitehead's metaphysics parallels the Leibnizean monadology, and Russell's first major book is *A Critical Exposition of the Philosophy of Leibniz* (1900). Leibniz believed all reasoning could be assimilated to a universal calculus of human knowledge. The resulting "universal grammar," or *characteristica universalis*, would serve to formalize in a deductive way all reasoning, including scientific proofs. The Leibnizean science of symbols was to establish and foster the organized unification of scientific research within a single system of combination and permutation. To this end Leibniz also worked on various models of the calculating machine throughout his lifetime. Appropriately enough, it was Leibniz's binary number system which was to be used centuries later by John von Neumann in developing electronic computers at Princeton.

In an early work, Heidegger analyzes the logic of Leibnizean rationalism as the precursor of modern thinking.[10] Heidegger argues that the logic of total systematic management was present already in the logical principles of such founders of modern rationality as Leibniz. Leibniz's plan for a symbolic logical calculus of total analycity was the forerunner of contemporary formalism in computer logic, and Leibniz himself, besides developing the binary logic, worked on some primitive models of a computational engine. Heidegger's treatment of modern logic in Leibniz was prescient. The Leibnizean logic of binary digits has become the basis of the encoding of language, thus creating a qualitatively different level of typification.

Writing converted to ASCII is fundamentally—as a phenomenon—different from handwritten manuscript or, say, the Morse code, though codified language in both ASCII and Morse code turns language into winged words. Digital reproduction of writing is as different a phenomenon in form from typewritten, printed language as digital audio reproduction differs from phonograph recordings and oxidized tape recordings. When a phenomenon has been digitized, it has been interpreted and processed. It has been transmogrified into a new form, a form that can be controlled by human beings with a precision far beyond that of other forms of reproduction. *Digital* is derived from the Latin *digitus*, or "finger." The fingers are the primordial counters, the first servants of human calculation. When something is digitized, it is interpreted as a sequence of numbers, numbers that have a precision that cannot be experienced directly in the original phenomenon, though the original phenomenon may have in itself a certain kind of precision that cannot be reduced to quantities or numerical relationships. Once a phenomenon has been digitized, it can be treated, as can all mathematical entities, as a series of relationships and proportions. The relationships between the wave lengths of acoustical phenomena can, for example, be calculated and modified, while at the same time the fundamental relationships between the wave lengths can be preserved. Wave lengths that have been digitized can be manipulated so as to improve upon the recorded phenomenon. For instance, recordings of the ocean may never sound really like the ocean until they have been interpreted digitally as quantities and then altered variously until the audio reproduction sounds real, like the ocean itself should sound. The impossibility of removing the flaws of the recordings of the original ocean sounds gives way to the creation of the real ocean sounds through digital manipulation.

Phenomena that have been digitized are new creations at the fingertips of human beings. Controlling phenomena as we experience them is itself a new kind of experience. The digital phenomenon is one facet of a totally controlled environment, an environment where what we experience is what we have created. The digits on which we count the world we experience come, through electronic amplification, to be the world we experience. The world on our fingertips becomes the world at our fingertips.

The temporal mood of total control and simultaneity is characteristic of the Enframing. This mood develops into modern technology over several centuries as modernity develops. In his study of Leibniz, Heidegger shows how the logic of formal systems is the modern continuation of the *visio Dei* (God's vision) in medieval Scholasticism. Leibniz strove from early on (in *De arte combinatoria* of 1666) to base the deductive capacity of human reasoning on a universal logistical calculus of human science. The logistical calculus was to foster a "universal grammar," a *characteristica universalis*, which was to promote the complete deductive formalization of all rationality and scientific justification. The temporality Heidegger finds in Leibniz's analytical formalism is the all-at-once simultaneity of totalizing presentness. The epistemological-ontological model behind the logic of Leibniz is, Heidegger shows, that of the *visio Dei*, the deity's omniscient intuitive cognition which was put into the philosophical tradition by the Aristotelianizing Scholastics. It is the knowledge of God, at least in its temporalizing simultaneity, that serves as a model for human cognition in the modern world as projected in the work of Leibniz.

The temporality of modern logic is seen in computer writing:

total control over all aspects of text, words caught in the dynamic system of electrified code. There is something here akin to the Enlightenment ideal of connecting all knowledge through a single code. The temporality or rhythmic tempo of the Enframing is instantaneous simultaneity, the logic of a total management with everything at one's disposal. The instantaneously managed world is not a world where humans evidently "dwell poetically," for the ambiguity and freedom of human "ingenium" (ingenuity or genius) must be mastered to fit the tempo of the Enframing. The specific temporality of technical systems supplies important clues which will be important in later chapters where the phenomenon of word-processing technology is disclosed directly and evaluated.

So far we have seen how Heidegger's notion of world offers an alternative to the transformation theory by countering the hope of a cumulative cultural memory with a notion of the existentially limited skills of the psyche. The ease and intuitive freedom of writing on a computer may mask, in Heidegger's terms, the revealing-concealing process intrinsic to the truth of the world. But the precise manner by which this darkening takes place in the specific technology of word processing is not made clear in existentialist ontology or theory of reality. Heidegger confines his remarks to noting the tendency of the contemporary world to reduce language to mere information to be managed; the primal history or existential events of human life are embedded in language while the current "Event" is the self-concealing of this history. Heidegger's treatment of technology tends to be—as is frequently found in the traditions of German Idealism—globally holistic and blind to particular phenomena.

Heidegger's global critique is, nevertheless, rich with insights for our purposes. The word processor will doubtlessly move language further into the mode of information exchange. Language is increasingly treated as information and is processed by the techniques of information management. Treated as information, language becomes a transparent vehicle for what is already determined existentially. That is to say, "in-formation" is already formed by the network of involvements in which it is exchanged; information takes place in a world that is presumed to have been already formed.

The informational mode of language may lead to the curtailing of the human ability to say, in Heidegger's terms, to call things freshly by name, by new names, to address the environing world poetically. The current integration of writing with information management is coming to be known as the knowledge industry. Such a development gives considerable corroboration to Heidegger's attempt to deduce from the principles of modernity the contemporary shift of thinking toward calculating. For Heidegger, being-in-the-world in its postmodern form is essentially an attempt to organize, systematize, and control the ensemble of things that constitute the human environment. Thinking, according to Heidegger's projection, is coming to be identified with speed, accuracy, and limitless calculation.

The so-called information industry includes professionals who must condense enormous amounts of textual information under exacting deadlines: attorneys, medical professionals, academics, executives, and financial analysts. Managing things today almost always includes personal computers; the use of microcomputers for text manipulation is not limited to clerical amanuenses delegated to type and finish documents. With the development of appropriate software, accessing and organizing information with microcomputers is increasingly done directly by those responsible for defining things linguistically; the computer closes the gap between writing and managing. Heidegger's projection of a language machine, which comes to dominate in the major employments of words, may not be far from the truth.

Heidegger points out another side to the Enframing or, rather, hints at it vaguely in one of his essays. In "The Question Concerning Technology," he reminds us of the connection in ancient Greece between useful skills and artistic creativity; the

Greek term *technē* does not sharply disjoin the works of necessity from the craftsmanlike search for perfect beauty: "The arts were not derived from the artistic. Art works were not enjoyed aesthetically. Art was not a sector of cultural activity."[11] Heidegger seems here to indicate some small avenue of exit from the Enframing. It may be possible to find again, within *technē* itself, a new encounter with ambiguity and an open field for human responsiveness, a new kind of non-Romantic poetic dwelling. There may be areas of creativity which still feed on ambiguity and on the human response to the unknown.

Looking into the Enframing: *Framework* the Program

Equipped with a revised transformation theory, and anticipating the description of the phenomenon of word processing in the following chapters, we might pause to look for a moment at one particular state-of-the-art instance of word-processing technology to see just how closely Heidegger's global approach fits certain aspects of the phenomenon.

The computer program on which much of the first half of this book is being written is called *Framework*.[12] It is advanced as part of "the new technology of information management." Such systems combine in a single integrated program several aspects of writing on microcomputers: word processing, "dynamic outlining," or "idea processing," database management, electronic spreadsheet, and telecommunications. As such, what is said about the program can serve very nicely as a synecdoche for word-processing software in general; *Framework* may also serve as a metaphor for the Enframing as it pertains to the intimate realm where written language is composed. A brief description can illuminate the extent to which Heidegger's premonitions about information management have been on target in the area of word processing.

Framework speeds up the processes of writing and communicating on the computer by using an abstract element, a frame, to identify and put a boundary around each work fragment. By using frames and subframes, each fragment can be manipulated: moved around, edited, added to, partially removed, combined with other segments, copied completely or in part, formatted, printed, and filed for later use. In this way, ideas can be developed through words, graphs, spreadsheets, or databases within frames and then stretched, combined, and arranged as building blocks in an almost infinite variety of ways. Each operation is placed in a frame that separates it from the rest of the program. Each frame is automatically placed in an outline form, which one can modify or rearrange at any time. *Framework* also utilizes a desktop format that permits viewing several operations at once on the screen. A zoom function permits instant expansion of any frame to fill the entire screen. *Framework* also features access to the disk operating system (DOS), and there is also an underlying high-level programming language called FRED (*frame editor*) which allows for the development of custom applications that can perform an indefinite number of specialized operations.

Acting intentionally upon the text as it is being written is directly connected to bodily gestures in *Framework*, a feature I will depict later in the description of the phenomenon in general where keyboard redesigning is treated as intrinsic to the new writing. The Point-and-Act Command system embodies an action on a frame or on part of the contents within a frame, first with the cursor to indicate the items you wish to affect, then with the press of a key or selected menu operation to execute the command. With this system, in the words of one guide to the program, "handling of data quickly becomes intuitive."[13] Operations, including storing and retrieving files, can be performed with a one-key command. Formatting on the page is done before your eyes as you enter it ("what you see is what you get"). Databases can be searched and sorted almost instantly.

The advertising claims, sprinkled with the usual dose of "hyperbole," declare more than was intended to be said: "This system doesn't just process numbers—it processes ideas. *Framework* makes it possible for knowledge workers to manage information in wholly new ways.... Because of its unique frames technology, you can create and manipulate ideas, words and numbers the way the best of the last generation software let you handle only numbers."[14] The handling of text in the modality of data manipulation would seem to corroborate Heidegger's notion of an Enframing technological world within which written language is now entrapped.

But such a writing technology is not—as we have seen in previous chapters—simply an external tool, something which we may pick up or let alone as we wish, something toward which we remain essentially indifferent. The proponents of programs like *Framework* speak of "a computerized extension of the mind" and emphasize the adaptability of such tools to helping create other tools: "Another way to think of *Framework* is as a software machine tool. That is, *Framework* is a kit full of software tools which can, in turn, be used to create new work tools."[15] Here the reference to adaptable tools implies a mind with a separate set of intentions outside of the framework of the Enframing. On the other hand, the proponents of programs like *Framework* speak of "a computerized extension of the mind":

> *Framework* not only speeds work, it can actually help
> expand your thinking. And as you become proficient in
> manipulating the mechanical aspects of *Framework*, you will
> probably begin to think WITH the system, conceiving new
> tasks that can be accomplished with it, organizing your work
> more systematically, and developing your own unique style
> of using *Framework*.[16]

Here, in the language of manuals, is the notion that computer software can attain a relationship more intimate to the thought process than any physical tool in the external world. *Framework* not only enframes the outer symbols of written language; it also enframes the thinking-composing mentality.

By placing the process of bringing things to word into manipulable frames, *Framework* presents an instance of Heidegger's claim: "The fundamental event of the modern age is the conquest of the world as picture. The word 'picture' (*Bild*) now means the structured image (*Gebild*) that is the creature of man's producing which represents and sets before."[17] And to this "objectifying" presentation of the world Heidegger adds that human activity is constantly "provoked" or lured into the production process of the Enframing.[18] Appropriately enough, the intended result assumed by most of the guidebooks for writing programs is the enhancement of "personal productivity" for "knowledge workers." As cited above, "*Framework* makes it possible for knowledge workers to manage information in wholly new ways." To do so, *Framework* "induces more systematic thinking about work."[19]

Many of the features of the *Framework* program described here serve to exemplify, in a specific way, Heidegger's claim that the world of modern technology tends to objectify and modify the communication process. The mode of composing language comes to reflect the whole existential world as a set of involvements attuned to a particular epochal mood and tempo. The mood and tempo of the Enframing is an all-at-once systematic network providing complete control and manipulation. The human is provoked to enter and is then entrapped by the Enframing, where acts of freedom are modified by the techniques of communication and become incorporated into the network. The linguistic act of creative metaphor is brought into the digital system of information processing and is managed within the format of digital communications. Such is the case, briefly, which Heidegger's thinking might make concerning the specific technology of word processing.

Some evident features of the new technology, however, give us pause in applying this particular wholesale assessment to word processing. If we look for the dimming of metaphor in general—as opposed to specific individual acts of creative speech—the computer industry itself seems to be a rich source of creative energy and originary naming. While still centered around the hardware and software of technology (themselves new verbal creations), the terminology of computers is rife with new meanings—or, better, with old meanings half-transposed and half-invented. The new technological poetry is the alien tongue that the newcomer must appropriate—perhaps more an active, spoken vocabulary than would be suggested by that vague phrase *computer literacy*, which confusedly applies an earlier model of understanding to the current transition. The world of computer involvement is first a language in which things can appear. These things, or new realities, include automatic reformatting, block operation, centering, cursor movement, file management, menu-driven programs, on-screen pagination, soft hyphenation, split screen, widow and orphan control, on-line database searches, electronic shopping, peripherals, interface. These new linguistic acts become customized as the programs and software become comfortable to the particular user. The ambiguity inherent in natural language makes possible words both sufficiently reminiscent of past usages and semantically precise enough to indicate the new, and then the alien new becomes the familiar. The process we observe today can be expressed in Heidegger's terms as follows: the Enframing itself emerges in a vocabulary of new metaphors.

The inventors of this new language do, in fact, sometimes regard their work as a kind of poetry.[20] Within the technology itself arises a new language of metaphor. That language is, nevertheless, one which is always on the verge of becoming a new brand name or solid product which comes to dominate and control acts of creation. What was innovative freedom experienced in a new name becomes the tag for a fixed commodity. The commodity deprives the environment of personal poetry and signals an end to creative response. And as the user learns the new system, the language installs the user in the system. The system offers powerful possibilities. But those possibilities are purchased by placing creativity into the system as input or as a software peripheral to the system. As writing becomes a kind of software, or system-oriented information, the human free act becomes peripheral to the system.

These remarks might seem to be true of any writing system or of any technology, perhaps even true of language if we regard language as a technology. But Heidegger's philosophy of historical drift maintains that only in modern rationality does the systematization become itself systematic. It becomes so systematic, in fact, that no longer is there any notice of the systematization as one procedure among others. Nevertheless, it does seem that the new technology has opened up new kinds of responsiveness and metaphorical activity in the human interface with computer writing, and it may well continue to do so.[21] That, for example, humans now frequently refer to "programming the mind" should not obscure the fact that making metaphors—including and especially metaphors that refer to ourselves—by using the language of computer technology is an act of creative appropriation.

The human peripheral, then, clearly comes forth into its own with the use of metaphors. And metaphor is an act of freedom (seeing something new) which is directly related to saying in Heidegger's sense of dwelling poetically, articulating the world around us as our own. The Enframing is a blend of enframing network and of artistic creativity. But only at the interface of human and computer does this ambiguous quality of the Enframing become evident as a phenomenon for description and evaluation. The metaphor itself may or may not persist as freely responsive act; it easily degenerates into finished things or objects of reference. By focusing on the phenomenon, we can preserve the ancient connotations of the meaning of *interface*. In ancient Greek, *interface (prosopon)* means literally a face that is facing, or toward, another face; it refers to a living mutual relationship that is itself a third state of being. The ancient word was a source of religious awe and mystical meaning in the description of the nature of a Trinitarian Godhead in which the Father and the Son subsisted together in the interface; the ancient religious word described a relationship between time and eternity. Interface, employed in the environment of computer writing, is the technical name for the physical connection and electronic circuits that connect the computer to a peripheral; in this context, adapter is another name for interface.[22]

The metaphor of interface may be more appropriate for the investigation of digitized writing than the notion of the Enframing, for there is a factor of free creativity not accounted for in the holistic notion of the Enframing. Interface is the space in which a phenomenon appears. Our attention is called—by this metaphor interface—to the place of human responsiveness where man and machine meet. That place is the realm of the phenomenon, in this case, the phenomenon of word processing.

For the total Enframing, nothing can arise as a phenomenon to be investigated. Human responsiveness and reflection on the technological interface is precluded by the analysis of technological Enframing. The phenomenon of word processing would be obscured by an exclusive analysis based on the Enframing, for the peculiarly human peripheral vanishes in that analysis. Nonetheless, Heidegger's philosophy of the finitude of existential worlds does serve to correct the optimism of the transformation theory by suggesting that writing skills may possibly become peripheral to the computer network; the existential analysis of the Enframing, at the very least, suggests the adaptation of human skills to the new writing technology. The adaptation will be described in the next two chapters as a trade-off in psychic framework of human thought.

The existentialist observations on the corresponding modifications of human language through technological Enframement do provide several important clues by which to guide our reflections on the interface in which we work. These include the connection between the origination of reality apprehensions and language skills, the temporal disposition (mood) of reality apprehensions, the typification inherent in modern technology, the tendency to interpret all writing under the rubric of information management.

PART TWO

DESCRIBING THE PHENOMENON

Chapter Four

The Psychic Framework of Word Processing

How do I know what I think until I see what I say?
—E. M. Forster

Psyche is ever in motion and continually moves itself.
—Plato, *Phaedrus*

Thought flows. This Heraclitean truism invariably becomes the first vivid impression for the beginner on a word processor—at least after mastering the initial procedures. The ostensibly fluid, liquid, and dynamic movement of digital writing establishes for the first time the central import of the element—as opposed to the medium—in which we formulate thought in symbols. The experience of the element of symbolic fluidity calls for a texture of new terms by which to address the phenomenon of writing in general. The terms for rendering it must bring the phenomenon forth in all its dynamic fluidity. Rather than analyze symbolization through the notions of form and content, message and medium, tool and communication, we must look now at the kind of element in which symbolic life is nurtured. At the same time, the articulation of the full phenomenon must also offer directions for evaluation, both positive and negative.

Once we grant the plausibility of the transformation theory— that basic intellectual changes accompany widespread innovation in symbol manipulation—and once we concur with existential analysis that human existence today is enframed in a fundamental way by technology, then our questioning presses to: How do we describe what actually changes in the transformation? What is it that we can examine consistently and fruitfully which will allow us to perceive the unique challenges to reality apprehensions that are raised by word processing? No matter what answer we reach for straightaway, the terms by which we formulate the answer hold in themselves the potential richness of the subsequent investigation. The description of what it is that changes will inevitably determine the mode and character of any later evaluation. To put the query in a less misleading way—because less suggestive of ontological assumptions postulating a world of things (individual substances) and stable objects: On what level of analysis shall we look for the transformations, on the level of biology, neurophysiology, or perhaps psychology? Or is there a still more fundamental level of description? How do we come to terms with the phenomenon?

The terms in which we articulate the phenomenon—inasmuch as there is truth to what we say—must belong to the phenomenon itself. Yet to state the truth, to find appropriate terms, is not easy. Simply to fetch from one of the sciences a ready-made terminology falls beneath the effort to disclose the phenomenon in its unprecedented novelty. The way technology enframes us affects our analysis of it, as it affects all reality apprehensions. At the same time, reciprocally, the way technology enframes also depends on the way we construe our interface with it. So everything depends on the manner in which we begin to speak of the interface as we interact with it. The heart of this book, in fact, has to do with the way we show our care for the symbols through which we formulate the realities we apprehend. That care, as we shall see in later chapters, is currently being transformed by a symbolization far removed from the book culture where we linger at the moment.

Languages of inquiry have been emerging rapidly, evolving directly from studies of the user interface. Today human-factors engineering seeks to approach human-computer interaction from the viewpoint of an engineering science focusing on human access to machines. This scientific inquiry is based on the recognition that systems engineering cannot achieve its proper goals without considering nonmechanical, nonprogrammable dimensions of system control. Engineering too has begun to understand itself as a study of the interface where human and digital computer amplify intelligence. The new human-factors research is concerned primarily with the confluence of human and system. Yet a hardware approach that takes into account the human factor remains at bottom a hardware approach, still a kind of calculation that factors in the input of the human user.

In his history of the development of the personal computer, for instance, Howard Rheingold frequently uses hardware language, not only in citing others in the computer design community but as part of his own terms of comprehension:

> Human information processors have a very small short-term memory, however, which means that while all computers and no humans can extract the square roots of thousand-digit numbers in less than a second, no computers and all humans can recognize a familiar face in a crowd. By connecting part of the computer's internal processes to a visible symbolic representation, *bit-mapping puts the most sophisticated part of the human information* processor in closer contact with the most sophisticated part of the mechanical information processor.... Creating new kinds of computer input and output devices to help human pattern recognition mesh with mechanical symbol manipulation is known as 'designing the human interface.'[1]

Here eyesight, or optical sensation, becomes, in Rheingold's terms, "the most sophisticated part of the human information processor." This is a representative instance of what Hubert Dreyfus, some years ago, warned against:

> Usually no argument is given for this new dogma that man is an information-processing system functioning like a heuristically programmed digital computer. It seems rather to be an unquestioned axiom underlying otherwise careful and critical analysis. There is no doubt some temptation to suppose that

since the brain is a physical thing and can be metaphorically described as 'processing information,' there must be an information-processing level, a sort of flow chart of its operations, in which its information-processing activity can be described.... Although psychologists describe that function called the mind as 'processing information,' this does not mean that it actually processes information in the modern technical sense, nor that it functions like a digital computer, that is, that it has a program.[2]

There exist dimensions of the interface that remain unapproachable through the procedures of engineering. As long as the human is conceived as peripheral, without psychic depth, human-factors engineering must necessarily bypass the problem of the interface. By trying to close as smoothly as possible the gap between human and programmed system, human-factors engineering preemptively designs interfaces where thoughtless peripherals can be plugged, like smart modems, into the system. Such a science cannot afford us the proper terms for word processing.

The terms we use to describe the phenomenon of writing-and-thinking on the computer will set up the way in which the phenomenon becomes visible. Our initial approach, since chapter 2, has been guided by the transformation theory. What terms does the transformation theory provide for grasping the phenomenon?

It should be first noted that the transformation theory employs no single consistent terminology. There is operative in it, however, a distinctive set of implicit philosophical assumptions, as we have seen in chapter 2. Each set of terms we might use brings with it peculiar problems of its own, problems that arise as the full implications of the terms, and their connection with other terms, unfold. The full meaning of the terms is implicit if thought is indeed connected intimately with language and if language in turn allows us access to the emergence from chaos of finite but definite things. "Poetry and philosophy," Heidegger maintained, "dwell on neighboring mountaintops." Both poetry and philosophy operate at a remove from daily life in that both work solely with the disclosure of things in natural language. For philosophy, moreover, language consists of terms and their consistently formulated connections. To seek to make connections fully explicit and coherent is the fate of philosophy, making it stand alone and apart.

With changes in writing techniques, as the transformation theory sometimes puts it, "consciousness is restructured."[3] The term *consciousness* resonates with the social-political philosophy of Hegel and his followers, as discussed in chapter 2. The notion of consciousness-raising becomes particularly strong in the modern period. In modernity the assumption is frequently made that society is constituted by a unitary universal reason, a social rationality evolving slowly through struggle and conflict. Through a struggle between diverse interests, ever greater freedom is generated—which freedom is usually interpreted as doing what is necessary under universal reason or, as in Marx, under the ethical-material imperative of a classless society. The strife of history, it is argued, brings about an expansion of consciousness whereby the interests of individuals are realized harmoniously. Precisely how are we to understand this consciousness? Is it an awareness accessible to the individual or is it available primarily to those who understand best and who then interpret to others the dictates of universal reason? Clearly, there are serious implications for any philosophy based on the ambiguity of the word *consciousness*. The transformation theory does not pursue the tangled set of meanings sufficiently to uncover the complex problems hidden behind the term.

The term *consciousness*, because of its philosophical-historical connections with social theory, also seems to suggest that symbolic environments can be most properly understood to be forms of media or communications. Writing understood as a social medium for information storage and retrieval is a limited interpretation of symbolic environments. It is an interpretation with roots in classical rhetoric, the study of public speaking or communication.

Against this narrow perspective on symbolic environments I earlier posed the notion of the element in which symbols persist. A medium denotes the tool for transferring symbols from point A to B, that is, the flow of information. The element—while not completely separate from the media—is not a tool for symbolization but the significant backdrop or horizon in which symbols move. The element of symbols is a certain aspect of their mediation of thought. *Medium* emphasizes the instrumental method for communicative interchange. *Element* emphasizes the conditions of symbolic experience and the implications of the mode in which things are represented.

Further, in the transformation theory the emphasis is on storage and retrieval. *Storage* is, of course, derived from the classical rhetorical concern with memory, or *ars memoriae*, which, in the transformation theory, becomes the retrieval of information for purposes of social communication and group survival. The transformation theory conceives the development of the human species as evolutionary. There is progressive evolution in the development of cultural-intellectual skills, and the progression in the development of skills is based on different modes of memory. Information is the underlying conception for this view of memory. The different modes of storing and retrieving information are indices for understanding a given cultural era. To be sure, classical rhetorical theory was far from understanding articulate knowledge as information, but the transformation theory updates classical rhetoric by inserting *information* where, say, Cicero might have said *sapientia*, or "wisdom."

The term *element*, as in electronic element, becomes clear only with computerized writing. The term brings out a different aspect of symbolic environments than does the mnemonic-communicative term *medium*. Only with digital writing does the interactive nature of the writing format and of the thought-symbol process become evident. Again, we want *symbolic element* to remain neutral with regard to the supposedly social purposes of writing and symbolizing. While the contemporary element is in general one which highlights the role of knowledge as information, the element must remain neutral so that the peculiarity of the contemporary element can be made to stand out.

Ong puts primary emphasis on the emergence of literacy from orality; his consequent attribution of more naturalness to public speaking tends to diminish the importance of the transition from the older writing element (chirography) to the electronic element. This can be detected in Ong's tendency to think about computerization of writing as a new transformation of literacy rather than as a shift in the element of thought and formulation. His occasional remarks about the impact of computerized writing are based on an analogy with the kind of impact literacy once had on thought.[4] The analogy dominates the transformation theory and shows a fundamental alliance with the classical rhetorical tradition. The latter emphasizes public speaking and the place writing has in developing the skills and mnemonic power for the purposes of public speaking.

Insofar as the term *consciousness* implies and reinforces the context where language is connected with social communication, it will not further our exploration of the new writing environment. Social interaction fails to bring out the ontological dimension of writing in different elements. The field of reality opened up by different symbolic elements is not merely governed by human needs and human purposes; it is the world itself, along with its human needs and purposes that is apprehended in different elements. It is this ontological dimension which must be brought out if we are to see how the world itself—and not just human interaction—is opened up through a certain symbolic element. The importance of the symbolic element itself, apart from social interactions, becomes especially clear when we consider the aims of the software and hardware designers who originally planned the new element. Their designs were surely intended to do more than create a new medium for communication, even though they may—

with a lack of philosophical precision—speak of designing a medium. In his history of computer development, Howard Rheingold recalls:

> [Alan] Kay began to understand that what he wanted to create was an entirely new *medium*—a medium that would be fundamentally different from all the previous static media of history. This was going to be the first *dynamic* medium—a means of representing, communicating, and animating thoughts, dreams, and fantasies as well as words, images, and sounds.... Alan wanted to create a medium that was a *fantasy amplifier* as well as an intellectual augmentor.[5]

Here communication is far from being a primary consideration in the design of the writing element. The software and hardware of the new writing technology were not designed so much to be a communication medium as a whole new element for the movement of thought. In the hands of the computer developers, it is as if the transformation theory were not a philosophically interesting thesis but an actual plan of action. It was precisely for the purpose of altering the thought process that the personal computer was developed. And computerized writing was the lever by which thought would change itself—using the computer for "bootstrapping," or self-enhancement.[6]

Another term frequently used by the transformation theory refers to the mental habits affected by changes in writing technologies.[7] The term *mental habits* seems a good one with a certain idiomatic flavor, and it seems to make, quite naturally, a connection between the intellectual aspects of symbolization and the presumably practical aspects of writing. The connection it makes results from its being a hybrid term made up of two terms with distinct histories. *Habit* by itself has specific philosophical roots in moral philosophy and in ethical theory.

The origin of the term in philosophy goes back to Aristotle's *Nicomachean Ethics*, where *habit*, or *hexis*, is used to designate a disposition of the human character. Habit, in the Aristotelian sense, is a proclivity for acting along the lines of certain potentials already developed through training and repeated practice. Character, in the Aristotelian sense, is an actual mode of behavior having an ultimate bearing on the completion or happiness of a human life. The term *habit* brings with it, then, a certain amount of historical baggage full of judgmental connotations with latent references to good and bad, right and wrong proclivities. Aristotle also locates habits in the practical sphere where individual human beings act according to their appetites—even though there are such characteristic dispositions as intellectual habits. The latter, though propensities for theoretical contemplation or scientific study, nevertheless originate in practical behaviorial dispositions which are essentially opaque to theory. Habit, in the traditional sense, is a property of individuals and cannot be attributed to a social body or group disposition. There is, too, since the advent of modern philosophies rejecting Aristotelianism, a consensus that habit is, to a great extent, blind lethargy and ignorant, unreflective repetition of routine behaviors. Habitual behaviors are considered subhuman insofar as they remain uncritical and thoughtless—at least where the honorifically human has come to mean progressively self-aware and able to enhance living with full consciousness.[8] While *habit* does suggest stability or reliability, it also has come to connote a mechanical social regularity without personal intensity.

The difficulties in saying what changes are evident too in the mental aspects of *mental habits.* Under the enduring influence of Descartes, *mind* has been a controlling term in modern philosophy. In the early twentieth century, the term continued to be synonymous with the object of philosophy; epistemology was still the central inquiry of a discipline which once embraced God, man, and world. Mind is the cognitive center of propositional truth or judgmental veracity. As the central locus of truth values, "the" mind is generally conceived to be unchanging, or at least change is considered irrelevant to the cognitive mental nucleus. Gilbert

Ryle's famous attack on "the ghost in the machine" examines the assumptions of this epistemological philosophy.[9] The notion of mind removes thought from the lively, changing, passionate realm of the body. In so doing, the notion enables us to refer to and stabilize an autonomous domain of cultural achievement. The term performs the important function of designating an interiorized state-of-culture. Apart from the transient life of individuals, the state-of-culture is an ideal or model according to which the stream of individuals can be guided, shaped, and given direction. The mind in this sense provides the criteria by which education and the dissemination of knowledge are defined and made possible through the channeling of cultural energies. *Mental* too calls up the disembodied, unalterable, essentially lifeless cognitive subject.[10] *Mental habits*, then, raises problems if we want to describe the mind's characteristic movements through different symbolic elements.

Terms such as *mind* and *intelligence* are frequently used to designate a statically conceived entity or a finalized package of capabilities. The cognitive nucleus of mind is often based on the model of a judgmental agency by which experience is sorted out and evaluated into different levels of propositional truth. The truth value of propositions is effectively either on or off, and the distinguishing mark of this binary intelligence is its disembodied neutrality or impartiality with regard to the process of evaluating experience. The activity of mind which culminates in the determination of true-false values keeps a distance from physical-emotional influence. The mind, unaffected by concrete involvements and by the ambivalence of feelings, passes judgment unswayed by extrinsic irrelevancies like feeling, situation, and context. Such a model draws sharp lines between the activities of intelligence and the sphere of passion and affectivity.

It is not merely in the old faculty psychology where the fixed bundle of human capabilities burdens the term *mind* and *mental*. The early designers of computer software also employed, as we have seen, terms such as *mind augmentation* and *intelligence amplification* to describe some of the applications they were inventing for computerized writing. If any individual can be said to have laid the foundations of word-processing technology from both a conceptual and an experimental standpoint, then Douglas Engelbart is the most likely candidate. Engelbart conceived and designed the first hardware and software for what we now know as word processing. But even Engelbart, in his seminal paper "A Conceptual Framework for the Augmentation of Man's Intellect" refers to human intelligence as the augmentation of "basic human *capabilities.*"[11] Engelbart does, however, emphasize thinking as a functional and organizational activity which can be altered in its "hierarchy of processes," and his central notion of the "Human-Language Artifacts Methodology System" (H-LAM System) bypasses at times the fixity of intelligence. Through the alteration of artifacts or methods on any level of the hierarchy of the thought process, thinking can be augmented, in Engelbart's terms. Because thinking is an organizational process having many different levels, and because the different levels affect the overall results by a kind of synergism, or mutually enhancing coordination, the introduction of high-powered electronic aids on the level of the man-artifact interface increases the human capability for thought.

Still, Engelbart's usage of "mind," "mental mechanisms," and "intelligence" seems frequently to suggest a substrate of static, unchanging human intelligence, an intelligence which, nonetheless, goes through natural and cultural evolutions but whose intrinsic, processlike character remains invariant. Through his intention to expand a given faculty in new ways, Engelbart comes across the "process hierarchies" of human thinking. But, as an inventor, Engelbart seeks to outline a *"conceptual* framework" for the augmentation of man's *intellect.* Once such an invention has been set into place it becomes clear, as we shall see, that there are also *psychic* frameworks at play, and these are held in continual motion.

Other current terms for the mind seem equally inappropriate.

There is the crude phrenology of our time that exploits the notion of a functional difference between right-brain and left-brain activities. Brain research has led to a conceptualization of a connection between hemispheric specialization and creativity; this speculation has provided some new ways of interpreting how *the* mind works. But however fruitful the application of the corpus callosum connections may be in explaining the preponderance of different cultural skills in different contexts, the tendency to take the bicameral brain split literally as a mental dualism leads to a barbarously crude notion of thought. Taken metaphorically and heuristically, the concept of hemispheric specialization can be useful. But, taken literally, these concepts foreshorten reflection on thought processes.

The notion of intellect carries with it connotations of a culturally shared intelligence. The term denotes more than the individual empirical mind, and in this way suggests itself for our purposes. *Intellect* can refer to the set of cognitive skills nurtured in the individual by the culture. Intellect, then, is an achievement of civilization and may enable us to connect modes of writing skills with thought processes and their way of opening to realities. Derived from the Latin *intellectus* (verb: *intelligere*), the word designates a repository of nonsubjective and binding cognitive skill. But the Roman-Latinate aspect of the term lends itself to the suggestion of a substantial thing that simply endures—especially where Intellect gets capitalized and turns into an object to be defended. Intellect can become a mere standard against falling intellectual standards, as it tends to become, for instance, in the terms of Jacques Barzun: "The alphabet is a fundamental form to bear in mind while discussing the decay of Intellect, because intellectual work presupposes the concentration and continuity, the self-awareness and articulate precision, which can only be achieved through some firm record of fluent thought; that is, Intellect presupposes Literacy."[12] Though Barzun is surely on to something here, we cannot properly watch the intellect transformed in the symbolic element of word processing if we first glorify "*the* Intellect" and then take up a stance of anxious defense.

Another term, one used by Ong, has a distinct philosophical origin in contemporary thought. The term *noetic field* is often used in the transformation theory to refer to the locus of the changes effected by new writing technologies. Noetics emerged with the Husserlian Phenomenological movement early in the twentieth century; the Phenomenological movement soon branched out into many domains of culture, affecting even the theater through Sartre and Marcel.[13] Deriving terms from the Greek *noesis*, or act of thought, Phenomenology treated the noesis and the noemata of cognitive activity. The term straddles the spheres of the human knower, complete with subjective qualities, and the objects known by the conscious subject. In other words, *noetic* as an adjective suggests an in-between resulting from the interaction of human subjectivity with the things apprehended by the human subject. As a composite notion, noetic field encompasses the structuring process by which human intentionality is wed to the things that become objects of cognition. The mind with its thoughts and the things in themselves are elements in a larger totality called the life-world. The notion of world, as discussed in the previous chapter, is an existential development of Husserlian noetics.

The term *noetics* is useful for the transformation theory. Because it infers the effects of artifacts on the symbolization process, the transformation theory naturally requires terms for bridging human conscious activities and the physical structures by which consciousness represents the things entertained by consciousness.[14] *Noetic field* is simply a better way to express the phenomena than any talk of *bridging*, since the latter already betrays a severance of human from the work environment and from the physical comportments governing symbolization. The term has been incorporated by computer designers in the form of *synnoetics* to indicate human-computer symbiosis. Louis Fein first used it to project a cooperative interaction of human intellect with automated mechanisms for creating a system whose "mental power" is greater than that of its individual components.

But the term's limitations are considerable. *Noetic* retains its genetic connotations from the original Greek, where its significance is purely cognitive. The nominative root, *nous*, is often translated by "reason." The cognate terms it has spawned contain a range of cognitive meaning. Terms such as *noetic* and *noematic* remain within the realm of consciousness, of knowledge and cognitive objects. The term does not suggest *sub*cognitive modeling which, as we shall see, underlies the symbolization process augmented by computers. Even when noetics is thought to undergo changes with different writing technologies, the term and its derivatives still carry connotations of the static presence of a cognitive subject.

One term that does succeed in avoiding the suggestion of static presence is *psychodynamics*, a term occurring with considerable frequency in Ong's vocabulary. With this word we come upon the phenomenon of word processing. With it we begin to symbolize the symbols that are charged with energy.

The term *psychodynamics* has even greater import than is recognized by the transformation theory. In the language of the transformation theory, psychodynamics is the characteristic movement of the mind as it is shaped by the various personality structures nurtured by orality and literacy, respectively. The psychodynamics of literacy is then defined by contrast with nonliterate, preliterate, oral modes of thought. In either oral or literate mode, human awareness possesses characteristic ways of attending to the ideational process. The transformation theory sees in primary oral cultures a distinctive movement of mind as it proceeds to articulate thought. In the psychodynamics of oral cultures, the transformation theory sees a repetitive, circularly redundant, and conservative movement of mind. It is a movement fully appropriate to the economy of oral cultures. Repetitive recurrence of the same thought—with perhaps minor variations— is not perceived by the preliterate mind to be redundant or repetitive. On the contrary, what is not repetitiously articulated must be either unintelligent or intrinsically mystical. For the economy of oral culture, the repetitive rhythm of thought insures a self-identity or continuity of truth where no such continuity can exist external to vocalized utterances. Central to the verbal economy of oral cultures is a stabilizing sense of eternity.

The transformation theory finds a further peculiarity in the psychodynamics of preliterate culture. In preliterate cultures, utterances tend naturally to be formulaic. In contrast to the analysis typical of literacy, there is in preliterate culture a drive toward the continual subsumption of many concepts under a single formula. When complexity is addressed, the traditional *topoi*, or commonplaces, tend to promote additive and aggregative styles of thought which resist internal articulation in favor of enumerations, listings, and what grammarians customarily label parataxis. In the relatively limited memory systems of orality, thinking that is subordinative, hierarchical, or hypotactic tends either to break down or to appear not at all. Literacy, on the other hand, promotes a sequential and subordinating style, which in turn leads to greater emphasis on analysis and to occasions for presenting complex relations. The consideration of this stylistic characteristic is often foreshortened by the correct but underdeveloped observation that writing promotes linear modes of thought. With the literate mind, the movement of thought becomes characteristically sparse rather than explicitly profuse. There is less dependence on ingrained, preservative memory and more respect for syntactical intelligence. Since the literate mind is freed from short-term memory tasks, there can be a reflective analysis of what is being thought out; the connecting relationships between things can be recognized as concepts and can be explored once the threat of losing forever the thread of thought is removed by the relative permanence of written text. In fact, one might say that only after the psychodynamics of literacy have taken hold can there be anything like a text in the original etymological sense of something whose value lies in being woven together by way of a complex texture of cross-references and systematic consistency. The resources of inscribed thought make possible new extensions of mental activity.

True to its origin in social communication theory, the term *psychodynamics* betrays in its content the contrasting duality of its context. Besides the more directly symbol-related features of psychic life, *psychodynamics* takes on a meaning which includes the structure of personality and interaction on the social plane. Ong includes in his enumeration of psychodynamic contrasts the "agonistic" posturing of oral culture. By this he means the new relationships to family and to self-development brought about by the transformative power of education for literacy. Psychodynamics changes as the individual learns to treat language as manipulable in script and no longer as directly engaging in the sense of what is orally and acoustically immediate and demanding. By "agonistic" Ong means certain deeply combative attitudes that have traditionally been fostered by educational systems established outside the parental home. The agonistic traditions of Western culture Ong connects with psychosocial attitudes toward sexual relations and the structure of the family. All these are seen to be connected with the notion of an intimate mother tongue and the eventual control over the mother tongue through the distancing process of literate symbol manipulation. The individual who learns to read and write undergoes changes in the situational "feel" for existence.[15] There is, too, a homeostatic trend in "primary oral cultures," a drive to harmonize, unify, and centralize. And for the transformation theory it is literate culture, with its potential for individuality, which provides the counterpole to orality and so makes visible the features of orally based culture.

I do not wish to take up the terms of the transformation theory and simply apply them to word processing. It has become increasingly clear that an unmodified transposition of that sort would bring with it an implicit anchorage in the classical rhetorical tradition of communication. Anchored in that tradition, our grasp of the phenomenon would necessarily project a social basis for the transformation of thought through word processing. I want, instead, to explore the ontological dimension of word processing where the mind apprehends reality in the life of symbols. The ontological dimension, though not separate, can be examined apart from the social-historical inquiry as another level of reflection. Since the transformation theory begins, in principle, with the vocalization of language, its understanding of symbolic elements will be bound by the understanding of writing as subvocal utterance and reading as a revocalization, always in reference to sound, hence always referred to socialized communication. This slants the transformation theory toward the natural condition of (Western) written language since only 2 percent of the roughly 3,500 languages spoken today have a literature. (Far Eastern literature enjoys a symbolic element that relies very little on acoustic or phonetic reproduction.) In order to take stock of the shift from written to electronic symbols, we must instead consider the symbolic element in abstraction from physical sounds and actual vocalizations. This level of abstraction is simply more appropriate to the highly developed nature of the phenomenon, though it would not have been possible, of course, at earlier stages of symbolization in Western culture.

Furthermore, because it is anchored in the difference between orality and literacy, the transformation theory is unsuited for extending the investigation of word processing. Constant reference to the emergence of literacy distorts the phenomenon by reducing the emergence of word processing to a new kind of literacy. The use of this metaphor from print culture is understandable when we are confronted by the profound novelty of digital writing. But if we lose sight of the weaknesses of the metaphor, we shall pass right by the phenomenon in our anxiety to treat it easily in a familiar, conventionally manageable way. The weaknesses of metaphors taken from the print world of literacy will be part of the subject of the following chapter.

The transformation theory does, however, offer a valuable key to the phenomenon in the notion of the psyche in the psychodynamics it describes from the viewpoint of social history. We shall take up the term *psyche* to unlock the phenomenon of word processing, but not, of course, from the angle of social history. Psyche is the place where language gives access to the new electric element of our symbolic life.

Psyche is used deliberately because the Greek word avoids misconceptions likely to accompany modern terms like *mind, intellect,* and *thought.* Traditionally, the psyche was the locus of inspiration, of manic drive, of the impulses of thought and emotion. The word *psyche* does not enforce divisions between the mind, the senses, and the emotions. *Psyche* connotes something like a disposition to a certain kind of awareness. It is a soft concept, one more adequate for assimilating the subtler aspects of thinking in and through computer software. If we speak of the organization and engineering of psychic frameworks through word-processing programs, we must be fully aware of the grand scope of the subject matter. We must keep in mind Heraclitus's saying: "You could not discover the boundaries [the *peras*] of psyche, even if you explored every path in order to do so; such is the depth of its meaning [*logos*]."[16] The purely cognitive notions of the conscious mind or intellect reinforce the form-content distinction by which we conventionally determine the same or identical concepts embodied in different media. The metaphysics of form and content is based on the abstractive power by which symbolization first arises. The ubiquitous success of such a metaphysic should not mislead us into reflecting exclusively within its boundaries. Outside the form-content distinction is an all-encompassing notion of psyche. The notion of psyche has been associated, since the ancient Greeks, with the unconscious dynamics of life, with nonmanipulable erotic drive, and with the hidden sources of symbol creation.

In speaking of the phenomenon, what we must consider is psyche—not psyche resting in itself, but psyche as Plato conceived it, as essentially in motion, as life-force. With the systematization inherent in various psychologies, it has become difficult to think of psyche in motion and outside the predefined connections of psychological theory. Psyche in this sense is hardly a familiar concept in contemporary thought, though there has been recent interest in rediscovering psychic processes along the lines of a renovated and revised Jungian psychology.[17] Ironically, it has been primarily the biologists today, such as René Dubos, Lewis Thomas, and Erwin Chargaff, who concern themselves philosophically with the psyche as it inhabits the mechanical interface. Biologists now push to the philosophical edges—no doubt because the violations of the living psyche have become most apparent in their field. In the last decades, biology and psychology have become part of the attempt to use electronic mechanisms to model parts of the nervous system. Inspired by the work of Wiener and others in the interdisciplinary field of cybernetics, biology for some time now has come to use mechanical models of living organisms to help create theoretical models of how organisms function. The main concern too of cognitive psychology has become the discovery of how the brain processes auditory and visual information. It is no wonder then that life-scientists today have become philosophical, having gained so vivid an awareness of the central event of our time: the symbiotic wedding of mind's life with the machine.

Now, according to Plato, the essence of the psyche consists in its being in motion. Plato defines *psyche* as that which moves itself. And this self-movement is born out of the conjunction of two principles: *peras* ("boundary"), or limitation, and *apeiron* ("boundlessness"), or the unlimited. The duality of both these principles is based on a polarity, the polarity between the unmoved One and the flowing continuum. The unchanging *peras*, structure, is associated with the Greek god Apollo, and is thus called the realm of the Apollonian; the principle of the continuum, limitless transience, is the realm of the Dionysian, the god of wine and unrestrained exuberance.[18] The combination of these two polar determinations comes to light clearly in every motion, for every motion is performed in the continuum, and yet it is still a particular motion because it has at the same time a definite order and a measure, or, as the Greeks put it, it has a rhythm. The first principle brings about form, limitation, and unity; the second leads to the dissolution of order, to limitlessness and multiplicity. The free self-movement of the psyche occurs only when both forces are in balance. If they come apart, the psyche is no longer moved by itself but by something else; it is no longer free. This movement is the temporality of experience in its most fundamental sense. Time occurs in the realm of the psyche. The soul, and the body moved by the soul, is therefore the sphere in which time or certain kinds of temporality appear. The problem of human life for Plato is how psychic energy might be directed into the best possible patterns of motion, something which I shall explore in chapter 7, where the critique of word processing takes its bearings from Plato—not the Plato whose *Phaedrus* apparently criticizes writing, but the Plato who helped Socrates turn the human spirit toward the contemplative realm of ideas.

The polarity of psychic motion and the qualitative levels of psyche are the keys for opening the investigation of word processing. When I conceive mind as psyche, I mean the thought-feeling, the life-force that meets and melds with mechanism. We must consider the psyche in motion at the interface. And the interface is more than mechanical: it is a psychic environment. To name this interactive environment I shall employ the term *psychic framework*. The term *framework* also suggests a continuity with the line of thought from the previous chapter; I shall note the ways in which electronic word processing structures the movement of the psyche. Rather than an innocuous neutral term, *framework* will put us on guard for those aspects of our finite situation which enframe the psyche in its current struggle with symbols for representing and conveying our thought life.

The symbolic element includes the physical interface where a psychic framework for symbols is in play. The psychic framework is developed by writing in an element. Intimacy between thought and things evolves within a psychic framework. Psychic frameworks are broader than conceptual frameworks, though the term is intended to suggest an extension of Engelbart's theory of the hierarchical structures at work in the process of thought formulation. Manipulation of symbols, as Engelbart notes, plays a role in the capabilities of thinking. Mathematical thinking, when it took up Arabic numerals, was altered by a removal of the limits inherent in the manipulation of the numerical symbols inherited from the Romans. But psychic frameworks, unlike conceptual frameworks, have intrinsic tempos or rhythms; psychic frameworks are guided by sensory motor skills. Conceptual frameworks establish relationships of deduction and of necessary connection. Psychic frameworks, on the other hand, inject a peculiar tempo to the three components of symbolic elements: manipulation, formulation, and linkage.

Before looking more closely at these three aspects of the electronic element, consider some general examples of what I mean by psychic frameworks. It is not difficult to find examples of the soft changes in psychic frameworks, though it is indeed difficult to put a conceptual finger on the precise changes involved. Suffice it here to point out some transformations which pertain to the subtler aspects of psychic life, without, however, going into the details required by a full investigation. The psychic frameworks of symbolic life are akin to those areas that have traditionally been neglected or even deliberately excluded by Western philosophy. Areas such as atmosphere in a conversation or in a discursive sequence have generally been relegated to the realm of the irrational or at best to literary or poetic interests, hardly worthy of analytical reflection. In the Far East, on the contrary, such categories as atmosphere play an essential role in intellectual evaluation and critique. Only where Western philosophers have begun to take seriously a direct exchange with the East have such psychic notions as atmosphere begun to find a vocabulary in Western language.[19]

But certain changes in psychic frameworks have become increasingly apparent in current Western reflections on culture. There is the encounter of traditional farming with the accelerating technology of the newly computerized agribusiness. Once upon a time, the farmer related in a poetic way to food production; there was a psychic framework that encouraged a sense of living on the soil, of a family bonding with the forces of the earth. The gradual industrialization of farming required the introduction of complex machinery, and this entailed a modification of what it means to live and work on a farm. Finally, there is now the demand for a highly trained industrial farm management team, one that can coordinate computers, satellites, and machinery in such a way as to bring an optimal yield and soil care to the farming industry. The social-economic transformation from family to corporate industry necessitates a shift in psychic framework as much as it requires a shift in investment strategies. Such changes drastically alter the psychic framework where human spirit meets with tool.

But more to the point is the shift in the psychic frameworks of cultural symbolics where, for instance, the power of visual impressions is altered by a new technology. The form-content analysis is inadequate for describing changes in the art-form of the cinema when the new technology of the personal videocassette is introduced. Though it may have the identical content, the film viewed through personal videocassette technology is not really the same film as that projected on the magic of the silver screen. There is a profound change in the experience of the art-form, in the sense of what is being seen, when the projected images are no longer bigger than life and are manipulable through fast-forward, freeze-frame, and every kind of fingertip control. Such viewing is no longer an occasion to which you must adjust your attention. With it, cinema culture comes to be on tap, manipulable at will. The videocassette provides a different psychic framework for the film.

Similarly with the psychic frameworks employed in our appre-

hension of everyday time. There are subliminal but faintly perceptible psychic changes as the technology for apprehending time
undergoes a shift. The most recent evident change has been from
the mechanical to the digital timepiece. The digital clock is a new
symbolic element for symbols of time—though it is not, of course,
interactive like the word processor; and, unlike the word processor,
it is not embedded in the ontological intimacy of thought and
language. The digital display of time effects a different atmosphere
in the apprehension of time. The element of time in which the
symbols are suspended develops certain dispositions to respond to
experience and, over time, develops certain dynamics of thought.

The difference between the new digital readout might be
ascribed to a simple changeover from analog to digital format. Such
a description remains, however, within the confines of hardware
engineering; it does not touch the psychic framework itself within
which there is considerably more at stake than a variant display for
a system of measurement. The psychic framework enframes a
different phenomenon of time itself or of temporality (experienced
time). The phenomenological interface of the digital timepiece
evokes a different dynamic pace than that of the mechanical watch.
The mechanical watch, with its actual physical motion of hands
through space, mimics the movement of bodies through an absolute
(Newtonian) space, with its secure up-down and right-left. The
digital watch, on the contrary, opens up an electronic element in
which we read our personal time on a discrete, information
interface; time is read out as information; it is not measured (as
phenomenon) in the continuity of movement. The mechanical
interface, by contrast, shows the visible movement through space
and thereby sets up expectations and an awareness of time as a
continuous backdrop of personal action. Such a psychic framework
can enhance personal action by providing a backdrop that is also
dramatic. This sense of continuous backdrop is minimized by the
digital readout. Read as information, time can be personally
appropriated on a subliminal level as less oppressively physical.

Further illustrations of psychic frameworks for symbolizing

time can be found throughout imaginative literature, for psychic frameworks etch themselves into the human imagination. Literature, the special domain of prescientific, prereflective imagination, offers many nice illustrations of the meaning of psychic frameworks using the example of interfaces for symbolizing time, transience, and temporality. One such illustration can be found in the form of exaggerated, hallucinatory magnifications of the mechanical framework of time in the writings of Edgar Allan Poe. His stories contain many instances of a reflection on the oppressiveness of time as experienced in the framework of mechanical clocks.

In Poe's nightmarish story "A Predicament" the hands of the clock in a Gothic church steeple literally cross one another slowly to decapitate the protagonist. Madness in its hysteria presents a truth that everyday sanity can but glimpse peripherally and then only cautiously and momentarily. The slightly deranged psyche of the protagonist seems to dream truths unmentionable by the reasonable mind. Nightmare has its basis in real anxiety:

> I observed that the aperture through which I had thrust my head was an opening in the dial-plate of a gigantic clock....I observed the immense size of the clock hands, the longest of which could not have been less than ten feet in length, and where broadest, eight or nine inches in breadth. They were of solid steel apparently, and their edges appeared to be sharp....As I was deeply absorbed by the heavenly scenery beneath me, I was startled by something very cold which pressed with a gentle pressure on the back of my neck. It is needless to say that I felt inexpressibly alarmed. There was no chance of forcing my head through the mouth of that terrible trap in which it was so fairly caught, and which grew narrower and narrower....I threw up my hands and endeavored, with all my strength, to force upward the ponderous iron bar. I might as well have tried to lift the cathe-

dral itself. Down, down, down it came, closer and yet
closer.... The ponderous and terrific *Scythe of Time* (for I
now discovered the literal import of that classical phrase)
had not stopped, nor was it likely to stop, in its career. Down
and still down, it came. It had already buried its sharp edge a
full inch in my flesh, and my sensations grew indistinct and
confused.[20]

Another hallucination of mechanical time occurs with the
"gigantic clock of ebony" in "The Masque of the Red Death," where
the ominous regularity supplants the dance music that is a
spontaneous, nonmechanical, expressive temporality:

Its pendulum swung to and fro with a dull, heavy, monoto-
nous clang; and when the minute-hand made the circuit of
the face, and the hour was to be stricken, there came from
the brazen lungs of the clock a sound which was clear and
loud and deep and exceedingly musical, but of so peculiar a
note and emphasis that, at each lapse of an hour, the musicians of the orchestra were constrained to pause, momentarily, in their performance, to harken to the sound; and thus
the waltzers perforce ceased their evolutions; and there was a
brief disconcert of the whole gay company; and, while the
chimes of the clock yet rang, it was observed that the
giddiest grew pale, and the more aged and sedate passed
their hands over their brows as if in confused revery or
meditation. But when the echoes had fully ceased, a light
laughter at once pervaded the assembly; the musicians looked
at each other and smiled as if at their own nervousness and
folly, and made whispering vows, each to the other, that the
next chiming of the clock should produce in them no similar
emotion; and then, after the lapse of sixty minutes (which
embrace three thousand and six hundred seconds of the Time
that flies), there came yet another chiming of the clock, and
then were the same disconcert and tremulousness and mediation as before.[21]

The rationality of conventional procedures and actions would seem for the most part to suppress explicit awareness of psychic frameworks: "The musicians looked at each other and smiled as if at their own nervousness and folly, and made whispering vows, each to the other, that the next chiming of the clock should produce in them no similar emotion." There is a difference between the rational explicitness of conceptual frameworks and the more subtle contours of psychic frameworks. Many hierarchies enter into the process of our discourse. There are levels, for example, operating on implicit subcodes of grammar and syntax, implicit because they function at a level we are not directly aware of. While we can be aware of the organized structure as a final result, the organizing itself is never experienced; about its actual modus operandi we can only speculate.[22] And the psychic framework is implicit at an even deeper level because it is more holistic, pervading all aspects of symbolic element.

These two samples from Poe show time apprehended in a distinctive symbolic environment. Though Poe's imaginative envisioning lives on exaggeration, the inexplicit becomes conspicuous, the mechanical interface of time being the necessary presupposition for such an apprehension and for such apprehensiveness. The pose of madness provides occasion for noticing what the daily apprehension goes right by. Our daily apprehension is inclined to treat the symbolic as a mere gauge of time, as a measure for something essentially external to the symbolic environment that shows us what time it is. Poe's mad magnification reveals the psychic quality of the interface.

While the psychic framework of time is a subtle, hard-to-reach corner of symbolic elements, the framework of writing, though elusive, does not so easily go unnoticed. For centuries, and in different cultural contexts, there has been careful cultivation and study of the psychic frameworks of written linguistic symbols. The motion or tempo peculiar to a given psychic framework can be studied for its own sake without reference to the use or purposes to which symbols are put or without reference to method or operational genesis. Such studies with regard to linguistic symbols have been done both in the Far East and in the Western hemisphere. In the East, calligraphy is inextricably bound up with writing, so that psychic motion is intrinsic to the subject matter of the written symbols. Japanese *sumie* painting, for example, is as much about the atmosphere experienced by the author and conveyed in the brush strokes as it is about the words themselves. In the ideographs of Chinese Ch'an drawings, the tip of the ink-dipped brush meeting the tissue-thin absorbent rice paper is an interface where the word and inner psychic motions are profoundly wedded to the point of being indistinguishable; such written symbols are not referred to sound or vocalization for their meaning. The traditions of writing in the Orient perpetuate such an interface by linking meditation with the movements of penmanship. From the Western point of view, this stance toward the written word makes every literate person necessarily a poet. In fact, however, our compartmentalization of the psychic realm may be due to the development of the metaphysics of type and the push toward the standardization and reproducibility of symbols.

In the Western hemisphere, a parallel exploration of psychic motion exists in what is known as graphology. The term itself means the logos of writing (Greek: *graphein*). Graphology has, however, concerned itself mostly with conjectural inferences about personality. It derives its conjectures from an analysis of the motion inscribed in written words. But because of its pretense to objective inferences and because of its penchant for subsuming individual samples under nomothetic generalizations, graphology typically blends the scientific with the spurious, or at least with the dubious. It is difficult for Western intellectual endeavors to maintain discipline and controlled insight without aspiring to strict, scientific systems which produce universal laws, like physics. The Western tendency is to objectify the subject matter as a hard and fast, even physical, thing, to seek out ways of measuring and classifying, and then to establish general laws that can be applied in a quasi-automatic fashion. Graphology assumes too that linguistic symbols are to be seen through, as transparent to ideational content. Like the everyday sense of the timepiece, graphology often approaches written symbols as an external gauge, in this case as a gauge of subjective personality factors. Still, however marred the path of graphology, its very existence, in both scientific and intuitive forms, indicates a recognition that psychic frameworks are to be found in the element of writing. Graphology finds in the element of handwriting something of the psychic motion inherent in thinking with linguistic symbols.

Graphology, calligraphy, the psychic framework of timepieces are guideposts to the psychic framework of word processing. They indicate no more than the direction our inquiry must go. *Psyche*, then, is our first term for word processing. It attempts to state the movement, the Heraclitean flow of the phenomenon. *Framework* is conjoined with psyche to indicate the technological enframing of language.

The Three Parts of the Phenomenon: Manipulation, Formulation, and Linkage

But *framework* should not be conceived in purely negative terms. As mentioned earlier, Engelbart's "Conceptual Framework for the Augmentation of Man's Intellect" provided the theoretical-practical basis for word processing, or more properly idea processing. While presented as a working paper for envisioning hardware and software development, Engelbart's theory offered a general framework for *conceptualizing* word processing. His framework is conceptual in that it attempts to stand outside the phenomenon in order to describe it constructively and ground it theoretically— even though his statements insist that they be understood provisionally. Engelbart's description is provisional because his statements maintain a deliberate openness to experiments with new and different setups for organizing symbols. As a conceptual framework, Engelbart's theory stands provisionally outside the phenomenon in order to grasp it.

Psychic frameworks, by contrast, can claim lesser theoretical distance. The psyche's unfathomable depths afford us analyses which can only open up further inquiry into the phenomenon. Analyses of this type do not establish the clarity and control of conceptual frameworks which first prescribe, prior to any interaction, the very terms and structures within which the phenomenon may emerge and by which the terms may come to modify themselves. The analysis of psychic frameworks has more to do with a new kind of criticism than it does with conceptual generalizations for their own sake. And there is need for a new kind of software criticism that goes beyond templates, keystroke counts, and questions of compatibility.

What makes the terms of Engelbart's theory highly appropriate is the conceptualization of what he insists on calling "structuring." The verbal form of his terminology dovetails with the phenomenon of word processing—though the latter term had not yet come into usage at the time of Engelbart's "A Conceptual Framework." Structuring is the axis of what Engelbart conceives to be the interface of human thought and symbol-enhancing machine, and he sees three divisions in the structuring that goes on in the human-artifact interface: mental, conceptual, and symbolic structuring. Mental structuring is the "internal organization of conscious and unconscious mental images, associations, or concepts which somehow manage to provide the human with understanding and the basis for judgment, intuition, inference, and meaningful action with respect to his environment."[23] Concept structuring is the further defining of mental structures that are "structurable in that a new concept can be composed of an organization of established concepts." In other words, the concept is a more sharply defined mental structure that can be internested and rearranged with other concepts in such a way that new concepts arise. Finally, symbol structuring is the flexibility to use "language by means of phrases, sentences, paragraphs, monographs, or charts, lists, diagrams, and tables for representing concepts." All these forms of structuring Engelbart conceives as being in continual process, and as a "hierarchical repertory of capabilities" in which changes of efficiency or efficacy in one capability entail changes in other parts of the hierarchy.

The structure of the psychic framework of word processing also has a tripartite division. The three subprocesses of the psychic framework of word processing we find in the phenomenon are manipulation, formulation, and linkage. These three are also connected and affect one another reciprocally. They appear as aspects of the electronic element of word processing and constitute the peculiar psychic motion of digital writing. Manipulation is the arranging of symbolic domains, and with computers it appears in the automation of writing and of accessing texts; the tempo and motion peculiar to this kind of manipulation can lead to the stress of enframed productivity. Formulation is the way thought attains focus and integrity in a symbolic environment, the way the writing instrument fosters a certain presence of mind; the mental form developed by computerized writing in the formulation of thought is characteristically dominated by information. Linkage is the psychic environment created by the networking of all symbolic life in a homogeneous information system; the linkage of computerized writing leads to a kind of psychic proximity that can endanger the privacy and the intimacy of thought. These three aspects of the psychic framework of writing will unfold in my description of the phenomenon of word processing.

Chapter Five

The Phenomenon of Word Processing

The screen is like a lens that moves at random over a text but is unable to apprehend the entire thing—like the Hindu allegory about the blind men who investigated an elephant and gave totally different descriptions: none of them saw God whole.[1]
—Remark by a computer user

How do you gain access to the new phenomenon on first encounter? Through a new language, of course. You learn to address yourself to unheard of entities. You learn to speak of files that possess no apparent physical dimensions, menus offering a selection of nonedibles, and monitors that provide a certain vigilance over your own words. You learn to navigate with wraparound and with a cursor—which some would more appropriately dub cursee as it becomes the recipient of their profanities. You may even learn the rudiments of RAM and ROM memory, mouse compatibility, and the ASCII code. At the very least, you must address yourself to floppies and to windows, to function keys and program documentation (read: instruction manual). As you write, you learn to edit simultaneously: you learn to address yourself to block moves, hyphenation zones, and soft spaces versus hard spaces. The vocabulary of the editor's cut and paste, which manipulates print on paper, becomes your own in electronic form. You learn not only to delete but also to unerase. Then to search and replace, and onward to globally search and replace. Automatic formatting and reformatting enter the daily routine of writing.

As you learn your way around the System, you come to feel literate in a new way—or, at least, so others would put it when, after a frenzy of frustration lasting anywhere from several weeks to several months (depending on your patience), you acquire enough skill to use word processing in your daily writing. *Computer literacy* is the terminology some people, especially educators, use when they want to indicate that something important is learned in the human-computer interface. The notion of computer literacy is no more than an awkward attempt, by borrowing a notion from another symbolic element, to bring computers rightfully within the purview of schools and scholarly consideration. Yet much of the new knowledge amounts to little more than the savvy required of a user when the device used is still in a primitive stage of development. The personal computer in the 1980s is still a very crude facsimile of a useful device, something like the Model T Ford with its hand-cranked starter and its user-coaxed engine.

Nonetheless, a certain self-masking is intrinsic to the phenomenon of word processing. It is more a built-in dissemblance feature than something which will pass away with the acquisition of skills and with advances in technology. The built-in dissemblance makes the phenomenon more elusive than other symbolic elements for writing. For dissemblance, or self-concealing, belongs to the phenomenon of word processing itself. To recognize the inherent self-masking feature of word processing is to begin the description.

Masking takes place in two ways. First, the very nature of our mode of apprehending the radically new masks its break with previous expectations. We necessarily grasp the new through metaphor, as was noted at the end of chapter 3. Human ingenuity taps intuitions we have already assimilated from our exposure to other procedures. Metaphors indicate newly emergent interpretations of existence; they are acts of freedom which also correspond to the demands of new situations.[2] By applying metaphors to what is new, through an act of human *ingenium*, we become one with the new, involved in it, and we exercise a finite freedom, a limited infinity, in that we have addressed, in a specific and irrevocable way, a process of continual unfolding. Our freedom is tied to previous practices, yet tied only in order to be loosened and projected anew. The electronic environment re-calls the older print technology by invoking its language. We assimilate the new electronic element of language through the older technology of print-on-paper writing, and even through technologies far older than print. This falls under the general cultural imperative to understand things by interpreting them; cultural life is inherently hermeneutical, a process of renewed interpretation.

When the new language teaches us to scroll through the text we write, then we are addressing the new by way of the ancient. Scrolls, unlike book pages, are continuous texts and are therefore addressed as an unfolding whole. Yet the nature of the electronic whole does not at all unfold the way a papyrus scroll unrolls. Here's how the *WordStar* manual describes horizontal scrolling: "The screen acts like a window to your document. The window, or screen, moves over the document to give you a full view of documents wider than 80 columns."[3] *Window, page,* and *scrolling* serve to get some hold on the radically new by using the handles of the familiar and even of the long past. This way of access, however, hides the calculational capacity of computers which makes it possible to assign pages to the text in an infinite variety of formats, before or during printout. And, of course, this way of access, through pagination, also seems to suggest that digital writing remains a permanent servant or tool for the purposes of print culture.

While different possibilities are opened up by the new element, our first grasp on it begins by covering up whatever goes beyond the familiar. What we highlight through metaphor simultaneously hides what we perceive in the phenomenon. This is clear today in the infant stages of the computer revolution when very few working writers actually think of their words as residing on magnetic media in digital format. Most still continue to print out their work at all stages of composition, save hard copy drafts, and even do revisions on the hard copy and transcribe them back to the computer.

Scrolling text on a computer screen differs from reading through a stack of manuscript pages as greatly as watching television differs from reading a book. You cannot juxtapose two finished pages and read them together when you are working with screen copy. A long manuscript is indeed a kind of video papyrus where a feel for the distinct steps and linear stages of thought is, of necessity, minimized. Certainly the sense of finalized sections is marginal as the transfer of portions (blocks) is always inviting. Automation of the writing element enhances the sense of unified document, in which you can, at will, search and replace any expression throughout the entire manuscript, regardless of what the written expression may denote. When a document is visualized as an entirety, you think of it as a single unit and can shift material back and forth without hesitation. As you become accustomed to the digital text, you grow inevitably impatient when trying to look up by hand certain passages in a printed book; it is so much more convenient to invoke automated searches when seeking out passages in digital text. The metaphor of scrolling takes us back centuries while propelling thought into wholly new relationships to language.

The metaphors for word processing are mixed and become explicitly, awkwardly, "ways of speaking": "The cursor is the blinking square or underline on the screen. The position of the cursor marks the 'point of action' where text or commands are entered or deleted. The shape of the cursor is a square in Insert Mode and an underline in Overstrike Mode."[4] The universal complaint about bad documentation for computer programs belies the struggle inherent in the articulation of the unprecedented, and the very fact of the user having to consult documentation—instead of, say, an instruction manual—indicates the novelty of the situation: the electronic element is the marriage of writing symbols and scientific technology. The old language breaks down before the direct experience of the new; playing around with the writing element supersedes speech about it—for a time, at least. And thus the profound truth contained in the simple advice of one pithy piece of computer documentation: "This is one of those computer gizmos that's easier to use than it is to explain. Just play with Up and Down; you'll get the idea."[5] The event of a new sense of reality calls forth the primary human learning response: play. Play belongs intrinsically to ontological discovery, to the defining of realities emergent from chaos, to the finesse of free discovery contained within the limiting constraints of our world, as we saw in chapter 1.

A second way in which the phenomenon is intrinsically self-masking is inherent in the nature of the technological framework itself. The intelligibility of, say, electrical light switches is both accessible (because we know it is man-made) and inaccessible (because it is connected to a highly complex electronic infrastructure). The automobile provides limited access to its operations, as does the airplane. But as the latter devices become computerized, they too will offer increasingly masked intelligibility and even more limited access to underlying operations. There will be fewer up-front gauges that encourage human assessment of what is happening, and they will invite a lesser degree of human intervention. Computational systems represent the apotheosis of automation insofar as decision making becomes converted to digital format. John Seely-Brown has called the inherent self-concealment of computational systems the "system opacity."[6]

System opacity is the fundamental disparity between the user and the engineered setup of the interface. No matter how much human skill becomes accommodated to word processing, the phenomenon will always remain partially hidden. Dissimulation is internal to the phenomenon because informational systems, unlike mechanical systems in general, are largely opaque, their function not being inferable from the underlying, chiefly invisible substructure. The types of physical cues that naturally help a user make sense out of mechanical movements and mechanical connections are simply not available in the electronic element. There are far more clues to the underlying structural processes for the person riding a bicycle than there are for the person writing on a computer screen. Physical signs of the ongoing process, the way the responses of the person are integrated into the operation of the system, the source of occasional blunders and delays, all these are hidden beneath the surface of the activity of digital writing. No pulleys, springs, wheels, or levers are visible; no moving carriage returns indicate what the user's action is accomplishing and how that action is related to the end product; and there is no bottle of white-out paint complete with miniature touch-up brush to betoken the industrial chore of correcting errors by imposing one material substance over another. The writer has no choice but to remain on the surface of the system underpinning the symbols. As we shall see when discussing manipulation, there are different levels to which writers can be drawn into the process of automation. But no level offers experiential penetration into the underlying opacity of the system; natural language and thinking in natural language are simply incompatible with the binary digits used on the level of machine-language—as any Assembly-Language programmer can testify.

As programs become powerful enough to exercise something of the discernment needed for automating more and more of the writing task, the system will acquire greater opacity. With present-day software, the writer must absorb acronyms and prompts as they are provided by the writing program: "When you see the familiar mark CM along with PRMPT, you know you're in XyWrite—these two markers are always present in XyWrite. The CM is where you talk to XyWrite, and the PRMPT is where it talks back to you."[7] With the eventual introduction of human voice input and synthesized responses, the above description may become literal: you will address the system and the system will respond to you. The disparity between automated physical symbol and human writing process will grow. In any case, current research on computer interface has shown that it is necessary for the user to develop a mental model or set of inferences concerning the underlying movement of the system.[8] However crude and un-sophisticated it may be, a mental model allows the user to build some basis on which experiences can be collected and from which the user can respond to the interactive processes of automated writing. A metaphor or sense-endowing map of the system is not provided ready-made by the technology, as was frequently the case with mechanical operations. Because of the indefinite number of its operations and because of the flexibility of any given software, the user can never wholly rely on a so-called idiot-proof system; it will always be necessary to manage problems as the system is applied to different tasks in the flow of information in thought and writing.

The human user, then, confronts the opacity of the system by building a set of metaphors for making operational guesses at the underlying structure. These are not, of course, explanations in any strict scientific sense. They provide the basis around which to organize responses for continued interaction with the system. To counter system opacity, the user comes to visualize, on a conscious or subconscious level of awareness, the system as a one or another kind of flow of information. When learning to write on a computer, for instance, you begin to imagine physical storage areas, such as disk drives, ram drives, and read-only memory. In order to save and organize files securely, you learn to conceive of them as physical locations, as imaginative places, however phantomlike they may seem. Otherwise, disaster is near. The most elementary case is the neophyte watching in astonishment as the text disappears when scrolled off the screen; some primitive model of storage begins to replace the first sense of irretrievable loss as the user learns to handle the vanishing writing. Users devise increasingly complex stages of building up a model, as the following example shows.

As I am writing with a word-processing program, I decide that the current additions to a chapter are exploratory and may not be appropriate for the final version. I want to keep going, however, in order to get down the ideas that are occurring to me here and now. I want to use sections of what I have written in an entirely different way and I want to add new ideas to them. The resulting material might be valuable in another context. So, I visualize what is on the screen as a second file, existing apart from the first material I was working on. In order to interact properly with the system to achieve my goals, I must first hit a save button to preserve what I have already written, identify the file I am working on with a new and different name, and then remember to save the second file and retrieve the first when I want to proceed with the chapter. Saving the file means noticing the light on the disk drive go on, hearing the whir of the floppy disk, or seeing the program return a saved message with a storage drive and subdirectory location assigned to the hard drive. If, on trying to save the explorations, the error message "File already exists" comes up, I must have formed something of a model about the way a computer stores information by using a set of unique characters to identify and keep track of a volume of information. If I have developed no such model, it will be a total surprise for me to discover later that there is only one file stored with my chapter on it, and the version I wanted to save is gone, vanished forever. This insight implies no technical knowledge of the File Allocation Table (FAT) or the bits set for file identifiers on the level of machine-language bytes, nor does it require awareness of the tracking system on the disk drive. What I do need is a sense of the unique file identifiers accompanying any block of information to be stored. Otherwise my second-draft explorations might obliterate the more satisfactory version I wanted to keep.[9]

Needless to say, this type of learning is usually of the hardest kind: trial-and-error experiences. Most likely, error and then trial. Being restricted to the surface of technological devices, the user generally develops an operational interpretation of the system's inner workings only after first mistaking the system's procedures. Recovering from errors is the primary resource for learning how to interact with the computer. This gap of necessary misunderstanding highlights the second sense in which the phenomenon of word processing is self-masking.

There is something reassuring, then, about those word-processing programs that emphasize What-You-See-Is-What-You-Get, affectionately called WYSIWYG (wizzywig) by the computer industry. WYSIWYG programs help stabilize—and conceal—the untamed power of digital writing by approximating to a high degree the printing metaphor as it applies to word processing. Such software focuses almost exclusively on the polishing and production of a final document, that is, of a text formatted in pages and then printed on paper. By perfecting the conjunction of computer technology with stand-alone automated printers, programs such as *Multimate*, *WordPerfect*, *XyWrite*, and the older *WordStar* synthesize the metaphor of writing on a computer as writing on a high-tech typewriter.

Before *WordStar* and the later WYSIWYG programs, computer terminals were regarded as "glass teletypes."[10] When you type a page on a typewriter, what you see is what you get. This is not necessarily true in the case of word processing, where a text can be formatted for hard copy in any number of ways. In the electronic element, the computer text in itself is not at all graphically visible to human eyes nor is it essentially inscribed. Text remains resident in computer memory at varying locations and in various degrees of volatility. So-called screen-oriented word-processing programs, such as *Leading Edge* or *Volkswriter Deluxe* or the others just mentioned, go to great lengths to make smooth the transition from computer text to clean, pagelike views of the text on screen so that the real, final, or printed copy mirrors a pagelike text on screen. (Beginners on word processors are troubled by the fact that the viewing area of the monitor cannot accommodate the full size of a printed page.) Some programs, such as *Professional QWERTY*, even attempt to emulate the typewriter with an interface designed to ease the transition from mechanical to electronic elements. Considerable time and skill were needed to develop programs that preserve the correspondence between text in the electric element and the physical end product of the printing process. Not only must correspondence between the radically different elements be internally adjusted by the software, but the commands to the mechanical printer must also be somehow contained (embedded) in the text without actually appearing. Simultaneously, the hidden commands to the mechanical printer must be accessible at all times to the writer of the text. The complexity of such a feat, achieved in varying degrees by currently available software, points to one of the three aspects of the new writing element, its distinctive way of manipulating symbols.

Manipulation of Symbols: Automation

After the first five months, most people who write on computers are enraptured: "This is bliss. Here is true freedom. No more cutting paper and pasting, no more anxiety over revisions. Now I can get to work without the nuisance of typing and re-typing." They feel the thrill of the electric speed of automation applied to the production of printed pages. Yet, in order to achieve such automation, writing has to be removed from the element of inscription and placed in an electronic element. This migration of symbolized thought to the electronic element signals a broader change than merely that of a further phase in the automation of the printing process. Besides a new association of writing with algorithmic modes of thought, there is the automation of older metaphors used for writing. Metaphors are human attempts at consummating a changeover into a different element. The automation of writing has opened new ways of manipulating the symbols of thought.

The integrated circuits and central processing unit of the computer await metaphors, creative human interpretations. It took, for example, a metaphor from routine business practice to propel the personal computer into the marketplace. Before 1979, the business spreadsheet was a necessary but cumbersome tool for analyzing any kind of routine data that can be put in rows and columns. Then Dan Bricklin, Bob Frankston, and Dan Fylstra applied the first electronic spreadsheet, *Visicalc*, to the Apple computer. It became possible to accelerate and streamline the traditional spreadsheet, so that it came to serve a whole range of calculational purposes. The spreadsheet became a program for specific uses in accounting: balance sheets, income statements, profit-and-loss statements; a program for general calculation: regression analysis, correlation, statistical functions; and a specifically business-oriented program: derivation and prediction of salary costs and merit budgets. The result was a new quality level of calculative thinking due to greater functionality and an extraordinary advance in ease of manipulation. With the advent of the electronic spreadsheet, spatial and intuitive thinking could be conjoined again, as they were in the age of the abacus, with calculation.

At the same time, all aspects of life fall increasingly under the imperative for accelerated productivity. The automation of life processes—mechanisms for augmenting or even supplanting biological animation—proceeds to encompass further domains of activity so that life becomes more productive, or at least product oriented. The psychic processes are perhaps the last domain into which automation is proceeding; I referred in chapter 3 to the psychic framework of word processing as a technological enframing of our process of symbolic ideation. And it was suggested in the previous chapter that the original metaphors launching the development of word processing were not taken primarily from the printed page or the book culture. It has been precisely a sense of the constraining limitations of bibliocentric culture that inaugurated the research on word processing.

Still, *word processing* is often taken to mean programs which emulate the functions of the typewriter with its production of manuscript pages, not to mention the so-called dedicated word processors, which attempt complete transparency to the printed page. Before WYSIWYG, there were program editors designed for the creation and editing of single lines of text—which were, originally, programs; some software programs, such as *Edix* and *Edlin*,[11] exhibit vestiges of these older line editors. But symbol manipulation in the electronic element is of a degree altogether different from the mechanical order of the typewriter. The encoding of the alphabet in ASCII and the storage of electrical impulses on silicon chips engenders possibilities of manipulation unheard of with the typewriter and printed pages. Through the reduction of natural language to encoded information, new ways emerge for manipulating symbols as they come to be formulated, arranged, and distributed. To a great extent, the page-oriented word processor masks the new phenomenon. For word processing, taken in its essential import, endows thinking in symbols with a processlike, automated psychic framework.

In the previous chapter, I noted that there are different psychic frameworks for seeing what you think, just as there are different ways of seeing what time it is. The manipulation of symbols, the arrangement of symbolic domains, has its own special time and motion. The temporal motion of calligraphy effects a different psychic framework than the arrangement of typography. The reproducibility of the latter, its inherent multiplication, establishes a different psychic framework than calligraphy with its aesthetic uniqueness. With word processing, the manipulation of symbols is characterized not only by typification but also by a typification that is automated. What this means is that control over the typification procedure is so great that symbols can be manipulated as they are produced rather than afterward. The inscription procedure is bypassed through electronic storage, and the actual inscription can then be expedited at any time, in any format, automatically, that is, without the inscription procedure dominating the composition process. Hence automation leads to the feeling of freedom and of flow.

Considering the concealment intrinsic to any new phenomenon, it is not surprising that word processing has been seen through metaphors dictated by earlier symbolic elements. The automation of the inscription process is experienced as bliss precisely because it brings the domain of symbolization into step with the productivity of technological enframing. The relative bliss of automated formatting and printing can hide the qualitatively different ways that text is experienced. Some word-processing software now uses metaphors other than that of printed type on paper. These directions enable the writer not only to bypass the labor of inscription but also to apply computer automation directly to symbolic ideation. One outstanding qualitative shift in this direction is the recently developed outliner programs for writing on personal computers. These programs have been popularly heralded as "the first small step toward fully computerized thought processing."[12]

Outliners are programs which apply a metaphor taken from the tool kit of traditional composition. As Ong has shown in his study of Peter Ramus, outlining came to prominence in the modern period with the application of Ramist logic to pedagogical theory, and this in conjunction with the growth of mechanical printing. Outlining constituted the essence of the Ramist structure of knowledge, and the application of simple outlined schematics to all of knowledge was the thrust of Ramist educational reform and of the first encyclopedias. Outlines once elaborated the structure of knowledge for the schools and became part of the academic repertory of methods for teaching complex written composition. In short, outlining was a kind of simplified scholastic logic for the early modern period. Later, outlining also became an aid for learning to deal with complex ideas in all areas of life, including business and commerce. The traditional nonacademic milieu of outlining came to include lawyers, scientists, and technical writers. It is this language of outlining, taken from predigital writing, that provides one of the first nonprint, noninscriptional metaphors for word processing.

Outliners display automated writing as it opens up unprecedented kinds of manipulation for the process of symbolizing. Outliners apply automation directly to the process traditionally called *inventio*, the conceptualization and connection of thoughts as they occur in composing them. But outlining in the electric element is a different kettle of fish from outlining in pen and paper or in printed schematics.

For one thing, outliners facilitate a different kind of exploration of digital text. Outlines do wonders for overcoming the sense of a restricted scope for viewing the text on screen. They enable word processing to overcome the limitations of the window scrolling over words. Take an extreme example: word processing on the Model 100 notebook portable computer. In order to accommodate large, legible letters on a small, liquid crystal screen, along with a human-scale keyboard, the Model 100 has only eight rows by forty columns of visible text. (Its lightweight portability—under four pounds—also limits the screen size, given current technology.) Now, with outliner programs, such as *THINK* or *IDEA*,[13] the screen of the Model 100 can manage large amounts of text under headings and subheadings; text can be collapsed into manageable chunks, moved about on a small screen, put into different relations. And this maneuverability is even greater with the desktop computers as the outliners can command greater resources of memory and access to huge amounts of text.

Besides breaking out of the page-bound metaphor where the screen is always hiding half of the page, outliners enable you to see what you think in different ways. They deal not with a finished result for printout, but they explicitly bring automation to bear on the thought process in the early stages of composition. Hence their marketing as idea processors. The power of the digital outliner indicates one of the ways in which word processing brings about a different relationship to symbols rather than merely automating in a more efficient way the older relationship to symbols.

What goes under the name of outliner here should not be simply identified with the pen-and-paper outline. The structuring of writing electronically both before and as you write provides a different experience from that of the outlining taught formerly in schools or used for presentations in industry and the professions. Computer outlining programs treat words as manipulable, fluid information as you write them. Such outliners as *ThinkTank* and *Freestyle* have, consequently, become a symbolic element for planners, decision makers, and managers. The text becomes a dynamic yellow pad where you can move headings and subheadings and hide large amounts of text behind them. Additions can lead to changes in the organization of headings; copying parts and erasing is instantaneous; you can show hierarchical levels to any depth; you can expand, collapse, promote, and demote ideas. Viewing dominates over the verbal event, over the emergence of thoughts; the language of filmmaking and cinema is used in the software: "zooming," "focusing," and "ordering a flow of ideas," "seeing a thought in context," "idea assembly."

A brief look at specific software environments will show how the psychic framework of word processing was acknowledged early on by the developers of software. For instance, the first outliner for personal computers, called *KAMAS* (Knowledge and Mind Amplification System), was written for CP/M computers by Compusophic Systems, a group of former philosophy professors who saw the outliner as a vehicle for furthering and inculcating a certain way of thinking. They wrote *KAMAS* under the influence of the Chicago school of philosophy as it was shaped by the neoclassicism of Leo Strauss, Richard McKeon, and Mortimer Adler in the 1940s and 1950s. The aim of *KAMAS*—the "classic vehicle," as the advertisement calls it—is to help the writer structure thoughts in hierarchical levels. The hierarchical classification scheme encouraged by *KAMAS* is derived originally from the Aristotelian logical principles of the *Categories* and of the classification scheme of genera with specific differences. (The bibliography of the *KAMAS* manual lists *The Material Logic of John of St. Thomas*, along with

Henry Veatch's *Two Logics: The Conflict between Classical and Neo-Analytic Philosophy* and Robert Pirsig's *Zen and the Art of Motorcycle Maintenance.*) *KAMAS* integrates ideas as they come to you by subordinating them under one general idea and then differentiates them by splitting ideas into several specific ones:

Vehicles
    Motorcycles
    Cars
    Stagecoach
    Roller skates

easily becomes

Wheeled Vehicles
    Nonmotorized
        Animal-drawn
        Skates and Skateboards
    Motorized
        Motorcycles
        Automobiles
            1932 Lincoln

And so on in Scholastic-Aristotelian fashion.[14] While the advertising suggests that "the user is in the driver's seat," the program is clearly intended to further hierarchical logic in the classical sense. It does succeed at creating a vastly more flexible way of organizing hierarchies than the primitive pencil and paper. With the latter, every shift in the hierarchy, every addition, requires a redoing of the entire drawing or at least of a great part of it. The digital text is infinitely more flexible and adjustable for the purposes of hierarchical organization. Nevertheless, since writing on a computer invites direct composition by adding and collapsing, expanding and rearranging text, a common response to top-down, hierarchical outliners is: "But I don't think that way." This objection is usually accompanied by the rejection of hierarchical logic in favor of a more expressive approach.

In fact, the more traditional kind of outlining is not the model for most computer programs. The metaphor quickly gives way to something of another kind altogether. In the early beginnings of word processing, Engelbart insisted: "The course of action which must respond to new comprehension, new insights, and new intuitive flashes of possible explanations or solutions is not an orderly process. Existing means of composing and working with symbol structures penalize disorderly processes heavily. It is part of the real promise of the automated H-ALM/T systems of tomorrow that the human can have the freedom and power of disorderly processes."[15] Confirming Engelbart's vision, a number of people today find outliners indispensable for putting free-association thinking into a coherent, usable form. One business person said, "I can write proposals in about fifty percent of the time it took previously. I can organize presentations better—I use it for just about everything. It has become as much a part of my computer use as a second skin." Today the psychic framework of word processing installs the manipulation of thoughts at a deep level of symbolic ideation, and it does so through a variety of outliners which automate the initial phases of composing and organizing ideas.

Outline environments differ in their temporal structures and in their movement as you write. *ThinkTank*,[16] for years now a staple for computer users, provides something like a floating hierarchy. The program accepts ideas as they arise without the requirements of a previously fixed order. It is then very easy to build on, elaborate, and add subordinate ideas to the initial lists created by brainstorming or lateral, as opposed to top-down or deductive, thinking. As the details become more complex, the outline can be collapsed into major headings at any or all points. Finally, the hierarchical structure of the organized text can be reformed in any way at any stage. Being without an intrinsic logical structure, such outliners—and there are several in this design[17];—offer a two-phase process for the manipulation of ideas. First is a phase for freely flowing creative imagination, with all judgment suspended.

Once the ideas have been put into the symbolic element, a second phase allows for a consideration of the relationships and connections between the ideas and their implications. In the first phase, something like a free association of the mind prevails, in which the critical faculties are not invoked; in the second, random thoughts are easily manipulated and even seem to invite structuring through a software that stimulates a kind of playing around with different hierarchies. This psychic framework is a far cry from the time and movement suggested by Aristotle's *Categories*, where subordination is based on the durable, even timeless, nature of each respective higher level.

A different framework for time and movement is suggested by outliners like *Freestyle*.[18] *Freestyle* is a real-time outliner; that is, text is outlined or placed under general headings as you enter text. Headings and divisions need not be introduced to a text before composition. Rather, the time of composing the text is the same time in which the outline is generated. In effect, the outliner is a feature of the word-processing program—not an appendage or mere skeletal order, but a constantly abstracting background which reveals the order of what is (has been) written. You can consult the outline at any point, either to reorder or to examine the logical progression. Of course, there is still the need for user decisions and control over how the hierarchy is to be assigned. But the intent of such a program is to allow maximum freedom of text entry without the intervening concern for organization. At the same time, the program automates the abstraction of the anatomy of the text that is entered. This variant of the outline metaphor brings out a different side of automation in the electronic element. On the opposite pole of automation, a project is under way to construct an outliner which will, from the skeletal anatomy of an outline, generate a complete text with little or no human intervention. Obviously, the range of complexity in textual content will regulate the extent to which production can be automated and the extent to which the writer will have to oversee the production.

I have discussed some specific outlining environments in order to highlight the way language becomes manipulable in the electronic element. Outliners exemplify an essential quality of composing on computers; they show how the process of composing thoughts is inherently modular. The electronic element differs from the other elements in that manipulation in it is automated. But for want of space, we could just as well have examined another important example of a metaphor used to gain access to the new symbolic element. The database is another metaphor, and many programs make reference to textual databases, employing further metaphors such as file cabinets, drawers, indices, note cards, and even the Rollodex. These approaches organize written words through search functions using Boolean logical operators. What results is a retrieval and cross-referencing system that only faintly resembles index cards and paper files. Some programs even use more flexible cross-associative algorithms that can go beyond identical symbols and can locate themes and networks of possible connotative connections.[19] Database is itself a metaphor taken from information gathering, and its suitability for writing on computers is obvious as long as we keep in mind the peculiarity of writing in a digital element. But there is another aspect of the psychic framework of word processing which has to do directly with the computer-based manipulation of symbols.

In discussing the psychic framework of word processing, I necessarily make frequent reference to programs and their various environments. Because of its programmability, the computer is not, strictly speaking, a machine, or single-purpose device (the Greek *mēchanē* means as much). Flexibility is intrinsic to the logic switching and electric energy of computers, as much as singleness of purpose is built into the cogs of a mechanical wheel. Computers are information centers. Since they provide such flexibility in assisting the manipulation, formulation, and linkage of thought, computers become awesome centers of power for the human user. In discussions with users—especially at this early stage of the social assimilation of computers—it is not uncommon to hear traditional theological terms applied to the way computers "take over" the lives of users. As a center for intelligent, unifying control over experience, the computer seems at times to assume an importance far beyond that of any single-purpose tool or machine. As a center for gathering meaning, the computer is at times discussed by users in the traditional terms of God. While no personality is attributed to the computer—something which is also true of certain Buddhist notions of the divine—there is reason for such an analogy. For the power of the computer, from which word processing emanates, lies in the infinite number of applications to which its electronic switching and memory can be applied. Rather than predefined for a specific task, the computer's power can be tailored down to the finest detail for any number of tasks. It has thus been called "a tool for the making of tools."

One level of flexibility is, of course, the indefinite number of applications for the computer, of which word processing is one. A further subset of applications is the flexible customization of the computer within the word-processing program itself. Programs differ in the way they enable you to customize the writing environment. Many word-processing programs, such as *XyWrite*, *The Final Word*, *WordPerfect*, *Framework*, and others, can be considered kits for the building of a writing program all your own. There are also keyboard enhancing programs that create macros, such as *Prokey* and *Superkey*. Keyboard enhancers enable you to define the keys as you wish according to specific tasks and preferences. Whole libraries of phrases and words can be assigned to individual keys. The execution of complex operations can also be assigned to the pushing of a single function key. Called a macro, this type of customization requires the repeated exercise of algorithmic patterns of thought. Because of its basis in the computational environment, the psychic framework of word processing fosters affinities with the same algorithmic thinking that stands hidden behind the manipulation of verbal symbols.

Algorithms, being step-by-step instructions for computational procedures, are human thought patterns isomorphic with electromechanical operations. Algorithmic instructions, originating on a variety of levels or interpretive stages, are assembled and converted to machine language so a program can be executed. The logic of instructional procedures is an analytical breakdown of the flow, or direction, of one or more operations. Hence the term *flow chart*. For the user, this means that the adaptation of the program to specific needs and the actual employment of the software initiates a certain kind of reflection on procedures in the interface, a kind of analytical reflection that is continuous with programming: "Any time you arrange your procedure for using a word processor or spreadsheet into a logical progression of steps, you are programming. In fact, even when you arrange your procedure into an illogical sequence of steps, you are programming. So the question is not whether you should learn to program, but whether you should learn to program well."[20] What this means is that the psychic framework of word processing is an environment that fosters the analysis of spontaneous motion in sequential terms. Human motions are scrutinized for repetitive, potentially programmable sequences. And to prefer programs that require no customization whatsoever, perhaps in the name of "user friendliness," is to trade the essential power of word processing for a "crippled" version of it.[21] To put it simply, word-processing programs invite programming.

Word-processing macros are programmed subsets of the algorithms of a particular program; they are commands automated so they execute at the push of a single key to which the macro is assigned. To automate the task of manipulating symbols, you must first analyze your writing and computer use in such a way as to perceive whatever motions are repetitious or follow regular patterns. Once the pattern is perceived, executing the movement can be computerized by creating a macro for the specific task. What was a spontaneous motion becomes interpreted as a sequence of programmable steps to be performed by the computer. Consider a simple example.

Say I am using the program *WordPerfect* and find myself more than once going through a file to strip out the footnotes from a text I have written. I want to gather the notes out of the text and put them into a separate file for closer examination or correction. First, I must observe each step I take as I pull out the footnotes by pushing the right keys. I need to regard my practice as a step-by-step procedure and rehearse each step until a memory of the sequence of actions is established. I press the Macro Define key and type in a name or key for the macro assignment. Then I must execute the following: (1) shuttle to a second screen, (2) give a top-of-file command, (3) place the header from the main text into the notes file on the second screen, (4) hit the margin key and set the margins for the footnotes, (5) hit the spacing key and set for double spacing, (6) make some space, hit Centering key and the Bold key and type "Notes" with some space beneath it, (7) call Mark Text command and then Define in order to set the kind of enumeration I want for the notes, (8) return to main text and invoke another separately created macro which pulls out the footnotes one by one and places them into the separate note page. Moreover, several of these steps require a number of decisions from complex menus. Forgetting a step when composing a macro, which is easily done, means I will have to redo the whole macro. Redoing means going over each step once again in sequence. Once it is created, the macro can be used an indefinite number of times and will save much time. But in creating a macro like the one above, a person will have spent maybe an hour thinking in algorithmic terms.

Obviously, macros are desirable for automating complex procedures. But in order to automate, there must be a prior analytical thought process through which the step-by-step procedure or algorithm is brought to full awareness. There is an involvement with algorithms. And you actually do have to go through many repetitive, algorithmic steps in order to *test* a macro. You need to retrace the steps in order to debug the keyboard enhancements.[22] Gradually it comes about that you begin to observe your own movements in writing as potential targets for improvement through algorithms. Each activity is regarded as potentially replaceable by an algorithm or programmable command. This fosters calculative thinking.

A good example of how word-processing programs elicit and develop algorithmic thinking is the genesis of a software package called *Nota Bene* (the first writing software to receive in 1985 the endorsement of the Modern Language Association). *Nota Bene* is a highly, perhaps even excessively, enhanced version of two other programs, the word processor *XyWrite* and *FYI 3000*, a free-form database for indexing text. *Nota Bene* is a licensed modification of both programs so that they work as a unit. It provides a keyboard with many features welcomed by academics, such as foreign language characters; it also handles footnotes, bibliographies, various style formats, such as Turabian and Chicago style. To complement it, the program includes a text-retrieval system for texts written with the program. None of these features is intrinsically lacking in the original programs combined by *Nota Bene*; they are merely latent or have not yet emerged through customized program macros. *Nota Bene*, published by Dragonfly Software, originated with a Yale philosophy student, Steven Siebert. Siebert began working on his doctoral thesis—titled "The Hermeneutics of Suspicion"—using a word processor but found the software too primitive.[23] After examining many programs, he began customizing *XyWrite* and *FYI 3000*, writing small programs in XPL (XyWrite Programming Language) and finding extensive applications for all the features contained but not explicit in *XyWrite*, which at that time had minimal documentation and was presented quite raw to the user as a lean but powerful program. Siebert became engrossed in the programming, turned his attention from the dissertation, and eventually made *Nota Bene* available in the marketplace. Today the program has perhaps the most complete, exhaustive, and logically detailed documentation of any word-processing program available. While other word-processing manuals may illustrate formatting and margins by showing pages from *Alice in Wonderland*, *Nota Bene* is the only computer manual that displays pages from a discussion of the philosophy of Jürgen Habermas.

Most word-processing programs have their own programming languages available in the background, always inviting an increase in speed and efficiency. Creativity is easily channeled into tinkering in algorithmic patterns of thought, certainly to the extent of learning at least the operating system. This again introduces the ontological dimension of play where things reveal themselves spontaneously. But the horizon of understanding in the play locates things within the algorithmic environment. *XyWrite*'s lightning speed and efficiency depend to a large extent on its still perceptible connection with the programming command language, XPL.[24] *Framework* has an internal programming language called FRED (*FRame EDitor*), which gives intricate control over screen windowing and rapid access to text files. Even the most popular and longstanding *WordStar* runs well only after the user has made certain program modifications. The modifications are publicly known, but you must do the programming. Word processing is rooted in programming, which is based on algorithmic thinking, which is in turn powerful in that it enables you to operate on data or information. With the automation of, say, *WordPerfect*, you are distanced from immediate physical keystrokes when you create an underline: you need only press the Escape key, the number 80, and Return, and there you have an underline across the screen. You are free of repeated individual strokes. Automation means speed.

With the promise of the increased speed of automation, there is the constant lure of getting into the system. The computer, unlike the typewriter, is a system, that is, a whole whose parts are alterable in such a way as to reconstitute the nature of the whole. A certain amount of identification with the system takes place as the keyboard motion and macros become a second skin and alter responses, like the instrument on which one learns to play expressive gestures. Just as the instrumentalist on the viola or 'cello becomes one with the instrument through continual practice and identification with it in public performance, so too a specific word-processing program with its customized procedures becomes your own. In an on-line discussion of the relative advantages and disadvantages of various word-processing programs, one user wrote,

> It's true that one's relationship with a word processor is a very personal, private, and emotional one; rather like wearing boxer shorts or jockies. It just boils down to an intangible "feel." At one time I was a professional musician, and I've spent countless (albeit enjoyable) hours discussing the merits of Rogers drums versus Ludwig or Pearl—and heard the brass players doing the same thing with Schulkie and Selmer. I have no doubt carpenters talk hammers and plumbers talk plungers. Professional writers spend more time with their word processors than they do with their spouses and, in the process, they develop very specific relationships and loyalties. We come to identify with them. Therefore, when someone says *WordPerfect's* the best thing since rubber wheels, *I* feel a little better. And when it gets dumped on, you might as well dump on me.[25]

The additional power obtained through saved keystrokes and automatic file manipulation is seductive. It is nearly impossible to avoid some amount of fooling around with the power of pro-grammed, automated writing. The inherently efficient nature of this temptation is accompanied by the thrill of algorithmic succes-ses. To streamline any process comes to be regarded as a primary virtue. This is more than merely passive automation, and it leads to the accelerated speeds which make possible a distinctive way of formulating thoughts in public format.

Formulation: Thinking in Electric Language

The accelerated automation of word processing makes possible a new immediacy in the creation of public, typified text. Immediacy is the sense of there being no medium quod, no instrumental impediment to thinking in external symbols, only a medium quo, or pure transparent element. As I write, I can put things directly in writing. My stream of consciousness can be paralleled by the running flow of the electric element. Words dance on the screen. Sentences slide smoothly into place, make way for one another, while paragraphs ripple down the screen. Words become highlighted, vanish at the push of a button, then reappear instantly at will. Verbal life is fast-paced, easier, with something of the exhilaration of video games. For this reason, children, we are told, prefer writing on a computer to writing with pencil and paper.[26]

Because this playful way of putting things is immediate, enjoyable, and less constrained by materials, it encourages on-screen thinking, that is, thinking in a typified, public element. The new immediacy does presuppose, of course, a modicum of keyboard skills—at least for those systems that are not talk-writers. And keyboard skills can be acquired all the more quickly when the computer makes considerably smoother the transition from thinking to (type)writing. As to the management of physical material (something relatively subconscious until the advent of word processing), digital writing is nearly frictionless. It invites the formulation of thought directly in the electric element. Formulation is the FORMation of words, conceptualization; it is the shape in which we articulate thought. The psychic framework of word processing develops formulation as ideational flow.

Of course, not only the frictionless electric element stimulates more direct writing: vast increases in the power of the editing facilities on computerized word processors have lured users anew to write spontaneously. The availability of immediate revisions and rearrangements of text without further externalization, or printout, attracts writers to make spontaneous drafts. Writers who are still adjusting to the new technology, as mentioned earlier, tend to prefer frequent hard copies on which to write revisions, which they then later transcribe back into the computer. Yet even these writers find getting started easier on the computer. Revision in the sense of reconsidering and recasting thought in a separate step is unnecessary on the computer. This leads to a sense of freedom which many writers praise. In a way, it's like being able to crumple up a piece of paper with your scribbled notes on it, throw it away and start over, and then, ten minutes later, fish the original idea out of the wastepaper basket and display it once again in its pristine form. You feel free to put things down as they occur to you since everything can be reworked or else used in another position or context. You can jump to the bottom when you have a thought, jot it down, then go back (using a special character marker) to where you were before. Sketchy drafts can be developed and polished later. Writing becomes more interactive and the computer becomes a place to think things out in a formal, typified way, yet without the constraining format of typewritten pages.

The marked change in formulation of thought is evident in the changes in rhetorical theory, at least in recent studies of the teaching of English composition.[27] The thought process previously called prewriting can be carried out on screen because the physical impressions of handwriting and typewriting are removed from the immediate work environment. When fluidity is emphatic and graphic, the psyche feels nothing is written in stone. The preliminary phases of composition are less likely to daunt the person beginning to set down some initial thoughts. What is entered as the first sentence on a word processor need not be considered first in any permanent or logical way. Automated editing functions—for example, search-and-replace, move-text, delete, typeover—generate quite a different sense of the risk involved in committing oneself to writing. Thinking, especially thinking in writing, is always bound up with an existential commitment, which is to say that our thought establishes and reflects an identity and a distinctive life-project. In removing the sense of words being carved in stone, the word processor eliminates the blockage caused by anxiety about how one will finally appear. In some cases of writer's block, for example, the simple act of scrolling text up the screen literally gets things moving again because of the inner bond of thought and symbolic element.

Still, at times a sense of the finished page comes to obtrude on the electric element. Writers who become stuck and are unable to continue easily with what they were trying to write often turn to local editing. That is, they belabor and fidget with what they have already written, and this playful editing is greatly exacerbated by the sheer delight of the technology. The immediacy of composing on computers can make even a small degree of frustration an excuse for writers to turn from composing to picayune editing. Such counterproductive work habits have been analyzed and treated by composition teachers in the form of either invisible writing or freewriting.[28] At certain stages in the composition process, the writer is to turn off the screen and keep typing away. The aim of invisible writing is to encourage the writer to get it down, even if it is not just right. Unable to look at the radiant words, the writer must concentrate on the ideas and let them flow into the fingers and thus into the computer memory. The drive to perfect the text as it is electronically produced is short-circuited. In freewriting, the writer continues typing without pause and can see the text being created on screen, but as soon as the writer pauses for a few seconds, the program begins to blink the screen till the writer continues. Corrections and revisions must wait until the first draft is completed. Both developments in rhetorical *inventio* promote a kind of composition that approximates dictation. The immediacy of formulation in digital writing is akin to the immediacy of speaking.

We see, then, that the formulation of thoughts in external, typified symbols in the electronic element promotes greater immediacy or directness. And this is possible because computer hardware and software can more closely approximate the speed of human thought. Computers can have a nearly symbiotic relationship with the human thought process, as science-fiction fantasies have frequently noted.[29] With word processing, this means that writing tends to become more writer-based, as opposed to reader-based. Writer-based writing proceeds with little reflection on the needs of the audience, on the *captatio benevolentiae* typical of the rhetorical tradition. The tradition prescribes careful analysis of audience and situation, an attempt to establish rapport. Writer-based writing carries out the directness typical of digital writing. (Chapter 1 of this book was first written largely as a sample of writer-based writing.) Without heeding the claims of the audience for meeting their particular needs, writer-based writing reinstates some of the formlessness of conversation or soliloquy. To observe the directness of writer-based style, you need only watch several learners as they begin writing on computers. Invariably some will type thoughts such as, "So this is how you open a file" or "Here are my first sentences on the computer." Many books written about word-processing programs and about how to use computers were written as expressions of a first infatuation with the direct style that the writer was finding at the moment—and finding on the computer. Many books on computers are first of all books *on* computers.

In terms of formulation, too, there is a notable increase in acronyms and in abbreviated formulae for things. Just as the manipulation of word processing fosters algorithmic thinking, so too the formulation of word processing promotes thinking in formulae and acronyms. This trend is concomitant with a more general relationship to language in contemporary society but originates specifically in word processing on two counts.

1. The involvement with vast material requires foreshortening for the sake of indexing the information. Giving names to files is a clear case where the writer must develop systematic acronyms for organizing videotext. Technical considerations are leading to a

general increase in acronymic symbols. One author says of his program, "In the case of our present program, which is called Racter, the language is English. The name reflects a limitation of the computer on which we initially wrote the program. It only accepted file names not exceeding six characters in length. Racter seemed a reasonable foreshortening of *raconteur*."[30]

2. Word processing encourages the use of shortened formulations which can later be expanded by automated search-and-replace operations. In writing this chapter, for example, I can type *wp* wherever *word processing* is meant. Later on, a one-time search-and-replace operation can in seconds insert the full phrase in every instance. I would not then be writing down symbols for language but responding to a mechanical set of decisions determining which replacement string should be inserted, *word processing* or *word-processing*, that is, determining whether the usage is nominative or adjectival. Or the replacement can also be automated to varying degrees, either with a mechanized insertion of the full text symbols after the completion of texts, or, as automated artificial intelligence becomes available for grammatical discernment, the decision procedure of the program itself may sort out the relevant grammar and apply my key words.

Abbreviated symbols, like acronymic file names, are neologisms which exhibit no direct natural-language base. That is, such word formations, since they do not have in them the history of cultural experiences, possess an arbitrary clarity and univocity; they can suit the writer's fancy—as long as algorithmic consistency is maintained for the search-and-replace; they are code words or signifiers pure and simple. Acronyms and abbreviations in word processing are part of the automation of symbols and support the efficient manipulation of text. Before their abbreviation, words display a linguistic cultural history, offering to the trained mind a fund of historical experience. The words of the English language, for instance, exhibit semantic events from many nations and from different periods. Fresh experiences are continually added to the semantics of the English language as vocabulary is embellished, new words made current, and certain phrases dropped. It was once customary for college students in the United States to study the Latin language in order to learn to perceive the experiences packed into English. Today students are urged to develop skills with the computer. Acronyms and abbreviations affect the formulation of symbols by removing language momentarily from the shared world of common experience. Both file handling and search-replace automation affect the formulation of symbols in the writing environment.

Computerized formulation, then, cultivates abbreviated symbolization as well as immediacy and writer-based style. Automated customization inserts this new mode of thought formulation on a deep level of the psyche as the computer becomes an expressive instrument to be played. The symbiosis of digitized symbol and human thought has significance for knowledge because knowledge is, among other things, publicly modeled (typified) thinking. The intuitive grasp of things in computerized writing develops a distinctive sense of what knowledge is. Word processing reveals knowledge to be a flowing process, a process parallel to ideational flow.

Knowledge in the mode of process distinguishes thinking on the computer from other characteristic modes of knowledge. The knowledge emerging from dialogue, by contrast, is a knowledge based on speaking and listening. There is a give-and-take, a search for the formulation of thought that calls the attention of the other person and that corresponds to the needs of the other. Listening is a difficult part of the formulation of knowledge in dialogue, as is the effort to truly respond and, in so doing, to call forth the full presence of the other person as a person or agent in a social drama. With the knowledge characteristic of the psychic framework of word processing, the flow of ideation prevails over the dialectical back-and-forth of personal conversation, though, as we shall see, the electronic element provides an extraordinary *linkage* for cooperative and communicative texts.

The knowledge characteristic of reading and writing books also differs from the formulations fostered by word processing. In written and printed formulation, knowledge is shaped by the form of argumentation. That is, a propositional claim is first made and then supported by a sequential reasoning with evidence which provides a warrant for the claim and which anticipates counterclaims. Such knowledge, structured linearly as claim and warrant for the claim, is formulated in terms of arguments and counterarguments. Reading and thinking in this element contrasts with knowledge as a process of ideation.

Knowledge, then, in its recognizable (typified) presentation, becomes unambiguously process. The process appears as a flow of manipulable information. It is true that with pen and paper you can also add in, draw marginalia, and write over; with the typewriter, however, you are limited. Typing requires consecutive formulation and linear organization of thought. The computer, on the other hand, provides a nonlinear formulation along with the public typification of formed letters.

Just as system opacity masks the radically different nature of text in the electronic element, so too the ideational fluidity of formulating words on the screen hides the mode of language inherent in word processing. The mode of language on the word processor is information. InFORMation is a very specific type of FORMulation. To formulate means, traditionally, to give shape to attention, to show the outlines or form of what we see intellectually, to put things in their limits, to delineate them. (Here I anticipate a theme of the following chapter, where I examine the semantic motion of the traditional theory of ideas.) By fostering formulation as continual process, word processing makes thinking open-ended, quite literally. For a protean process has of itself no form or limits. It simply moves on and on. Information assumes that the formulation of something is neutral or has already been accomplished. Information precludes the struggle for formulation. It is, presumably, already formed and formulated. As a result, the mode of formulation in word processing minimizes the struggle for formulation as it increases the flow of ideation.

Now, the generality of this notion of information should not eclipse the fact that the psychic framework of word processing already enjoys rich variations. Software environments treat the flow of information diversely, each seeking to make its own particular contribution to the life of the mind. Again, *mind* here means something like what William James called "feelings of relation, psychic overtones, halos, suffusions, or fringes" throughout the stream of consciousness.[31] For software environments are subtle aesthetic creations and deserve the care bestowed on art forms. In the space here, I can only suggest a new kind of criticism or perception of software—not the literary criticism of books, nor reviews about keystrokes and quality of documentation, but the critical perception of the specific frameworks where the psyche lives its active symbolic life in a technological culture.

Take, for instance, the most dramatic atmospheric difference between two word-processing programs: *Nota Bene* and *ZenWord*. *Nota Bene* is certainly one of the most thoroughly engineered pieces of software available. It is meticulously documented down to the finest detail and presented with stringent logic; the manual contains several hundred pages packed with instructions and advice on customization. Moreover, the editing program is internally wedded to a second program, a textual database. Working within this environment, you have the sense of an elaborate and bulky structure held together by slow and exhaustive menus, marvelously detailed with style menus for automated formats like the *Chicago Manual of Style*, the "Turabian Manual for Writers," and the "American Psychological Association Manual." The very weight of the structure of capabilities gives *Nota Bene* a serious gravity. The structure seems that much more elaborate if you are already familiar with the underlying word processor, *XyWrite*, which is known for its lean speed and its ability to fly. In speaking of *Nota Bene*, one user employed the term *baroque*, for there is even a sense of something weighty, top-heavy, ponderous, maybe even unstable about it. To feel this by way of contrast, you have only to spend ten minutes with *ZenWord*, which, as might be gathered from its Buddhist-inspired name, strives for intuitive simplicity and clean austerity. ZenWord achieves a splendid simplicity, even in its documentation, which is a slim, light pamphlet of twenty or so pages. The program can be learned quickly and simply through interaction once you learn to press the Escape key for the labels to appear on the blank, naked screen. The elegant charm of this editing program lies in its empty receptiveness to user movements. The sequence of keystrokes needed to operate most functions is learned quickly, and the learning offers the pleasant sensations associated with habits that seem to build naturally. It is similar to certain pieces on a stringed instrument which lie well for the fingers, while other pieces of music will never belong to the instrument in the same way, even though they were written for that instrument. So it is with *Nota Bene* and *ZenWord*. But the latter limits the user's output. *ZenWord* places a limit on the size of the files it can manipulate; *Nota Bene* not only handles any size but it can index and search any number of files. *ZenWord* does not allow full customization of the keys while *Nota Bene* excels in providing key combinations for every imaginable operation, including keys for scrolling two windows at once and for reversing the position of letters, words, sentences, or paragraphs. It is not clear yet what, if any, relationship there is between program limitations of software and the psychic framework engaged at the computer interface by the writer.

Linkage: The Network of Text

The distinctive features of formulating thought in the psychic framework of word processing combine with the automation of information handling and produce an unprecedented linkage of text. By *linkage* I mean not some loose physical connection like discrete books sharing a common physical space in the library.[32] *Text* derives originally from the Latin word for weaving and for interwoven material, and it comes to have an extraordinary accuracy of meaning in the case of word processing. Linkage in the electronic element is interactive, that is, texts can be brought instantly into the same psychic framework.

Automated spelling checkers, proofreaders, and thesauri are the simplest examples of linkage. As you type, for instance, memory-resident spelling checkers will beep whenever you type a misspelled word. (Many writers dismiss these programs as "nags.") They will then provide alternatives which can replace the misspelled word at the push of a button. A thesaurus, like *Word Finder* or the one built into *WordPerfect*, gives instant access to many levels of synonyms offered for automatic replacement of the words you write but find vaguely unsatisfactory. Far more intriguing than any book thesaurus, such aids are themselves lures for exploring connections of meaning in the English vocabulary. The electronic thesaurus invites the writer to enter as many different levels of synonyms and associated words as desired. With memory-resident linking programs, such as Borland's *Lightning*, joined with state-of-the-art compact disk storage, whole encyclopedias, law dictionaries, and medical references can be at the fingertips for consultation with reference to any word or phrase you write—as you write it. The text in progress becomes interconnected and linked with the entire world of information.

Texts can be accessed instantly as coresident ingredients of the psychic framework of word processing. (Surely, the current usage of *to be accessed* can be traced to the ubiquity of computerized information.) Windows, or split screens of any number, can be opened on the monitor to bring several texts into view simultaneously and, unlike printed books, interactively. Through the use of optical character readers (OCRs), the written texts of printed books are rapidly being digitized so they can be accessed by videotext and manipulated as information. This includes the written corpus of texts from all historical time, as the *Thesaurus Linguae Graecae*, for instance, the entire library of Classical Greek literature, becomes available from the University of California at Irvine.

Combine automation with the flow of information and new connections of interactive text emerge. Cross references then become identical with textuality, not just proximate and mutually influencing texts but texts coresident and in the same interactive element and capable of being directly juxtaposed or superimposed. This is more properly called intertextuality. The sense of a sequential literature of distinct, physically separate texts is supplanted by a continuous textuality. What Ted Nelson calls links can create, for example, computer-dynamized footnotes.[33] Instead of searching for a footnote or going to find another document referred to, the dynamic footnote, or link, can automatically bring the appended or referenced material to the screen. The referenced material could be a paragraph or an article or an entire book. A return key brings the reader back to the point in the original text where the link symbol appeared. This interactive textuality has been dubbed hypertext. The word might be interpreted to mean the text of all texts or simply the text of texts. Hypertext also includes access to previous versions of writing, whether the writing is literary composition or notes for decision making.[34] With economical and virtually invisible storage of multiple versions of documents, the whole notion of an original text shifts.[35] In magnetic code there are no originals.

Currently, the access to windows and hypertext requires either large amounts of memory (which are now in the millions of bytes already for microcomputers) or else on-line modem connections with larger data banks. Modems, of course, are modulators for transferring digital information over common-carrier lines. In the United States, telephone lines are being rapidly converted to digital signal carriers, which will mean that all communication will soon be more compatible, more compact and economical. Computers will then no longer need modems (modulator-demodulators) for accessing the telephone lines and thereby large databases. At the same time, however, the new optical laser and compact disk technology will soon provide virtually unlimited access to stored information on the personal computer. As orbital satellite technology develops, digital linkage will bring all text—complete with images and sounds—into a generalized and unified signal.

With linkage, digital writing enters a network of symbols, even vocal, graphic, and musical symbols. Already there exists computer linkage through electronic mail systems, both locally and nationally; business has developed computer teleconferencing over common-carrier lines with national links to facilitate deliberations; there are computer conferences, which move the flow of scientific knowledge more efficiently and with less lag time than printed journals. Information services bring writing from across the country and from overseas to the screen of the personal computer, where the formulation and composition of individual thoughts takes place.

What does this open window to society mean for the psychic framework of word processing? Colette Daiute of Harvard has done extensive experiments on the psycholinguistics of computerized writing and its effect on the "social dimension" of writing. In *Writing and Computers*, she concludes that "communicating with others via a [computerized] bulletin board highlights the communication functions of writing. Because the bulletin board is displayed in the same screen space as the writers' texts on the computer, the entire writing environment—the keyboard, the screen, and the computer operations—is associated with general communication." And: "Writing on a computer is more public than the traditional writing environment—and more noisy, in a good sense of the word. Although any writing environment can be designed to include discussion and sharing, the classroom with computers may be most appropriate for interaction.... The shared tool, which displays the text upright, invites group reading as well as group writing."[36] Pamela McCorduck in *The Universal Machine: Confessions of a Technological Optimist* concurs: "One salient fact of computing, and one of the most important world-wide effects of computing might be its introduction of a new ethos of cooperation."[37] And the research of Patricia Marks Greenfield leads to a similar conclusion: "The screen makes an individual's thought processes public, open to others who can also observe the screen. It makes writing into an easily observable physical object, which can be manipulated in various ways by other people. Thus, the computer makes the private activity of writing into a potentially public and social one."[38]

It is appropriate that the psychic framework of word processing, linked as it is with a homogeneously encoded information base, should foster collaborative interaction. There is not only a new technology available in word processing but a gradually emerging sense of a new kind of community. And in such community, psychic life will be redefined. As digital interactive writing spreads and is no longer restricted to sociotechnical groups, it may behoove us to inquire further about the ontological dimension of computerized writing: what does it reveal of our apprehensions of reality, of the world which we are coming to inhabit and in which we make our choices? In short, how is our grasp on things changing as we move away from previous forms of writing?

PART THREE

EVALUATING THE PHENOMENON

Chapter Six

The Book and the Classic Model of Mind

The Moving Finger writes, and, having writ,
Moves on; nor all your Piety nor Wit
Shall lure it back to cancel half a Line,
Nor all your Tears wash out a Word of it.
—*The Rubaiyat of Omar Khayyam,* trans. Edward FitzGerald

Books are not absolutely dead things, but do contain a progeny of life in
them to be as active as that soul was whose progeny they are; nay, they
do preserve as in a vial the purest efficacy and extraction of that living
intellect that bred them.... Who kills a man kills a reasonable creature,
God's image; but he who destroys a good book, kills reason itself, kills
the image of God, as it were, in the eye.... A good book is the precious
lifeblood of a master spirit, embalmed and treasured up on purpose to a
life beyond life.
—John Milton, *Areopagitica*

Even the transposed, groping metaphor of computer literacy
indicates a latent concern for something more in the notion of
literacy than the sheerly instrumental value of an alphabet that can
aid communication. Literacy, or the reading and writing of books,
has fostered psychic life in ways that go far beyond the subservient
utility of a means of communication. True, political democracies
often concern themselves with the skills and social instruments
required to maintain a flow of communication, or, more accurately,
to further a noncentralized interchange of information. There is
hope of self-rule only where people feel genuinely knowledgeable
about the forces affecting their lives. But, on a deeper ontological
level, the reading and writing of books has significance beyond the
merely instrumental. The book defines a certain way in which
access to the things in the world is fostered, a certain modeling of
the way things are held up to attention. Literacy is as much an
expression of the way a person inhabits the world as it is an

instrument within the world of human concerns. The reason literacy can be invoked with all the confidence of a shibboleth is precisely because the book, like all symbolic elements for natural language, reaches to "the fathomless depths of the psyche," as I recalled through Heraclitus in chapter 1.

A classic model of the mind subsists in the symbolic element of books, both in premechanized form and in the print form which makes wider distribution possible. To consider, somewhat retrospectively, the psychic framework of the classic book is to begin drawing an alternate, contrasting model for assessing the trade-offs contained in the world of word processing. This model will aid us in navigating the currents of historical drift.

In examining the psychic framework of the traditional book, I will be reconstructing the "classic model of the mind" and alluding to the intelligence as it has been understood in the long-standing tradition of Platonic Realism. Platonism is often taken to imply, in principle, or metaphysically, a separation of the mind from physical existence. A separate, "unearthly soul" is often postulated by Platonic thinking. Such a Platonism would, taken naively and literally, deny that the physical context of symbols induces different states of mind, or at least that the physical context ought not—in a quasi-moral sense—be regarded as a determining factor in mental states. Platonism, in this sense, was the "rational psychology" referred to and attacked by William James in the following passage:

> *Mental facts cannot be properly studied apart from the physical environment of which they take cognizance.* The great fault of the older rational psychology was to set up the soul as an absolute spiritual being with certain faculties of its own by which the several activities of remembering, imagining, reasoning, willing, etc. were explained, almost without reference to the peculiarities of the world with which these activities deal. But the richer insight of modern days

perceives that our inner faculties are *adapted* in advance to the features of the world in which we dwell, adapted, I mean, so as to secure our safety and prosperity in its midst."[1]

But James's remark seems to suggest that the adaptation of faculties is, according to the simplified hypothesis of evolution, the narrowing of consciousness and psychic life to the empirico-material world of "nasty details." Some of James's "butcher-shop categories," such as "tough-mindedness" and "tender-mindedness," might lend further support to this interpretation. In other words, James's redefinition of the psyche might be taken for a denial of transcendence, for a rejection of the need to go beyond the sequential routine of mundane experiences. We know from his other writings, however, that James did not wish to deny such transcendence.[2] The point here is not what William James did or did not hold. The point is rather that certain adaptations of the mind to the physical environment have been successful precisely because of the leverage they provide for transcending the immediate mundane environment. Literacy is more than the mind's convenient adaptation to the felt needs of communication.

The classic mind, in the Platonic mold, does indeed "set up the soul as an absolute spiritual being" to be studied in abstraction from the surrounding world. And of this abstraction modern thought is properly suspicious. The clean arrangements of such a Platonic metaphysics must be continually reestablished in and by experience and in the confirmation of experiment. Modern philosophers reject the tidy metaphysics of separate minds, and in so doing they become aware of the unending nature of the adaptation human beings must make to the world. There is a continual process in which we project ourselves beyond the immediate particulars of any and every given world. Part of "adapting to the world in which we dwell" is the effort to redefine and recast the things in the world. And redefinition means that the world itself must be thought out and revised anew before the things within it can be reworked.

James's "safety and prosperity" in the midst of the world must be construed much more broadly than the simple utilitarian compromise with things already given in daily experience.

Sometimes our understanding of the world itself needs to be reviewed and revised. *Adaptation to the world* may mean that the things given in day-to-day experience must be reconstituted by a new articulation of the world. As we see in the understanding of the world being brought about now by high technology, we need at times to reformulate things by using fresh metaphors. The old concept, for instance, of proprietary rights based on the possession of an original creation no longer permits us to adapt ourselves to a world where the technological basis of creative work makes copying easy and inevitable; protecting creativity in such a world requires adaptation on the part of the mind as it must envision a wholly new order of creative ownership.

The absolute spiritual being postulated by traditional Platonism is—far from being a dry assertion of metaphysics—the postulate of potential transcendence from the flurries and confusions of daily experience. Taken in the context of its characteristic symbolic element, the Platonic tradition nurtures the culture of the book, the reading and writing of it. This nurturing is not due to the historical accident of Plato's lifetime happening to coincide with the advent of the book and literacy. Platonic philosophy nurtures book literacy, pace the transformation theory, because the model of psychic intelligence the philosophy promotes has its element in the book. The Platonic notion of intelligence fosters intelligence not as information processing, not even as computational capacity, syllogistic or otherwise, but it promotes the contemplative consideration that forms the basis of both calculation and argumentation. Whereas in chapter 5 I provisionally characterized the printed book as furthering linear thinking and thus providing a symbolic element for the claim-evidence structure of argument, we shall now see that the psychic model of the book, in the classic sense, ultimately depends on a deeper level of stasis, of contemplative awareness upon which argument itself and logical sequence must be based. From the standpoint of Platonic philosophy, argumentation is not fundamental since every true argument must be based upon a mental vision or understanding of primary forms whose self-evidence is the ultimate support for logical linearity.

When John Milton refers to the book as the "purest efficacy and extraction of [the] living intellect," he is attaching to the book and to the notion of intellect psychic qualities not reducible to information, communication, or merely logical argument. Milton was convinced of the sacrosanct preserve of psychic insight and energy in the form of the printed book. Inscription has been regarded since ancient times as a preserve of spiritual force. That force is attested to by Horace's famous lines in *Odes* III, "I have completed a monument to outlast bronze" (*Exegi monumentum aere perennius*), which are later echoed by Shakespeare's: "Yet do thy worst, old Time; despite thy wrong,/ My love shall in my verse ever live young" (Sonnet 19). The traditional notion of literacy goes beyond political necessity, instrumental value, and even private purposes. Books provide a psychic framework for symbols by which the psyche learns to transcend mundane familiarity with things, to go beyond routine realities. Classical metaphysics was immersed in and supported the literacy of the traditional book, even to the extent that book literacy became the framework and standard of philosophical thought. As we shall see, the philosophic mind became identified with certain qualities of the book.

My aim, then, is not to advocate classical metaphysics pure and simple as a description of the eternally true reality according to which I might want to criticize the psychic life fostered by word processing. My aim is not to return to the philosophy of the ancients in a literal sense, however pleasantly distracting such a romance might be. Nor do I, as do the modern philosophers, seek to denounce as pretentious idealism the classical philosophy based on the ancients; I do not define philosophizing by way of an opposition to the ancients. Nor is the attempt, in Hegelian fashion, to assimilate both ancient and modern philosophies in a single, overarching contemplation of all historical time. Rather, my approach is postmodern inasmuch as classical metaphysics serves to provide an alternate model or counterpoint through which I can begin a contrasting assessment of word processing. The psychic transcendence fostered by the book cultivates three facets of psychic life corresponding to the manipulation, formulation, and linkage found in the psychic framework of word processing. The tradition of the book is, accordingly, constituted by three facets: the scribal hand, contemplative transcendence through the formulation of ideas, and the integrity of the private mind.

The Scribal Hand: Manipulation as Contemplative Care

In a previous chapter I noted that calligraphy does not stand in the mainstream of the symbolic element of Western writing as it does in the Far East. Western alphabetic symbols serve to inscribe, roughly and approximately, the phonetic contours of spoken language, leading many to the conclusion that written symbols cannot be considered apart from their vocalization. As such, the visual symbolization of language appears merely to serve as notation for the spoken word, a point developed by the transformation theory. But this subservient role does not exhaust the ontological dimension, where the way a person inhabits the world is expressed and where a distinctive way of inhabiting the world is cultivated. For many centuries before instrumental thinking enjoyed its current prestige a cultural premium was placed on writing by hand—and its high esteem was not due to the purely functional value of inscription as a means of communication or as an aid to memory.

The scribal hand was related, to be sure, to the spoken word as a repository of speech. But, more important, the scribe was from early on respected as the vessel of a higher, transcending activity. Writing and reading conferred special status on the few who mastered the skills. The status was not based on power or convenience or efficiency. Someone who possessed the skills was deemed to be closer to a higher realm of thought than was found in everyday existence—even if the person was of low social standing and even if the scribal hand was primarily in the service of another. Consider, for example, the epitaph for Xantias, a sixteen-year-old Greek slave who served as stenographer for his Roman master in an early Roman settlement in Cologne in the second century A.D. Xantias died in Cologne and was buried with a young Greek flutist by the name of Sidonius. Both these young men were regarded as artists, as "servants of the Muses." Their shared tombstone, recently discovered, is exhibited in the Roman-Germanic Museum in Cologne, next to the Cologne Cathedral. The epitaph reads,

You who love songs and the Muses,
regard this, this grave.
And read our names to be mourned
on a shared tombstone.
For we two young slaves
were of the same age, but of different arts.
I am Sidonius, who blew loudly in high pitches on the double
flute.

This epitaph, this grave altar, these ashes
are the grave of the slave Xantias
who was kidnapped by sudden death.
He was already skilled [doctus] in writing down
many short forms of letters and names
with his speedy pen,
and he could take down rapidly what was said;
no one surpassed him in reading aloud.
At the first sound of his master's voice
he had already begun taking rapid dictation,
ready on demand to read back what was written.
Alas, through an early death he passed away,
the only one who was to know the secrets of his master.[3]

Here Xantias the scribe is regarded as dwelling close to the Muses, the goddesses of, among other things, music, drama, poetry, and song. Protectors of noble leisure, the Muses were emblems of inspired activities of the psyche, behaviors based on charm and dream and love. They represented, even for Aristotle, states of mind so elevated that they cannot be construed as essentially subservient to utilitarian purposes or extrinsic aims. Musical activities are, for Aristotle, paradigms of those activities which are ends in themselves, among which, of course, Aristotle advances theoretical science as the first and foremost.[4] Here the scribe, Xantias, is identified with the musician, the servant of the Muses. Writing by hand did not belong to the banausic type of labor the ancients associated with tools, useful handwork, and machines. The scribe was not regarded even as an artisan or laborer but partook of the fine arts of the Muses. The secrets of his master, the inner recesses of the mind (of his master) were committed to the inscribed element by Xantias, and Xantias's handwriting was thereby more than a tool for his master's purposes. His scribal hand was the intermediary between psyche and the symbolic element. He was a person of culture (in Greek, musikē) through the exercise of a skill that transcends everyday purposes.

If ancient Greece and Rome attributed noble leisure to the scribal hand, the Jewish-Christian stream of Western civilization applied far greater solemnity to the skills of working with the book. The conception of the sacred book (*Bible* itself meaning *ta biblia*, or group of books) connected literacy with a special entry to revealed truths through contact with the sacred book. Christians invented the book, or codex, as we know it, although the Christians who invented it had not yet become the powerful institution known as the Church. Groups that were later declared heretical played an important role in creating a sacred literacy through the copying of books.[5] Because of the notion of the Word of God, the natural universe as a whole could become, metaphorically, a book in which the believing eye reads what the hand of the Creator wrote. Recent scholarship has dwelt on the Renaissance shift from God's book of nature to the modern effort to examine or read nature directly, finding genetic codes and other forms of information in nature.[6] The sacred book was the center of institutionalized religious life, and the transmission of its contents was an apostolate for those who administered the books as well as for those who promoted the Gospel by copying sacred texts. The importance of the scribal hand in Jewish-Christian scholarship is doubtlessly connected with proselytizing communication, and communication in turn with the increasing power of a unifying institution. But for this study of psychic frameworks what must be emphasized is the fundamentally contemplative nature of scribal culture.

The cult of books in the Christian West, far from being an exclusive concern with proclamation (*kerygma*), was also essentially contemplative. Manipulation of the inscribed symbols as manuscript—both terms containing as a component the Latin word for *hand*—was a special kind of handiwork. Not only handy for the missionary apostolate of an expanding Christianity, the cult of the book was at the same time the cultivation of a transcending state of mind, of a distanced and composed contemplative attitude. The book was a psychic framework for personal transcendence. During the many onslaughts by barbarians, it was the monastic tradition that preserved books. Monks and dedicated ascetics used the book to preserve states of awareness beyond the mundane routines of necessity. The personal care and contemplation given to books in monasteries were more than a merely subjective piety and more than the religious zeal for processing information for propagating the faith. This can be seen in the monastic understanding of reading.

Books in the medieval period were far from indifferent receptacles of information. Reading was a *practice* in the strict sense of the term, a discipline and a way of life. Active reading was connected with prayer and the transformation of the spirit. The inscription of the book, held in the hands and read aloud with the lips, was meant to inscribe thoughts in the mind and heart:

> In the Middle Ages the reader usually pronounced the words with his lips, at least in a low tone, and consequently he hears the sentence seen by the eyes—just as today, in order to learn a language or a text, we pronounce the words. This results in more than a visual memory of the written words. What results is a muscular memory of the words pronounced and an aural memory of the words heard. The *meditatio* consists in applying oneself with attention to this exercise in total memorization; it is, therefore, inseparable from the *lectio*. It is what inscribes, so to speak, the sacred text in the body and in the soul.
>
> This repeated mastication of the divine words is sometimes described by use of the theme of spiritual nutrition. In this case the vocabulary is borrowed from eating, from digestion, and from the particular form of digestion belonging to ruminants. For this reason, reading and meditation are sometimes described by the very expressive word *ruminatio*.... To meditate is to attach oneself closely to the sentence being recited and weigh all its words in order to sound the depths of their full meaning. It means assimilating the content of a text by means of a kind of mastication which releases its full flavor. It means, as St. Augustine, St. Gregory, John of Fecamp, and others say in an untranslatable expression, to taste it with the *palatum cordis* (the heart's palate) or *in ore cordis* (in the heart's mouth). All this activity is, necessarily, a prayer; the *lectio divina* is a prayerful reading.[7]

The book was not solely a means for spreading the faith but was heaven itself, or at least a discipline for practicing heavenly states of mind. One authority on monastic culture says, "This deep impregnation with the words of Scripture explains the extremely important phenomenon of reminiscence whereby verbal echoes so excite the memory that a mere allusion will spontaneously evoke whole quotations and, in turn, a scriptural phrase will suggest quite naturally allusions elsewhere in the sacred books. Each word is like a hook, so to speak; it catches hold of one or several others which become linked together and make up the fabric of the whole."[8] Reminiscence is not the same as memorization, or the medium for storing items to be communicated. The book becomes a world unto itself; the mind and the heart—the psyche—become modeled on the book.

So strong was this sense of contemplative relationship to writing, including the calligraphic embellishment and illustration of texts, that monastic leaders defended the values of the scribal hand long after the proliferation of printed books began with the mechanical press. Five hundred years ago, at the end of the Middle Ages, the invention of printing was eroding the medieval art of copying by hand. Yet the raison d'être of manuscript, or hand-writing, was defended by some who argued that the printed page could never replace handwritten texts. At times the disagreement was on psychic grounds, on the qualitative spiritual difference between the thoughtful presence of mind that can be bestowed on texts written by hand and the more rapid, but potentially ephem-eral, efficiency of the printing process.

One of those who championed the handwritten page was John Trithemius (1462–1516), an early Renaissance humanist and the Benedictine abbot of Sponheim and St. James at Würzburg. Trithemius was an avid reader, a recognized scholar in the republic of letters, a polyhistor and serious teacher. The gradual erosion of handwritten texts was the occasion for his *In Praise of Scribes*. Printing was becoming the means for relatively rapid communica-tion. At the time, the medium for conveying news and for expressing personal moods and attitudes was still the handwritten letter. Letters between learned humanists constituted the foremost means of communication, and the personal letter brought forth its own literary genre, which, when later fed into the mechanical printing presses, began to connect the private self of the individual humanist with public readers other than the addressee. But Trithemius was at a crossroads where the trade-offs of the printed book culture became manifest to the manuscript culture.

In his *In Praise of Scribes* Trithemius wrote,

> He who gives up copying because of the invention of printing is no genuine friend of holy Scripture. He sees only what is and contributes nothing to the edification of future generations. But we, beloved brothers, shall keep in mind the reward of this sacred occupation and not slacken in our efforts, even if we were to own many thousands of books. Printed books will never be the equivalent of handwritten codices, especially since printed books are often deficient in spelling and appearance. The simple reason is that copying by hand involves more diligence and industry.[9]

Many of the reasons Trithemius gives in defense of the scribal hand have to do with the qualitative dimensions of hand-writing. Writing by hand imprints thought content—not on paper but on the soul: "As the scribe is copying the approved texts he is gradually initiated into the divine mysteries and miraculously enlightened. Every word we write is imprinted more forcefully on our minds since we have to take our time while writing and reading." Trithemius also sees in careful, contemplative reading the psychic qualities of a transcendent, more satisfying life: "Books sustain us in our desire for future bliss, soften the misery of our present exile, drive away vice, implant virtue, give strength in need and make tangible the fruits granted by the passing of time. How much would we know besides the things of this world if our consolation were not found in Scripture?"

Trithemius's argument for the priority of writing by hand includes not only the personal presence and care of a contemplative attitude, a respect for the sacredness of written symbols, but it includes, as could be expected of a missionary tradition of the Word Incarnate, the joint goal of bringing sacred truths to others: "In carefully considering the history of times past we are amazed to learn of the solicitude the ancients and the holy Fathers devoted to the copying of books, even with their own hands. They were quite aware of the twofold nature of this skill, which was both profitable for their own body and soul and also promoted the upright life of those who were to follow." This joint goal, which includes both the edification of others as well as personal transcendence, is connected with the outstanding trait of finely written and embellished texts, that is, their relative permanence: "The printed book is made of paper and, like paper, will quickly disappear. But the scribe working with parchment ensures lasting remembrance for himself and for his text." And: "All of you know the difference between a manuscript and a printed book. The word written on parchment will last a thousand years. The printed word is on paper. How long will it last? The most you can expect of a book of paper to survive is two hundred years. Yet, there are many who think they can entrust their works to paper. Only time will tell."

Formulation: The Book and Transcendence through Mental Forms

The temporality of the scribal presence of mind, the monumental dignity conferred on writing intended for future generations, affects also the psychic framework of the classic book in terms of the formulation of thoughts. While reading and writing books is, to be sure, configured with the outer world of communication and with social efficacy, on a deeper level books develop a solidity and fixity of thought in the psyche. This contemplative stasis is not instrumental but serves purposes of awareness and new levels of attention—that is to say, serves intrinsic purposes. Since the last century, it has become customary for philosophers after Nietzsche to trace the genesis of the value of moral stability and personal constancy to the socially useful or instrumental value such qualities have as ingredients in the "herd instinct." On such a suspicious but perceptive reading of Platonic aspirations, society accords high esteem and social reinforcement to behavior that is self-consistent, predictable, and therefore dependable. Such high evaluation of self-consistency and personal identity is inseparable, according to the Nietzschean critique, from a defensive wall set up by society against all self-transformation, relearning, and personal change; the latter threaten the inertial tendencies of social lethargy and diminish the organized, controllable behavior of the whole group.[10] But tracing the genesis of ideals such as self-consistency and steadiness of mind should not blind us to the *potency* of the Platonic model which generated so much of Western culture. If it is true that we must read Plato after Nietzsche, it is also equally true that reading itself—whether it be of Plato or of Nietzsche—must be examined anew and in the light of that alert and steady attention which has been the hallmark of the book. The book supports the cultivation of intellectual forms in the formulation of ideas.

The deliberate care and presence of mind exercised in the production of relatively permanent writings, as underscored by Trithemius, reflects a philosophical tradition that supports a distinctive approach to the formulation of ideas in language. In fact, ideas and the (intellectual) forms in formulation constitute the heart of this approach to thinking in symbols. Ideas and forms are, indeed, the very terms Platonic idealism contributes to our language, along with its other frequent contributions of cultural energy and desire for transcendence. The medieval advocates of the scribal hand buttressed the Platonic approach to formulation by emphasizing the resistance of the material element of writing and by stressing the artistic craftsmanship needed to overcome recalcitrant materials. The cost in time and in deliberate discipline was great, especially for producing elaborately illuminated manuscripts and calligraphic texts. But what is purchased by the painstaking care of craftsmanship is a sense of endurance, patience, and clear-eyed longevity. My treatment of formulation in the psychic framework of the book begins with this resistance and permanence of book materials as they relate to the philosophy of ideas as the source of mental wholeness and intellectual integrity; I then consider formulation in terms of the authenticity involved in the act of writing.

Hardly a mere tool, the scribal manuscript mirrors, at least in its general aspirations, the Platonic drive first to encounter and then transcend physical resistance. Physical resistance is transcended by being overcome or surpassed in the sense that physical resistance is transformed: the recalcitrance of the materials becomes, through craftsman's labor, the stable basis of relative permanence and durability. The transformation of materials, turning obstacles into the very means of perpetuation, demands and evokes psychic intensity. What Plato first called the idea (Greek for mental vision or formal identification of something) is the product of great inner intensity. In the *Dialogues*, psychic insights or ideas are frequently seen to be grounded in mania, frenzy, and obsessive fascination. Greek philosophy was rooted in love, or passion. Passionate attention, according to Plato, is the basis for Socrates' fatal enthusiasm for defining things, for seeing clearly and deeply behind appearances into the essences of things.

Plato gives us, in the *Symposium*, a picture of Socrates as "the great lover," on his way to a feast of discussions about love and passion: late for the beginning of the festivities, Socrates is found standing alone on a doorstep, rapt in thought, lost in contemplation until a servant comes to fetch him to the dinner.[11] During the lengthy discussions at the symposium, and especially after the speech of young Alcibiades, it is Socrates who appears to have attained the greatest mastery of love, both in practice and in understanding the highest sources of passionate attention. Socrates' love—at least as suggested by his story of Diotima— culminates in a passionate attendance to the ideas or in a lingering among stable mental visions.

In the *Symposium*, Plato grounds the ideas, the search to formulate and define through thinking, in the passionate nature and destiny of human beings. The drive for permanence that elicits human sexuality is continuous with the high intensity of art and contemplative thought, so much so that, in Diotima's speech in the Symposium, animal reproduction is made to parallel the creative intellectual drive for immortality. The constancy of attentive fascination (beauty) is common to both love and the psychic grasp of an idea. This conjunction of sexual regeneration and self-perpetuation was taken up again and again in the Platonic tradition. The full realization of human powers and creativity emerges in love and in contemplative attention to ideas.

Intellectually, the idea is what embraces and brings together the particulars of life and experience. Intellectual comprehension is a mental act that embraces many things in a single holistic focus. As such, the idea provides a greater wholeness than mundane experience of its own accord permits. To come to a conceptual understanding of something both distances one from the existing instances and simultaneously draws one to a closer intimacy with the lingering intellectual form of the thing. The intensity of this inner conceptual approximation the Greeks called Eros. And the ancient Greeks in general considered Eros to be a fascination with the perfection of form: clear, stable identities—a general trait of classical Greek art and literature.[12] In the book, both for the author and for the reader, the psyche can find a locus for symbols that offer occasions for the contemplation of clear, stable ideas and that nurture the love of ideas.

From this point of view, Plato's critical remarks about the book, as found in the Phaedrus, are ironically diversionary. They relate to the book sheerly as material object rather than as the psychic framework of thought. As object, the book may be understood to be a repository of information and a preserve of previous insights; it may be regarded as surrogate interlocutor. Compared with the personal intensity of Socrates, books do, of course, lack the direct erotic intensity needed for grasping true or stable ideas. The transformation theory, dependent as it is on the notion of media as communication storage, repeats Plato's criticism of the book when it comes to computers; the transformation theory, taken consistently, even views Plato as trapped by the ironies of his own medium. But Plato carried on Socrates' work, albeit in a slightly less dangerous way, by relocating the intensity of intellectual discovery within the psyche. The point is not to apply to computers what Plato said about the book; the point is rather to look at what Plato does with the book and what he does with the theory of ideas through the book. While some scholars note how Plato's dialogical style extends the structure of writing,[13] it must not be forgotten that Plato moves the Socratic act of philosophizing into a different element. Since Plato, Western philosophy could become a series of footnotes (to Plato) precisely because philosophic intelligence became identified with systematic, linear, and comprehensive intelligence—modeling its intelligence along the lines of a written book.[14] The book supports the contemplative formulation of ideas. It serves to aid the mind in finding a steady focus in the psychic flow. The book aids in the transformation of experience by raising attention from the mundane level in order to transcend to an encompassing wholeness.

The idea as a focus of contemplative concentration becomes the source of steady forms.[15] Around it perceptions and vivid experiences can gather to be organized. The idea is a felt point of attention wherein a thing becomes something, begins to matter, has definiteness and import. Ideas provide continuity for the constant stream of experience and for the fragmentary succession of life events. Insofar as ideas are cultivated, the inner psyche achieves greater wholeness within the contours of experience than mundane experience permits.[16] This inner landscape, when accompanied by respect and resolute consideration, is termed intellectual integrity. By drawing the energies of the psyche into the point of central fixity called the idea, the inner forms of things help shape the characteristic patterns of psychic energy. Through learning to focus on ideas, the mind itself grows more steady, more clear and definite in itself.

Platonism projects a model of the psyche, not a metaphysical entity, but a model for transcending the vagaries of daily experience. Where Plato speaks of the divine, we may speak of an aspiration to a Platonic or Socratic self-identity. Plato compares the psyche to the sea-god Glaucus, who is covered with seaweed and barnacles, dismembered by the rough seas, so that he seems more like a monster than what he is by nature. Beneath the tangle of mundane concerns, how shall we then find the soul? Plato answers:

> We must look to its love of wisdom. And we must note the things of which it has apprehensions, and the associations for which it yearns, as being itself akin to the divine and the immortal and to eternal being, and so consider what it might be if it followed the gleam unreservedly and were raised by this impulse out of the depths of this sea in which it is now sunk, and were cleansed and scraped free of the rocks and barnacles which, because it now feasts on earth, cling to it in wild profusion of earthy and stony accretion by reason of these feastings that are supposed to be happy. And then one might see whether in its real nature it is manifold or single in its simplicity, or what is the truth about it and how.[17]

The divine is the stable, "immortal," serene existence. The psyche becomes like the divine, stable order it contemplates:

> For surely, Adeimantus, the man whose mind is truly fixed on eternal realities has no leisure to turn his eyes downward upon the petty affairs of men, and so engaging in strife with them to be filled with envy and hate, but he fixes his gaze upon the things of the eternal and unchanging order, and seeing that those things neither wrong nor are wronged by one another, but all abide in harmony as reason bids, he will endeavor to imitate them and, as far as may be, to fashion himself in their likeness and assimilate himself to them. Or do you think it possible not to imitate the things to which

anyone attaches himself with admiration? Then the lover of
wisdom associating with the divine order will himself
become orderly and divine in the measure permitted to man.[18]

Intellectual integrity, as it is interpreted by the Platonic tradition,
is often associated with the moral-ethical quality also called
integrity. While there may be some latent connection between the
two meanings, our concern here is with the nonmoral, ontological
dimension of psychic integrity. Integrity in the ontological sense is
a wholeness of mind expressing a definite kind of apprehension of
the things in the world, and at the same time it expresses a standard
or model of intelligence for understanding the world. The way
things are seen and defined mentally, with contemplative care and
psychic coherence, reflects a truth or genuineness of the mind that
sees things. Plato expresses this by saying that the truth of things,
their firmness in apprehension, affects the truth of the mind that
sees them, so that the mind that contemplates truth becomes itself
more truthful, more like the stable identities it contemplates.

Obviously, the mind here is not understood as a passive
receptacle or blank slate on which things can write or make an
impression. The mind is, rather, an active and productive agent in
various modes. The mind is part of the living psyche. Through a
focus on ideas the mind becomes true, enjoys greater integrity and
wholeness. So the formulation nurtured by the book is also the
formation of the mind through expressions based on intellectual
form. Literacy in its bibliocentric element is, then, not constituted
primarily by the skills of information handling. The activity of
forming, of ideational focus, belongs to the kind of insight fostered
by the book. Information handling, the management of pregiven
data that is already essentially formed, is a fundamentally different
psychic activity. The value of literacy, in the Platonic tradition,
resides in the fact that literacy produces literate minds. Far from
tautological, the notion of a literate mind includes psychic qualities
such as wholeness of attention, contemplative presence of mind,

and a distance from the mundane pressures which scatter and fragment human experience. The literate mind is an achievement of the book—but not the book as a mere repository of communicative information or as a physical object.[19]

The Solitude of the Book and Mental Privacy

The notion of psychic integrity shades into that of mental privacy. Since formulation is a personal and contemplative activity, there is in it a felt sense of being the locus for the origination of an idea—idea in the sense of a mental vision of considerable intensity and focus. At least in its genesis, the idea arises and is formulated through the exercise of the powers belonging to an individual person. The resistance of materials in handwriting enhances the sense of felt origination. The genuine formulation of an idea is always one's own, no one else's; it is a child of the psyche: the very words may belong to a commonly shared and universally viewed idea, but the words themselves, their specific formulation, is my own. The stamp of characteristic ownership marks written thought as my own, acquired through the struggle with experience and with recalcitrant materials. Handwritten formulation thereby enhances a sense of personal experience or an integrity pertaining to the private, personal self.

The portability too of the printed book enhances the sense of private contemplative space. Because reading a book opens up a space for private thought, psychic transcendence through the book comes to include a certain purity in the sense of felt origination in the thought process. The purity is a felt sense of being a source, a free point of origination for a thought process. Purity is the figurative corner mentioned in the famous lines of Thomas à Kempis: "Everywhere I sought tranquility and found it nowhere, except sitting apart in a corner with a little book."[20] The notion of purity is especially germane in a mass society, where the external public realm is constantly assailed by claims that capture attention, through entertainment and through endless external stimuli. In such a polluted environment, the privacy of book reading and writing adds a pure sense of self to the origination or participation in the psychic framework of symbolized thoughts. This intimacy of thought with itself, this personal privacy is something that appears in the "one pure act" of the budding writer described in a novel by Henry Miller:

> Instead of rushing out of the house immediately after dinner that evening, as I usually did, I lay on the couch in the dark and fell into a deep reverie. "Why don't you try to write?" That was the phrase which had stuck in my crop all day.... In the darkness I began to work my way back to the hub. I began to think of those most happy days of childhood, the long Summer days when my mother took me by the hand, led me over the fields to see my little friends, Joey and Tony.... To write, I meditated, must be an act devoid of will. The word, like the deep ocean current, has to float to the surface of its own impulse. A child has no need to write, he is innocent. A man writes to throw off the poison which he has accumulated because of his false way of life. He is trying to recapture his innocence....

> The best thing about writing is not the actual labor of putting word against word, brick upon brick, but the preliminaries, the spade work, which is done in silence, under any circumstances, in dream as well as in the waking state. In short, the period of gestation. No man ever puts down what he intended to say: the original creation, which is taking place all the time, whether one writes or doesn't write, belongs to the primal flux: it has no dimensions, no form, no time element. In this preliminary state, which is creation and not birth, what disappears suffers no destruction; something which as already there, something imperishable, like memory, or matter, or God, is summoned and in it one flings himself

> like a twig into a torrent. Words, sentences, ideas, no matter
> how subtle or ingenious, the maddest flights of poetry, the
> most profound dreams, the most hallucinating visions, are
> but crude hieroglyphs chiselled in pain and sorrow to com-
> memorate an event which is untransmissible.[21]

Here Miller, in Romantic fashion, emphasizes the gap between symbols and the contemplative act prior to symbolization. He brings out the chaotic openness which drives toward the realization of distinct entities. This too has its correlate in Platonic tradition. Plato insists on a distinction between the silence of the idea gazed upon by the mind and the verbalization through which the idea is formulated.[22] This distinct gap protects the transcendent distance of the idea; it prevents the symbolization of language from degenerating into a state of trivialized and overly worn tokens of communication. Such a gap is experienced especially during the formulation of ideas as one undergoes a period of gestation. To give birth to a true brainchild, a genuine conception, there must be a prior period of silent gestation during which speed and manipulation are beside the point. Without the distance of silent, contemplative awareness, language in symbolic form becomes merely a social code of trivial tokens devoid of psychic depth. And what Miller calls innocence is the felt awareness of being a locus for the formulation of an idea, an origin from which words proceed and gather meaning. Being an origin for formulation is to be original in the truest sense.

As the felt locus of the origination of an idea, the temporality and solitude of the book foster the self-identical presence of mind known as authorship, or, in its passive aspect, readership. Originality occurs in the intimate privacy of the creative act, including the re-creation of an author's ideas in the reader's integral act of thought. The first grasp of an idea has been related, by Plato, to the experience of reminiscence, whereby something stirs deeply from within the psyche and allows one a sense of coming into one's own, of reclaiming what was always present in the inmost recess of the mind but only now emerges out of silence. With originality arises the author formulating an idea, bespeaking an eternal creation, as it were. The powerful sense of illumination and realization is what is behind the so-called authorial voice. The authorial voice is what Vladimir Nabokov calls "an anthropomorphic deity impersonated by me."

This special sense of psychic authority makes the writer, and the true reader, particularly vulnerable to every organized attempt to totalize social-political control over human beings. The author as well as the contemplative reader seized by an idea is a potential deviant from the administrative authority of the state and its managers. Totalitarian political philosophy witnesses, indirectly and by way of suspicion, to the power of the book as an important preserve of personal thought. Philosophers of totalitarian bent even go so far as to ascribe "bourgeois private consciousness" to the book, especially to the characteristic art forms of book writing, such as the novel; from the standpoint of totalitarian politics, the book, with its leisurely pace and concentration on individual feelings, threatens the efficacy of a well-maintained social consensus or "universal reason."[23] In a society concerned increasingly with total management and productivity, the person of books plays the dual role of one who is living out the heritage as well as the destruction of the book culture.[24]

Contemporary writers often use the fate of the traditional book as an emblem of personal thought under threat by a totalitarian network of human beings. The fate of the book in an age of collectivism is the theme of Ray Bradbury's novel *Fahrenheit 451*, later a film by Francois Truffaut. The protagonist of the novel is employed as a fire-starter in the official bureau of book-burners during a period when possessing or reading books is illegal (paper burns at 451 degrees Fahrenheit). In this putative future, reading is outlawed as a decadent form of individual self-assertion. Books threaten the benevolent, well-engineered State by introducing discontent and dissent. Old books are nevertheless preserved by a clandestine group camped just outside the cities. One day, the protagonist happens to meet a member of this group and notices the spontaneous, vivid way an individual's words can invest experience with significance and insight. He is fascinated and seeks exposure to the individual voices speaking through books. As he begins to break from the mechanical routine of book-burning, the protagonist reflects:

> Last night I thought about all the kerosene I've used in the past ten years. And I thought about books. And for the first time I realized that a man was behind each one of the books. A man had to think them up. A man had to take a long time to put them down on paper. And I'd never even thought that thought before. It took some man a lifetime maybe to put some of his thoughts down on paper, looking around at the world and life, and then I come along in two minutes and boom! it's all over.[25]

Finally, the former book-burner escapes, flees the city in search of the hidden enclave of readers and preservers of literature. The novel ends with a melancholy description of that esoteric but collective literary organization: each of its members commits to memory an entire book or set of books of a given author or period; each spends a lifetime rehearsing the words aloud and reciting passages on request; communication between and among members of the group is minimal and serves only to perpetuate the cult-activities of the secret organization. Like the organized culture in Hesse's *Glass-Bead Game*, the different social context of the book gives it an altered meaning. What once stood for intellectual integrity and the authority of personal formulation is now only a faint facsimile of the psychic truth of the book.

The reflections in this chapter have been cast deliberately in a historical and primarily retrospective tone. No single world properly incorporates within itself the totality of reality apprehensions.

We can only strive to recover something of the awareness we are about to release from our own historical world. There are trade-offs in reality apprehensions, limitations inherent in human awareness. A different psychic framework for symbolizing realities was called forth by the demands of the world in which the scribe and the monk first developed the book. A specific psychic framework constitutes the world of the book with its special claims on human attention and concern. The book, as it has been known in scribal and printed form, will never be the same once linguistic symbols are routinely encoded as digital information. But the characteristics of the book, in terms of its essential psychic framework, provide a contrasting background on which I can begin to assess the impact of computerized writing on human thought processes. The trade-offs through historical drift will be all that much more apparent once I have established a clear philosophical counterpoint.

As we shall see in the next chapter, digital writing supplants the framework of the book: it replaces the craftsman's care for resistant materials with automated manipulation; deflects attention from personal expression toward the more general logic of algorithmic procedures; shifts the steadiness of the contemplative formulation of ideas into an overabundance of dynamic possibilities; and turns the private solitude of reflective reading and writing into a public network where the personal symbolic framework needed for original authorship is threatened by linkage with the total textuality of human expressions. The critical encounter of the two symbolic elements, themes derived from the juxtaposition of chapters 5 and 6, is the subject of my next evaluational stage.

Chapter Seven

Critique of the Word in Process

"The moving cursor having writ...can erase or copy all of it."
—From an on-screen tutorial, "Programming the Apple Computer"

When the project to computerize the commentary on Jewish law got
under way at Bar Ilan University in Israel, the programmers faced a
puzzle. Jewish law prohibits the name of God once written from being
erased or the paper upon which it is written from being destroyed. Could
the name of God be erased from the video screen, the disks, the tape?
The rabbis pondered the programmers' question and finally ruled that
these media were not considered writing; they could be erased. In other
words, electronic text is impermanent, flimsy, malleable, contingent.
Where is Truth in impermanence, flimsiness, malleability, and
contingency?
—Pamela McCorduck, *The Universal Machine*

Digital Manipulation and Handwritten Care

Writing is usually done sitting down and has nothing to do with
heavy lifting; it is not considered a physical burden. Yet a certain
amount of drudgery has always attached to the task of putting
words on paper, and some writers have even attributed great
importance to the physically resistant materials as they affect their
writing consciousness. Word processing promises the removal of
drudgery, and drudgery is usually associated with menial tasks
connected with physical procedures. Word processing appears as a
liberating force, allowing unprecedented speed and convenience for
the writer, precisely in that word processing is the computerization
of the physical procedure. The convenient speed of computerized
automation at the same time expresses the entire context of
involvements or holistic world wherein the writing takes place.
The automated world develops certain channels in which human
beings care about things, and the psychic framework of word

processing fosters certain dispositions to care in certain ways about what one writes and thinks in the form of publicly accessible symbols.

Anachronistic defenders of handwriting are not alone in attributing a special kind of care to handwritten script. One habituated user of the word processor, Pamela McCorduck, stops in her enthusiasm for computers and sighs: "I pen a letter and am appalled at my handwriting. The keyboard, through which thousands of my words pour each day, is obliterating this sign—this signature—of myself."[1] The graphic stamp, or personal character, of the writer is more than a merely subjective component of the element of handwriting, as we have seen in the accounts in previous chapters. The graphic stamp is the subjective side of a process which includes the physical resistance of the materials and a respect for materials arising from this resistance. W. H. Auden, the poet and essayist, also noted how subjective qualities are filtered out by the public effect of typification, and he recognizes the psychic effects on the formulation of thoughts:

> Most people enjoy the sight of their own handwriting as they enjoy the smell of their own farts. Much as I loathe the typewriter, I must admit that it is a help in self-criticism. Typescript is so impersonal and hideous to look at that, if I type out a poem, I immediately see defects which I missed when I looked through it in manuscript. When it comes to a poem by somebody else, the severest test I know of is to write it out in longhand. The physical tedium of doing this ensures that the slightest defect will reveal itself; the hand is constantly looking for an excuse to stop.[2]

Computerized writing combines the subjective immediacy of the private thought process with the public, typified look of written text. When I feel the ease of managing the nearly liquid electronic text, I experience my own private thought process as directly impersonal, presentable, public.[3] The "signature of myself" is subtly disowned by the writing element. The typified automation of word processing removes the graphic stamp of character and does so with no apparent loss of personal immediacy.

Many writers, such as the French philosopher, teacher, and journalist Alain,[4] experience the writing process as sculptural, as a carving in resistant materials. "My pen is always trying to go through the paper; my writing is like wood sculpture, and I have to make shift with the cut of the chisel; how can I revise it? When a man gives himself up to inspiration, I mean to his own nature, I see nothing but the resistance of the material that could save him from hollow improvisation and the instability of the spirit."[5] The materials provide stability of spirit and a certain necessary control of the free improvisation process. Style, for Alain, was a question of heightening the resistance of writing materials and of language. With digital writing, material resistance is nearly eliminated and is certainly not brought out by word processing except in the negative mode of impatience with materials.

For Martin Heidegger, too, the basis for handwriting has to do with the primordial embodiment of human awareness:

Human beings "act" through the hand; for the hand is, like the word, a distinguishing characteristic of humans. Only a being, such as the human, that "has" the word (*mythos, logos*) can and must "have hands." Both prayers and murder happen through hands, as do gestures of gratitude and salutation, oaths and summoning, but also the "work" of the hands, "handwork" and equipment. The handshake seals the bond of association. The hand unleashes the "work" of ravaging devastation. The hand becomes present as hand only where there is disclosure and concealment. The animal has no hands, nor are hands derived from paws, claws, or talons. Even in moments of desperation the hand is never merely a "claw" with which the human being "crawls." The hand has only emerged from and with the word. The human

being does not "have" hands, but the hand contains the
essence of the human being because the word, as the essential region of the hand, is the essential ground of being
human. The word as something symbolically inscribed and
as thus presented to vision is the written word, that is,
script. As script, however, the word is handwriting.

It is not by chance that modern man writes "with" the
typewriter and "dictates"—the same word as "to invent creatively" [*Dichten*]—"into" the machine. This "history" of the
kinds of writing is at the same time one of the major reasons
for the increasing destruction of the word. The word no
longer passes through the hand as it writes and acts authentically but through the mechanized pressure of the hand. The
typewriter snatches script from the essential realm of the
hand—and this means the hand is removed from the essential
realm of the word. The word becomes something "typed."
Nevertheless, mechanical script does have its own, limited
importance where mechanized script serves as a mere tran-
scription for preserving handwriting, or where typewritten
script substitutes for "print." When typewriters first became
prevalent, a personal letter typed on a machine was regarded
as a lapse of manners or as an insult. Today, handwritten letters slow down rapid reading and are therefore regarded as
old-fashioned and undesirable. Mechanized writing deprives
the hand of dignity in the realm of the written word and de-
grades the word to a mere means for the traffic of communication. Besides, mechanized writing offers the advantage of
covering up one's handwriting and therewith one's character.
In mechanized writing all human beings look the same.[6]

Here Heidegger sees a primary connection of thought and gesture in
that both are tied to living in a specific, physically conditioned
environment. He sees the connection between thinking and bodily
orientation broken by the intervention of mechanical devices in

those cases where the devices usurp the primary connection of thought and gesture as they are rooted in the physical environment. He focuses on the typification process brought about through the modern rationalist model of standardized intelligibility, which underscores the qualities of repetitious, formal specifications and instant clarity and certainty.

These criticisms of the typewriter, though far from irrelevant, are somewhat off the mark now that personal computers have made mechanized typewriters obsolete. The hand is drawn once again into a nonmechanical, nonimprinting process. The writing action of word processing is related again to personal bodily gestures, such as pointing and moving things, but the actions are done in an already typified element. Direct hand movements are no longer simply replaced by an industrial-mechanical mode of action; the gestures of word processing operate in a typified environment but do so in ways that have left behind the industrial machine with its cumbersome but efficient mediation of human actions. The electronic element shifts the personal quality of action onto another level. Formulation can establish impersonality while achieving a directness undreamt of with the typewriter. One writer avers: "The multi-windowed screen is a more accurate image of my mental process while I am writing and thinking than any linear typescript could ever be." Yet critics of digital writing are correct in connecting the decline of personal letters with the last stand of handwriting; there seems to be a synchronicity. One critic remarks:

> I write letters longhand when I really do want to communicate with someone. I love the physical process; I like to write, physically. I like shaping my paragraphs and sentences on the page. I revise and insert endlessly on the page and I get a sort of sculptural pleasure out of revising with my hands. I love the words that I use, and I like to have immediate contact with them. I love the English language and love the words as they are, letter by letter, and the shape of them, and

how I make them when I write, and I don't want to lose
touch with that.[7]

Here the hand is related to personal care, and the perception is
supported that computers have a place in the more public presentations of thoughts but not in the more intimate realm of personal
communication. The recurrent word *love* underscores the felt
intimacy of language, thought, and bodily motion.

Handwritten care, however, is seldom connected any longer with
the writing of personal letters. Nor is the advance of thought any
longer connected with personal correspondence. While there was
once a serious culture based on the exchange of personal correspondence, little is left of the cultivation of the personal letter. In
Europe, the death of the letter culture is a commonplace, and
Europeans should know, because much of their culture and
intellectual influence was once maintained by the exchange of
letters, going back to the humanists of the Renaissance who
championed personal thought while at the same time encouraging
the further publication of their letters through the printing press.
Today, however, even the most avid writers of personal letters
invariably join the phonocentric culture that surrounds them.
When Europeans speak of the death of the traditional letter culture,
they mean to convey something of the personal history and
frustration expressed by one American professor who describes
his personal experience in the following terms:

> From the ages of 14–21, I was a prolific writer of letters. I
> wrote volumes—volumes. Tons. Long, long letters, often 10 to
> 15 typed pages: to family, teachers, friends, newspapers,
> magazines, radio stations, scholars I didn't know personally.
> And I modelled myself on Goethe, Eckermann, Proust, Henry
> James, T. S. Eliot, Virginia Woolf, and other men and women
> of "belles lettres."
>
> But eventually, I wore myself out. I was hurt, frustrated,
> embittered, disappointed, disheartened. Why? Because I

rarely, if ever, got a response: almost never, in any event, a letter of equal intensity, equal honesty, equal literary effort. So I finally gave up. And, in fact, I've never resumed that kind of effort since.

Most of my letters are very brief. I avoid writing letters whenever possible. I much prefer the phone. I don't really enjoy writing letters. And I simply don't have the time or energy to put into that kind of effort.[8]

The notion that letters can be simultaneously individual, personal, frequent, lengthy, and imperishable seems to have quite vanished. The typed but personal letter, having changed from insult to propriety, is now giving way to the merged form letter, which knows only a typified, information-generated individuality. In place of the personalized letter there has emerged the cordial note or, even more commonly, the ubiquitous memo (connected etymologically with *memorable* but here in the sense of *reminder*). In the case of both memo and note, the semipublic quality of typescript yields fully to the increasingly official atmosphere of writing. Automation through computer writing is very likely the terminal point of the personal letter, at least the personal letter as a printed, individual, cultural form.

The personal letter conveyed a coherent, individual identity and addressed another; it had a physical kinship with the personal pleasures of the book. Many writers echo this sentiment when criticizing word processing, saying that word processing is simply unsatisfying physically and aesthetically in ways that books and papers are not. A tactile pleasure comes from the personal ownership of a book. A professor of education writes,

Aside from being easily portable and readable, in comparison to an electronic screen, and aside from its physical attractiveness, the book (with its pages) conveys a tactile quality and pleasure that no push-button circuitry can provide—even when one is only browsing or skimming through a book, or making marginal notations (preferably only on the pages of

one's own books). The physical attributes of a book and its
printed pages are far more personal than the computer screen
or printout, as indicated by the common practice of writing
one's name in a book to designate valued ownership, or of
writing an inscription when presenting a book as a gift to a
friend.[9]

This criticism is more than sentimental reaction, for it acknowledges the intimacy of thought and language and symbolic element
and it recognizes the psychic framework of symbols in the
transformation of human beings.

Yet these qualities of the book and of handwritten care may
become luxuries by the year 2000. Such, at least, is the argument
from economics put forward by those who, like Gary Kildall, are
currently envisioning and working to produce an actual version of
Alan Kay's "Dynabook," a notebook-size computer capable of
accessing and storing vast amounts of information.[10] Designers like
Kildall argue that on sheerly economic grounds the electronic
"book" accessing the equivalent of two hundred printed books will
displace paper books by the end of the century. With the advent of
cheap optical disk readers, the microcomputer can deliver information at a greatly reduced cost when compared with printed books.
Though art books may not come under this generalization, the
computerized book will be able to provide animated or dynamic
graphics and incredibly powerful search and locate capabilities.
Encyclopedias and dictionaries are already available on compact
disk. The paperless society may find the privately owned book a
charming memento of a more person-centered age.

That we are approaching a paperless society and that computers
minimize the involvement of the unique movements of the personal
hand are not trivial suggestions or sentimental criticisms. They
touch the ontological foundations of our world, the way we turn to
apprehend realities. The shift in economics is inseparable from a
different apprehension of truth. Today, what is true presents itself

within the drive toward greater productivity, better management and control, and increased organization through technology. Things present themselves first and foremost as things to be managed, organized, and scheduled. When reality is apprehended under the guise of Total Management (if we update Heidegger's notion of the Enframing), then thinking too falls under the heading "knowledge productivity." Today far more pages are produced as an ancillary function of corporations and of government agencies than by all the traditional book, magazine, and newspaper publishers combined.[11] Instead of what was traditionally called the intellectual, we are developing what Alvin Toffler calls, somewhat glibly, the cognitariat. This he defines as "a group possessing organized information, imagination, and other cultural qualities essential for production of more information. It owns what might be regarded as either an essential raw material, or, alternatively, a kit of mental tools."[12] The human being becomes part of the resources of an information system, including word processing, which spurs on accelerated productivity.

As a resource in the system of Total Management, the human being in the computer interface undergoes a transformation in the felt sense of time, as is commonly noted by novice computer users. A philosophy professor notes,

It is impossible to avoid the feeling, as one becomes more deeply involved in computer use, that one has been drawn into a world quite different from the world one once dwelled in. There is a phenomenological dimension of computer use which accompanies growing experience and facility: one learns to anticipate the computer's responses to various situations, and to predict its behavior, in a way which seems vaguely like the process of learning the customs of an unfamiliar culture. Computers are endlessly patient and stubbornly unyielding in their consistency, and as I have learned to accommodate their intolerance of ambiguity I cannot help but feel that the random access memory and the basic operating system of my own thinking have undergone subtle shifts. Moreover, one's sense of time is radically altered: a program which takes two or three seconds to respond to a command comes to seem intolerably slow, and printers which outpace the most skillful typist by an order of magnitude or more nevertheless seem to take an eternity to chatter out a paper.[13]

The other and darker side of entering the "unfamiliar culture" of a "world quite different" is the pathology known as technostress, a sense of stress due to a felt acceleration of time. The term appears as the title of a study by Craig Brod.[14] Brod writes of psychiatric patients who begin "internalizing the standards by which the computer works: accelerated time, a desire for perfection, yes-no patterns of thinking." These internalized standards combine to reduce the ability of the person to "perform creatively or to relate to others in a loving way."[15] Brod seems at times to refer technostress not to the *world* of the computer but to a certain aberration induced by computer use or by fear and avoidance of computer use.[16] At other times, however, he seems to refer technostress to the entire human condition in the contemporary world, as expressed by the use of computers, which are bringing about a "mental sweatshop":

Our expectation is that computer technology, with its split-second accuracy, will save time, make our work easier, and create more leisure time. But computers are anything but mere replacements for pen, paper, and typewriter. By offering us so much power, speed, and accuracy, they are expanding at a breathless pace our concept of what we can—and should—do. Equipped with a portable business computer, Sam Armacost, the forty-four-year-old chief executive of the Bank of America, stays in touch with a dozen other top executives of the bank. At Armacost's "suggestion," the other senior executives have been trained to run their systems at the office and home. They can "talk" to one another at any time, day or night. Do these executives really find that being constantly on-line has afforded them more free time?[17]

Brod defines *technostress* as a modern disease of adaptation—either an anxiety and unwillingness to accept computer technology or an overidentification with computers.[18] The primary symptom of overidentification is "loss of the capacity to feel and to relate to others."

> Those in this technocentered state tend to be computer pro-grammers and other professionals, but anyone who is intensely and constantly working or playing with computers is at risk. Technocentered people tend to be highly motivated and eager to adapt to the new technology. Unwittingly, however, they begin to adopt a mindset that mirrors the computer itself. Signs of the technocentered state include a high degree of factual thinking, poor access to feelings, an insistence on efficiency and speed, a lack of empathy for others, and a low tolerance for the ambiguities of human behavior and communication. At its most serious, this form of technostress can cause aberrant and antisocial behavior and the inability to think intuitively and creatively. In some cases, spouses report that their technostress partners began to view them as machines.[19]

So it appears that Brod attributes technostress to the psychological process of identification or overidentification. As both resource and participant in the altered time structures of accelerated produc-tivity, the human being begins to suffer under the pressures necessarily put on all materials so that maximum productivity can be achieved. Stress, then, becomes the prevalent pathology of our time, just as hysteria or neurosis was once the dominant pathology in the period of Sigmund Freud's first explorations.

But Brod's psychological observations may be deepened to touch on the ontological dimension: the psyche not only as pertaining to an arbitrarily afflicted individual but psyche as the comprehensive center of reality apprehensions. It is not that our tools come to dominate us along the lines of the Sorcerer's Apprentice, externally subjecting us to stressful pressures as we come to understand ourselves in the image of the computer. On the contrary, rather than being an internalization of the computer's instrumental qualities— as if the computer were a curse imposed from outside—the pathological impatience and yen for speed are expressions of the integral world of Total Management we increasingly inhabit. Not a mere tool to pick up or set down, the computer interface is, moreover, an instrument on which we express ourselves, just as the practiced musician becomes the viola or violincello, the sounds produced being as much inhabitants of the psyche as "results" of certain technical operations of hands, fingers, and muscles applied to an exterior arrangement of wires and wood. It is our mind and will which express themselves in the computer, and the gap experienced between mechanical response and electric impulse is less a personal impatience, an unwillingness to suffer, than the current limits of the technological implementation of complete control.[20] If word processing fosters an algorithmic perspective on physical operations, as suggested in previous chapters, it does so in the name of complete control and efficiency. Technostress is not a passing personal debility but a psychic disposition inherent in the abiding cultural trance, in the way things are apprehended and preserved, under the project of Total Management. Emphasis on productivity (even in the intimate sphere of writing and thought) is part of the pressure of the contemporary world, or, clinically expressed, part of the syndrome calling for a therapy for stress. Stress itself now also comes under the general rubric of stress management. No single object or set of circumstances is the cause of stress but the managed world itself has become inherently stressful and holds all things—including human beings—under constant stress needed to provoke and manage things for always accelerated productivity. The constant stressful provocation of human powers also affects the formulation of ideas.

Contemplative Formulation under Technostress

The integrity of the psyche under the stress of the technological world is affected too in its characteristic formulation of ideas. This is especially apparent once we have a fully developed notion of idea as it emerged and evolved in the Platonic tradition. The contemplative idea, as we have seen in previous chapters, is a focal point around which many lines of experience are related and drawn, as it were, into an integral whole. The integrity of formulation and its authenticity are affected by the automation of the symbolic element in several ways.

Insofar as managerial and calculative modes of thought are inherent in word processing, they effect a constant pull away from the focus of the idea in formulation. Calculative power can distract from contemplative thought even, and perhaps especially, when it has become second nature. Manipulative control requires a certain inner distance. What was once operative in physical resistance is transformed into the mental energy required for computerization. Whereas the culture of the book, especially in its scribal phase, emphasized the physical confrontation and transformation of resistance, digital writing supplants the physical confrontation with a different kind of thinking. In chapter 5 we discussed the proclivity for algorithmic thinking induced by computerizing writing motions; many professional writers today still resist word processing precisely because "it takes too much time and energy away from the actual writing." What Joseph Weizenbaum says about the seductive dangers of "compulsive programming" applies mutatis mutandis to the writer composing on the word processor with any but the most elementary, prepackaged writing program.[21] With the incitement of human powers under the stress of productivity, it is quite natural for many writers to speak of computer writing as addictive: "Like so many others, I'm hooked on word processors like I'm hooked on electric lights and a car. I know the spiritual benefits of living closer to the primal technologies that nature bequeaths us, but am seduced by the material gains granted by the grosser technologies of modern life."[22]

Yet the appeal of word processing comes not essentially from "material gains." There is a fetching new model of intelligence operative in computer-based writing, a model that pertains to the addictive speed in formulating ideas. It simply will not do to repeat the worn comic line as one holds up a pencil, "Here's my word processor!" This boast has about as much cogency to our world as the jester who brandishes a shoe and exclaims, "Here's my transportation!" The new way of managing intellect appeals more to the spirit than it does to material gains, and the spirit is a new one—or at least it is the latest implementation of the long-standing spirit of modernity. The appeal is to thoroughgoing productivity, a productivity that manages even the spontaneous meanderings of the mind. As stated by the documentation for the outliner *Thoughtline*: "Experience the joy of random thought ... Captured."[23] The idea-processing software discussed in previous chapters supports brainstorming, fact compilation, organizing, and reorganizing in ways that go far beyond the notebooks, index cards, blackboards, and appointment books of the precomputer world.[24] As life without electric lights now seems mean and backward, so writing without computers is primitive and crude. If the quill pen is gone, so is the typewriter. The crudity of other symbolic elements is comprised of the relative slowness and lack of control over resistant materials. Compared to working with traditional materials, writing on a computer feels like speedwriting, on a parallel with speedreading.

The speedy, interactive kind of thought formulation discussed in previous chapters has about it something of the electricity of thought, the instantaneous drive of intuitive ideation. This electric element for symbols is fun, in the sense of stimulating the human's innate physiological fascination with light and fire, with the joy of zapping, with the sense of holding absolute control over the symbolizations of thought. The book, on the other hand, produces a different kind of trancelike state where concentration and inner suggestibility are heightened. With the book, deep recesses of mind are reached through contemplative concentration and the sustained suggestions of stable symbols. The slight hypnosis induced by phosphorescent symbols effects a greater optical break with much of the everyday sensory environment, but this does not mean that concentration through radiant symbols is any deeper on the psychic level. Superficial glitter may in fact prohibit deeper assimilation. Those who defend the aesthetics of the printed page really intend to advocate something more than an appreciation of pleasant surfaces; they suspect the psychically different kinds of literacy.

The inner gestation of thought formulation is foreshortened. An increase in reading speed comes with practice at reading the rapidly scrolling computer screen, especially where data is interchanged in the form of messages and on-line communication. Verbal life becomes faster paced, ideational flow is emphasized over gestation, and what William James calls "the active expectation of the not yet verbalized" grows shorter in span. The FORMation of words in formulation is, consequently, truncated. The traditional activity of formulation seeks to halt attention by reaching toward terms that are richly laden with experiential content. The intentionality, or characteristic "movement of thought," belongs to a deep and unconscious level of the psyche. The speed of formulation and the foreshortening of the gestation period belong to the psychic framework of word processing.[25] This does not mean they are immediately obvious after a couple of sessions with a computer. In fact, the first impression of greater control makes it seem as though you are in complete control rather than being affected by the psychic framework of word processing. It is not easy to describe the precise way in which a symbolized idea is affected by a different psychic framework, just as the digital timepiece evidently gives us the same time that a mechanical timepiece does. But the difference between a fresh egg laid by a barnyard hen and an industrially forced egg is unmistakable, though subtle, to the palate.

Formulation in word processing is more immediate, resulting in sets of symbols that are less developed on the basis of sequential organization. With the word processor, the difficulty of getting started is less of a problem. Starting with random sentences and phrases, one finds it easy to begin writing, only later to elaborate and structure what has been entered into a file. With a word processor, the logical beginning point of a sequence is less dominant over the material it orders.[26] Because the writer can begin anywhere in a text, then effortlessly reorganize and restructure paragraphs, word processing offers to many a cure for the notorious writer's block that arises from the terror of the blank page. Immediacy reduces the terror of writing, since the screen can be continually revised and played with to reduce the frozen self that appears on paper. There is always room later for unlimited refinement and polishing—if there is time. By bypassing the anxiety of gestation, the user can overcome certain counterproductive attitudes. Yet immediacy leads also to a greater abundance of material of a less refined sort. Because of the ease of electronic automation, writers simply produce more without necessarily undergoing the refining process whereby experience is slowly digested and then structured inwardly. Paper writing traditionally offered a disciplined look at what you think; digital text is, characteristically, output.

The immediacy of word processing is due in part to the interactive nature of computer software, as I mentioned in chapter 5. The interaction of human mind and machine develops a certain kind of alert interconnection between what a person is thinking and the symbolic element in which thought becomes writing. The interactive nature of computerized writing can be seen in these critical comments from a writer about an automated spell-checking program:[27] "I just checked 'gypped' and *Light* said it was spelled OK when I asked it. I hit Escape, then pressed the spacebar—and it beeped at me. It also beeped at me when I quoted it—and it beeps at me when I spell beeped or beeps!" The physical symbols of language in the electric element are immediate in the sense of radiant, both to write and to read. Radiant means streaming out, holding direct attention, even tiring optical nerves with the sustained fixity of attention. Because they stream out, such symbols do not call forth the tranquil gaze of a reader to ponder words lying quietly on a page.

The immediacy and directness experienced by the writer has been aptly called "writing without barriers" or even "sprint writing."[28] Because automation enables the writer to clean up the text later in a thoroughly powerful and automated way, the formulation of thoughts in external, typified symbols occurs with great immediacy and directness, thus promoting what I referred to in an earlier chapter as writer-based text. One experienced writer and software developer says,

> Word processing lowers the barriers to full expression. A touch typist can compose far faster at the keyboard than with paper and pencil, and without fear of errors. If you consider a document as a "snapshot" of a writer's thoughts, then past technologies have suffered from a kind of Heisenberg effect, where the act of observation changes the thing being observed. Writer's cramp enforces economy. My own experience, particularly with letters composed on a word processor, is that electronic copy more closely resembles speech.
>
> Yet, there is still a major factor preventing a word processed document from being a snapshot of thoughts: a writer must consider the audience. A reader will share neither the writer's knowledge of facts, the writer's background knowledge, nor the writer's sentiments. Thus, a writer must in-

clude enough information to convey the thought effectively, which often interrupts the thought itself. Also, a reader's attention span is limited, and his concentration level differs from that of listening. The careful writer must take these concerns into account and must break up the thoughts. To me it seems that today's automated writers sacrifice economy for completeness. Perhaps our society's obsession with detail, combined with a general view of artistic expression as "inefficient" or non-utilitarian can explain these emphases.[29]

Here is the notion that word processing reclaims something of the direct flow of oral discourse. But, as a consequence, a certain step is bypassed in composition. Though the step of considering audience belongs more properly to rhetoric and communication, it might be added to the general erosion of the gestation period of formulation, the long inner ferment a writer must endure when working with physically resistant materials. While there is in word processing a closer approximation to oral-aural language, paradoxically, a certain "forgetting the situation" occurs in which any writing, as written and not spoken, takes place.

Allied to this immediacy is the writing pattern known to users of computerized telecommunications as flaming. Flaming is the tendency to write messages on the computer so directly that the usual norms of civility and politeness fall away. Like other forms of writing, electronic mail allows for leisure to read and consider what was written without the pressures of real-time replies. Like messages on the telephone, however, electronic mail arrives in less than an hour, and there is a freshness to it without the need for the exchange of small-talk that usually accompanies telephone conversation. The use of electronic mail, some researchers have found, promotes a "confrontational style."[30] Just as anger often brings forth words the speaker later regrets, so too does the directness of digital writing sometimes surprise the writer—and may even upset the reader. So writing without barriers can also prove to be writing without restraint. The formulation of electric writing is less contemplative than writing in other elements.

It has also been noted, especially by observers of telecommunications, that grammatical liberties and certain uncultivated aspects of informal spoken language are especially perceptible in digital writing. Vulgar or street talk infiltrates communication; there is greater in*form*ality—because less formation, less formulation. The focus of such writing ceases to be formal and is directed toward definite forms or ideas. If, as Ezra Pound suggested,[31] prose differs from poetry in that the former is "less charged," then we might say that digital writing differs from traditional prose in that the former displays a charge with less central focus and less mental integrity. In this sense, what Heidegger, Herder, and Vico before them say about the pristine power of original language is especially in danger of total oblivion. For these philosophers, the power of language lies in its pristine, evocative creativity, in other words, its poetry—something that is lost with the charge of digital prose.

The diminished charge of digital writing is related also to the simple abundance made possible by automation. Automation, because of its ease and speed, releases possibilities of productivity to such a degree that the writer is quickly overwhelmed by the actual amount of text produced and by the amount of text that can be accessed directly and drawn upon to aid composition. With so much text available, symbolized language acquires the ambiance of cheap, disposable consumer goods.[32] There is an inflation of text through word processing. And the glut of text produced, rather than being pulled together by integral vision or symphonic intelligence, is frequently the result of sporadic sprint writing. Fragmentation and incoherence have been frequently noted as characteristics of word processing. If creative abundance—what Erasmus called *copia*, or copious profusion—is the virtue of digital writing, then fragmentation in the formulation of ideas is the corresponding vice.

The vision of one of the developers of the notion of word processing has been described in this way:

> He yearned for more than a lazy man's typewriter. He
> wanted the freedom to steer thought paths in new ways. He
> wanted to have the freedom to insert and delete words and
> move paragraphs around, but he also wanted the computer to
> remember his decision path. One of the specs was for
> something he called "historical backtrack," in which the
> computer could quickly show him the various earlier alterna-
> tive versions of his ever-changing text. "Alternative
> versions?" From a place to store notes to a tool for sculpting
> text, his term project had now landed him in even more
> wondrous science-fiction territory, a place where it was
> possible to think in terms of parallel alternatives. Of entire
> libraries of parallel alternatives, and automated librarians to
> perform the most tedious of searches in microseconds. Why
> should we abandon any thought at all? Why not just store
> every variation on everything and let the computer take care
> of sifting through it when we want to view something?[33]

This superabundance of possibilities is comparable to Nietzsche's description of nihilism as a state of indetermination wherein everything is permitted—and as a result nothing is chosen deeply, authentically, and existentially. Boiler-plate text and reusable fragments haunt all word-processed writing as a constant lure and possibility. Fragments, the experienced user learns, can be used and reused, can be fit in somewhere and without much effort. The inevitable *mot juste* gives way to the more convenient *réchauffé*.

This is one of the senses in which word processing manifests truth destabilized. That is, if the mind is made truthful by the fixity of the stable idea, as Platonism maintains, then the volatility of the electric element insures that the felt sense of truth is undermined. The ephemeral quality referred to in the epigraph to this chapter is perceived as undermining the reliability and permanence attributed to the sacred word. Because its symbolic element is impermanent, flimsy, malleable, contingent, the word processor has provided a new metaphor for the eclipse of all absolutes. When in 1984 he was questioned about objections to a new tax proposal, U.S. Secretary of the Treasury Donald T. Regan said on the national television network NBC, "It was written on a word processor. That means it can be changed." The definiteness that was once the prize attribute of written symbols now shimmers on the flickering screen. What stands before the eyes is a continuous scroll with endless other symbols, going on and on interminably. The context of written words undergoes a sea change.

Possibility dominates over consistency of vision—at least as consistency was envisioned by the book tradition and by the philosophical mentality. But this is not possibility in any grounded sense of taking up a certain kind of existence based on a distinct context or felt necessity; it is not the possibility seized by the purity of one's own inner voice. On the contrary, such a proliferation of possibilities remains free-floating because they remain under the supervisory control of technical power. The possibility field is akin to the idle curiosity that can paralyze any effort to effectively come to grips with things. With word processing a creative superabundance prevails over the composure of the mind characteristic of traditional formulation. Mental excitement and stimulation supplant mental composure.

The glut of possibilities opened by word processing is akin to the *curiositas* condemned in the Middle Ages and to the existential *Neugier* inveighed against by Heidegger's *Being and Time*. Such a glut may lead to the disappearance of the authentic and determinate human voice or personal presence behind symbolized words. Some time ago the philosopher Henry Veatch raised the question about our culture's two logics: first a traditional (Aristotelian) logic with rules for the predicate inferences "natural" to the spoken and written word according to which the human being usually makes rational inferences in direct, everyday address; and second, a "spider-like" calculus which weaves logical relations of great technical power and abstraction without, however, being necessarily grounded in any particular individual human enunciation or intentionality, but rather solely in a mathematical logic of relations between terms.[34] How, asked Veatch, can we have two logics with such divergent—as he demonstrated—ontological bases? With the embedding of symbolic, relational logic in the circuits of the microchip, it only now becomes possible to see how this seemingly schizoid state of affairs, described as such twenty years ago, has reached an equilibrium, perhaps even something of a *telos*, or final realization. The manipulative, relational "spider logic" described by Veatch has become the vehicle for underlying code which is used to interpret the alphabetized assertions of natural-language logic. The language of direct assertion gets poured into the electric element, where the logic of manipulative power reigns supreme. It becomes possible to treat the entire verbal life of the human race as one continuous, anonymous code without essential reference to a human presence behind it, which neither feels it must answer to anyone nor necessarily awaits an answer from anyone.[35] The absence of personal presence so proper to the written letter will be not just absence but anonymity.

In the psychic framework of word processing, text is increasingly experienced as data. The computer's lightning speed in handling data enables the word processor to treat enormous amounts of textual material as a data base which can be searched and referenced with powerful indexing capabilities. Programs to create and maintain textual databases, such as *ZyIndex*, *FYI*, *411*, and the *Idea Processor*, all make it possible to access previously created writings with great flexibility, usually through the use of Boolean logical operators. Add to this the on-line databases that are continually growing, the new *ScholarNet* and *HumaNet* for the social sciences and humanities, and virtually any text can become the data for computer searches. As the writer or reader now controls the search process through a logically determined program, certain random and intuitive kinds of reading and consulting will no longer be possible in referencing procedures. Except where human error has caused the search to go off in totally irrelevant ways, what one accesses on line will tend to be precisely what one is looking for—always filtered in advance by the terms of Boolean logic. The thoughtful paging and browsing through tangentially related books, all done at a leisurely pace, will no longer be afforded by computerized writing and reading. Where the lawyer once took days to page through printed legal material to search through precedent cases and relevant statutes, the computer will now provide instant references with complete accuracy—and the computer user will have less occasion to consider and mull over tangentially related law and thus over the desirability of one or another course of legal action. The system of texts will be more accurately preserved but will afford less leisure of contemplative formulation. The legal system too is coming under the stressful demands of the technological world.

Textual database searches conceal as well as reveal what it is we learn. The Boolean search operations help hone our intentions and thought impulses as they begin to seek something. What is possible with the computer's logic defines in part what it is we seek. But, in so doing, the computer in fact hones down our intentions and impulses in the sense of making them narrower or at least different from the spacious meanderings that belong to the traditional looking up and leisure browsing. As more is revealed to us more accurately and with greater control, we lose something of the spontaneous thought process that does not happen to dovetail with the power of computerized writing. With time and increased electronic space for data storage, the event of concealment will become manifest, thus in a sense exposing the concealment. For, even though we will have more storage space, the problems of the finitude of personal time and the eventual copyright limitations inevitably placed on direct access will increase. While computer searching is far more powerful than paging through books, searching texts requires eventually some form of abstract or index—just as, analogously, a hard disk user needs a considerably more elaborate way of maintaining access to files than does the floppy disk user. When you search for information on where to find a text, for instance, you might find there also some notion of the contents of what you seek, perhaps in the form of an abstract created by an auto-paraphrase program, or some brief extracts, or maybe even a summary with a brief evaluation made by an evaluator. The way thought finds and then encounters a piece of writing available in digital form will inevitably limit the way a text is approached—even in ways the author may find objectionable.[36]

Linked to the Network of Texts

Digital writing turns the private solitude of reflective reading and writing into a public network where the personal symbolic framework needed for original authorship is threatened by linkage with the total textuality of human expressions. Anyone writing on a fully equipped computer is, in a sense, directly linked with the totality of symbolic expressions—more so and more essentially so than in any previous writing element. The printing press expanded the connection between private and public mind and did so by overcoming the material resistance that gave quality and public affirmation to what a person put into symbols. As the whole notion of publishing, of making public, is shifted by word processing, so too is the correlate concept of privacy. Digital writing, because it consists in electronic signals, puts one willy-nilly on a network where everything is constantly published. Privacy becomes an increasingly fragile notion. Word processing manifests a world in which the public itself and its publicity have become omnivorous; to make public has therefore a different meaning than ever before.

As described in chapter 5, digital writing fosters cooperative, group writing. The fully equipped computer develops this collectivist aspect of the psychic framework of word processing both with regard to atmosphere and content of thought. Criticisms touch both aspects.

The notion that the atmosphere of word processing is one that fosters a noncreative flow of overabundant, anonymous symbols is already to be found in the metaphors used in contemporary discussions of the way writing is handed down by tradition. Consider the metaphorical sense of *word processing* as one scholar uses it in describing the criticism of Homer's epic poetry. He is discussing the narrowing of Homeric criticism ever since Homer's writing has been taken primarily as an expression of the oral tradition (as does the transformation theory discussed in chapter 2):

> They lost sight of Homer's poetry, stressing the limitations of oral composition and the impossibility of invention within the Tradition, which they saw as monolithic. They concentrated on fixed elements and inflexibilities, on whatever oral poetry allegedly cannot do. The Tradition became a kind of data bank, and the bard or singer of tales, now anonymous, became a word-processing outlet.... [Adam] Parry's specific analysis is vulnerable, but his basic insight was acute and it has been more and more influential. Homer was not a teleprinter; he was both within his tradition and against it. He was, that is, the beneficiary of its store of diction, scenes, and concepts, and at the same time he questioned them and went beyond them.[37]

The oral tradition here becomes conceived by analogy with word processing and with the network of digital text. The criticism of the psychic framework of word processing is implied but clear, the implication being that word processing gives a wholly new meaning to *tradition*. The body of individually creative and deeply felt writings is a tradition worth venerating and relearning; the electronically automated body of symbolized meanings possesses nothing venerable in itself. All text is input, including the creative voice of the individual, which is itself homogenized by the total textuality of the network.

This omnivorous abundance applies as well to the individual microcomputer, especially as the dreams of the developers of word processing become reality:

> Everybody can create what they want and put it on the system, from sonnets to pamphlets to textbooks, and everybody can quote or cite any other document. Documents can consist of links. Compendia, guided tours, directories, and indexes will spring up as independent documents; order would become a valuable commodity. "The result is a seemingly anarchic pool of documents, true, but that's what literature has been anyhow . . . ," Nelson claims. "Its orderliness is not, as some would suppose, imposed by the computer or its administrators, but by something which arose long ago in the natural structure of literature, and which we are merely retaining." Just as literary critics and librarians have found ways to organize and categorize the apparently chaotic stream of traditional literature, people will spontaneously invent methods of organizing a hypertext-based body of literature.[38]

The abundance lies not only in the manipulation of text on one's own computer and data storage but also in the magical word which will replace libraries: *access*. As we have seen in previous chapters, the nature of digital text is characterized by linkage in an *essential* way.

The networking of written symbols via computer has led many to project a new kind of collective intelligence, one not possible previously because of the time constraints of postal correspondence and because of the scheduling and focusing problems of telephone conferences. The hope for this conscious use of the essential linkage inherent in digital writing is that it will create "an intelligence higher than any member."[39] The notion of collective intelligence and the potentially dangerous possibilities of controlling such a public voice has been a frequent topic of concern in the twentieth century. The political possibilities go back to Plato's *Laws*, where rational political planning dictates that

> The lawgiver should seek only the convictions which would do the greatest good for the city, and he should discover every device (*mechanē*) of any sort that will tend to make the whole community speak about these things with one and the same voice, as much as possible, at every moment throughout the whole of life, in songs and myths and arguments.[40]

After this passage in the *Laws*, the Athenian quickly adds, "Now if anyone thinks things are otherwise, let him not hesitate to carry on the controversy through argument." That is, the argument can continue in private between reasonable men who are not themselves identical with the one voice of the community.

The collective atmosphere of networking will doubtlessly facilitate the transmission and fortification of what is known as received ideas. Authentic thought that arises from inner resources of the psyche may itself become trivialized by absorption in the digital network. Received ideas are what Milan Kundera calls "a special modern kind of stupidity."

> Flaubert discovered stupidity. I dare say that that is the greatest discovery of a century so proud of its scientific thought.... The most shocking, the most scandalous thing about Flaubert's vision of stupidity is this: that stupidity does not give way to: science, technology, modernity, progress; on the contrary, it progresses right along with progress! The Flaubert discovery is more important for the future of the world than the most startling ideas of Marx or Freud. For we could imagine the world without the class struggle or without psycho-analysis, but not without the irresistible flood of

received ideas which—inscribed in computers, propagated by the mass media—threaten soon to become a force that will crush all original and individual thought, and will thus smother the very essence of modern European culture.[41]

These less than sanguine observations suggest that the general atmosphere of computer-mediated communication creates a psychic framework in which more text will become easily available but the text will be probably less intelligent, less carefully formulated, less thoughtful text. Computers may boost productivity, according to this criticism, only to have a greater production of written stupidity, even decreasing the likelihood of finding worthwhile material.

Computerized word processing opens up powers of self-publishing in a print format which imitates mechanical print but does so without the complex specialization and capital investment necessary for mechanical print. The individual with a laser printer can create virtually typeset manuscripts, with the user controlling more of the final product. Self-publishing in this sense is more direct: no editor intervenes; the author has hands on the final look and wording of documents without having to answer to copy editors.[42] The liberation of the typified, public document seems totally positive. But with the new approach comes more labor spent on controlling the look of the result; concern shifts toward technical problems; the price of freedom is greater responsibility for thinking out technical procedures. But the general linkage of digital text, aside from imitating mechanical print, occasions a different psychic atmosphere.

In such an atmosphere, the normal safeguards provided by traditional publishing will be rendered inoperative—or at least they will have to be greatly modified. While some authors speak of an "electronic Alexandria,"[43] with a profusion of sprawling possibilities in electronic publishing, our concern here is with the psychic framework. The authorial voice will deteriorate as a model of mental integrity. Fragments, reused material, the trails and intricate pathways of "hypertext," as Ted Nelson terms it, all these advance the disintegration of the centering voice of contemplative thought. The arbitrariness and availability of database searching decreases the felt sense of an authorial control over what is written. This is the other side of the superabundance attained by digital linkage. And there is ontological import to the network of word processing. Symbols can be used to bring things to awareness, but they can also, through trivialization and inflation, blend things out of awareness. Just as you can use speech to bring things into awareness, so too some things can be talked out of awareness.

On a limited basis today, so-called on-demand publishing is already being implemented, especially with regard to scientific articles, where instant access is valued over the sluggish publication process. Scientists in a discipline are linked by computer to a single network; someone does a research report, puts it into the network, and then anyone can call it up on their terminals to read it. More information is put out into the world at large with less delay. But this also does away with the quality-control mechanism of the professional journal or the published book. Peer evaluation and review are circumvented or rendered ineffective commentaries. Reviews too and summaries add further to the information overload.

With word-processing capabilities, new journals and homemade publications are springing up in many disciplines, thus opening up possibilities of expression that challenge the hegemony of the established channels that connect private thought with public mind. The marketing of publications based on scarcity, hierarchical peer selection, and the cost of scarce materials may lose place to the greater abundance of computer accessible material.[44] On-demand publication may come to mean that everything is available—which in turn places the burden of selection on everyone. Limited examples of this phenomenon are already showing up in the circulating files of in-house correspondence at large firms.

There, everyone becomes aware of what everyone else is saying—instantly and easily. This frequently leads to the nihilistic situation in which everything is available—and at the same time, a barrage of irrelevant junk mail causes things to lose poignancy and value.

The older print publishing is comparable to a medieval European city, where the center of the activity, the cathedral or church tower, serves to guide and gather all directions and pathways; the spire is visible to all and draws all other buildings toward a central model. The process of choosing texts to be printed did serve a similar function in print culture. Through a process of selection, a central model in typified form is presented so as to channel the creation of symbolized language. The new publishing resembles more the modern megalopolis, which is often described as a concrete jungle, a maze of activities and hidden byways, with no apparent center or guiding steeple. This is the architectural equivalent of the absence of the philosophical and religious absolute. In the electric element, the question of discrimination and of new metaphors for selecting information becomes urgent.

As the model of the integrated private self of the author fades, the rights of the author as a persistent self-identity also become more evanescent, more difficult to define. If the work of the author no longer carries with it definite physical properties as a unique original, as a book in a definite form, then the author's rights too grow more tenuous, more indistinct. The anonymity of continuous digital textuality reduces the felt sense of a definite physical original. Contemporary book publishing has already moved to a conception of ownership rights that goes far beyond the simple printed book, extending now to acquisitions and sales for specific media and markets, such as book club, paperback, serialization, television, film, video cassette, or cable-televised production. As mentioned, the electronic media pose unprecedented problems. As the authoritativeness of text diminishes, so too does the recognition of the private self of the creative author.

Besides the problems raised by the marketable nature of all

modern communications media, the digitally linked text shrinks the psychic solitude of author and reader. A certain amount of solitude is requisite for creative thought, for any innovative thinking that reaches beyond a mundane familiarity with things and beyond the margins of current terms and fashions. Creative artists, for instance, have asserted this essentially contemplative solitude in often emphatic ways. Consider this declaration of the usually meek Georges Braque, which conveys more than a hint of bitterness: "Those who forge ahead turn their backs on the followers. This is all that the followers deserve."[45] But the privacy gained by turning one's back may not be easily acquired in the electric element. There is always, with computerized writing, the possibility that one is on the network when there is no desire to be public. The ever-present possibility of digital writing being intercepted or in some way recovered creates an effect not unlike that of Winston Smith's telescreen in *1984*, which receives and transmits simultaneously.

> How often, or on what system, the Thought Police plugged in on any individual wire was guesswork. It was even conceivable that they watched everybody all the time. But at any rate they could plug in your wire whenever they wanted to. You had to live—did live, from habit that became instinct—in the assumption that every sound you made was overheard, and, except in darkness, every movement scrutinized.[46]

Computerized linkage can be made whether wanted or unwanted, and there seems to be no foolproof way to prevent unwanted textual linkage on microcomputers.

Signals radiating from a computer terminal screen can be picked up by very simple electronic equipment and duplicated by images produced on a television set.[47] Modem transmissions can be intercepted, and it is likely that digital signals will eventually be transmitted by wireless radio waves, which can be intercepted. The U.S. National Security Agency has tried to set up standards and hardware specifications for minimizing electronic eavesdropping. But data security is far from absolute, even under stringent measures. Computer users have long been aware of the ease of access that is inherent in digitized symbols. In earlier chapters we discussed the open quality of digital text that attracts group work. Where users have wanted a sense of creative privacy, they have often come to understand their privacy in terms of secrecy. Understanding the privacy of written symbols as a form of secrecy means using data encryption programs. Algorithms for data encryption rely on the underlying nature of digital text as code. Code can be scrambled and unscrambled through the use of stipulated keys. The National Bureau of Standards in 1977 set up the Data Encryption Standard (DES) which is based on a complicated coding algorithm.[48] The purpose of the DES is to provide an effective way of coding information with some assurance that the fluidity and accessibility of digital information remain under the control of computer users.

Codes can be broken. The DES algorithm itself is public knowledge, and so there is no mystery about what is used to encrypt the data. The key is what provides security. Since there are 56 relevant bits to a key, and each bit can be either one or zero, there are 2 to the 56th power, or 72,057,594,037,927,946, possible DES keys, which means a little over 72 quadrillion possibilities. Nevertheless, the computer itself provides the best means for breaking code that has ever been devised. The German Enigma code cracked by the Allies during World War II had over 50 million keys, and it was broken by hand. Code experts doubt whether any code can be perfectly secure.[49] If this is true, it means that the linkage of digital text is essential as well as inherently public.

The intimacy of thought and things, as it achieves presence in the contemplative framework of traditional reading and writing, is transformed by the new electronic element. The privacy of mind that must shift into secrecy is no longer inhabiting the same psychic framework as that of the handwritten page and the book.

Just as the formulation of word processing fosters an immediacy and superabundance of thought symbolization alien to the contemplative distance of the book, so too the inherent linkage of digital text places new challenges and conditions on authentic creativity in written symbols. Thought must now learn to live in a new element if it is to live at all.

Chapter Eight

Compensatory Disciplines

> The discipline of thought is not generalization; it is detail, and it is personal behavior. While the government is 'studying' and funding and organizing its Big Thought, nothing is being done. But the citizen who is willing to think a little, and, accepting the discipline of that, to go ahead on his own, is already solving the problem.
> —Wendell Berry, *A Continuous Harmony*

The illusion of progress is engendered by the limitations each epoch inevitably places on the range of its aspirations. Our study of the trade-offs implicit in the psychic frameworks of various symbolic elements makes this general observation specific. We can glimpse our own limits by contrasting current reality apprehensions with those of previous epochs. It would be, therefore, a glaring instance of the "pride of the living"—*superbia vitae* in the old Latin sense—to hope that a few simple prescriptions could open fully the new confines brought on by word-processing technology. Nevertheless, only a flat, one-dimensional determinism would exclude the opportunity humans have for interacting with their destiny, thereby reaffirming their essential humanity: animals do not have the privilege of resigning themselves to destiny; gods never need try. There are, then, certain directions we can examine in seeking ways to release the intensity of our hold on the world, to ease up our grip on things. The tension in our reality apprehensions can be modified in such a way as to create an openness that affords more possibilities than any unreflective grasp of things could allow.

One prominent approach to lessening the stress of technological innovation recommends "reversion activities." Games, humor, sports, gardening, creative artistic expression, and other leisure activities are prescribed to remedy what is known as "mind-work." Alvin Toffler, for instance, says,

The fact is that even those who work with information—i.e., in a world of abstractions—will also want to return frequently to the world of concrete experience. This means direct involvement with others. It means body care and health care. It means tactile, sensory involvement with the environment through things like manual activity, gardening, cooking, sailing, or, for that matter, touch-football, dance, or construction—building a home or a cabin in the mountains, for example.[1]

The supposition here is that the world as a totality can be divided into at least two subordinate worlds: the world of abstract information and the world of concrete experience. Rather than one activity affecting another by loosening its hold on realities, the two worlds coexist, each in turn serving either the calculative needs or the psychological well-being of the person. Reversion activities contribute to the human psyche at the interface only indirectly. Helpful as they may be as antidotes for preserving individual mental health, such activities do not redress the loss of psychic integrity at the interface. Instead, reversion activities regress to a wholeness, and thus they presuppose as such the fragmentation of our sense of the world. While such activities do open other possible worlds of involvement, they only release us from the world of the symbolic interface by causing us on occasion to let go of it entirely. Reversion activities do not provide a discipline within the interface itself; they offer no pattern of action serving to offset the transformation of the psyche.

Patterns of action to offset the automation of word processing must function as part of working within the electronic element itself, as an internal discipline. Traditional cultures are aware of psychic transformations and the subtle losses they bring about, and so these cultures sustain themselves through transformation by encouraging the performance of disciplines. A discipline is a conscious pattern of regular action that promotes the sense of wholeness or completeness. Without discipline, an activity involves attention only fleetingly, haphazardly, or arbitrarily. Of themselves, activities do not channel energies into a sensed perfection or fullness. Mastery comes from a felt sense of perfection or completion, and discipline is one condition of mastery. But even without mastery, discipline induces an appreciation of wholeness, of totalities that are not immediately useful but are appreciated for themselves. Only after a child has worked long and hard at memorizing a work of art under the guiding hands of parents and teachers, can he or she then later release structured energies into an expression full of beauty and rhythmic order; the poet Rilke compares this disciplining process to the wonderful liberation of springtime when things seem to rush outward and sing—but only after much deep and difficult inner hibernation has taken place through a long winter of suffering.[2] If it is the integrity of mind that word processing threatens, then we must look for disciplines which promote intellectual wholeness within the electronic element itself.

A sense of personal limitations and of the need for discipline is not usually thought to be a typically American characteristic. The notion of discipline is, nowadays, not a fundamental notion for most Americans. The lure of random possibilities in the New World has shaped a people that acknowledges immovable obstacles only with reluctance, that only very slowly concedes limitations to its will, its ardent enthusiasms and persistent ingenuity. Look closely at Americans traveling abroad and you will see a remarkable impatience with what is not yet organized, with what is still not fully managed or under control. In the context of most other countries, Americans appear hyperactive, overbearing, pushing organization to what seems at times the overmanagement of situations. At international meetings of scientists and philosophers, there is usually a general air of surprise when an American raises doubts about the possible trade-offs brought on by technological innovation. Europeans and Japanese, for instance, harbor a more tragic sense of history, if not publicly, at least in private. They generally believe Americans are technophiles with little awareness of the human cost of technological revolutions. Discussing the pitfalls of word processing is quite a different matter among European intellectuals than it is, say, among the computer enthusiasts of southern California.[3]

If we examine the philosophical traditions behind American attitudes, the overall difference in orientation is not surprising. A sense of loss and of the fragility of cultural continuity is not especially fostered by American Pragmatism. For John Dewey, the primary goal of education is not the constancy of formal modes of attention but rather "actual thinking as problem-solving." Actual thinking "always refers to a context, to an unsettled situation which lies outside of thinking."[4] But here "context-dependency" is not the embodiment of mind in the interface but what Dewey calls the "actual thinking" of individuals, found in problem-solving, overcoming obstacles, false starts, etc. Actual thinking is the process of meeting the challenges of experience, and "education deals with actual thinking of individuals."[5] Through meeting challenges and overcoming obstacles, Americans define themselves as persons who can emerge from groups to become distinct individuals. Education is supposed to direct the mind toward experience in all its diversity, and by surmounting problematic situations the person is supposed to grasp the opportunity to make oneself. Before the Pragmatic turn, American schools once knew something of the pure attention accorded subject matter as it has been cultivated in the European tradition; our graduate schools were once modeled on that self-forgetting dedication. Pragmatism advanced actual thinking by pointing out the abuses in that older traditional system, and the abuses were fair game: mindless repetition and the cultivation of tradition without individual thought.

In Pragmatic philosophy, making oneself in the face of problematic experience means less the fashioning of an existential-artistic identity than the habit of orienting psychic energy toward solving pregiven problems. Thought, according to Dewey, "always refers to a context, to an unsettled situation which lies outside of thinking."[6] This is because Dewey believes that "the need of thinking to accomplish something beyond thinking is more potent than thinking for its own sake."[7] So, for Dewey, the cultivation of the psyche is less concerned with autonomous practices than with picking up an unconscious, generalized skill at handling any and all kinds of external problems.[8] Pragmatic thinking, as a psychic practice, promotes a vague general habit applicable to a wide range of subjects.

Making oneself through skill at handling problematic situations is not a very good script for reflecting on the subtle losses induced by the transformation of past traditions. Dewey's powerful philosophical influence on American education eroded the idea of discipline as it was imported earlier from European schools. The repudiation of the priority and autonomy of psychic needs was precisely the novel appeal of Pragmatism. When Pragmatists insist on cognition as doing, as practice (from the Greek *pragma* or "action"), they do not mean by *practice* the inner work that shapes and channels psychic energy. On the contrary, practice in the Pragmatic sense is directed outwardly. The impact of Pragmatism on the schools led to an emphasis on communicative socialization. To be sure, the Pragmatist says, "while we cannot learn or be taught to think, we do have to learn *how* to think well, especially *how* to acquire the general *habit* of reflecting."[9] But *habit* for the Pragmatist is not an explicit or conscious practice full of presence and attention; it is rather an unconscious, unfocused engagement with the things that stimulate a person to think with regard to a certain obstacle or problem. The Pragmatist is concerned about setting up concrete conditions which stimulate and guide a succession of ideas but not about the practices that nurture the ability to transcend situations so as to appreciate them from an entirely different context. In other words: the disciplines of distance.

Traditional cultures are far more alert to the slippage of psychic nuances, and they try to reinforce some aspects of psychic life—if not with blind rituals then at least with cherished disciplines. More tradition-oriented cultures sense that the loss incurred by historical change cannot be easily recouped by good intentions or sheer will power. What is irretrievably lost can be recalled, or beckoned again, only through metaphors and through living transformations—not by simply conserving past dispositions, which can only be lugged along like heavy baggage.

While Pragmatism as a philosophical orientation frequently leads to the disparagement of intellectual discipline (in the name of practical experience), not all theoretical Pragmatists consistently suppressed efforts to discipline the psyche for its own sake. The young John Dewey once reviewed very favorably *The Art of Thinking* by Ernest Dimnet.[10] Dimnet's book is something of a classic concerning the daily discipline of intellectual habits, being a mixture of practical observations and edifying homilies. Throughout Dimnet consistently emphasizes the contemplative attitudes that foster wholeness and integrity of thought. Young John Dewey is attracted to the book's suggestions, which, he thinks, "will lead to improvements of mental habitudes." Nevertheless, Dewey wryly adds: "The suggestions probe deep, and unless one is willing to face himself he would do better to confine himself to the easier task of checking the list of qualities in some efficiency chart." Dewey also explicitly links intellectual with moral qualities: "No one can read the book in the spirit in which he [Dimnet] recommends that every book should be read, and not realize that sluggishness, parasitic dependence upon others, slackness of taste, and similar defects of character cause more deficiencies of mind than do lacks that are distinctly intellectual in origin." In its early phases, before scientific Positivism set in, Pragmatism could flirt with a moral and aesthetic conception of thinking as a discipline unto itself.

While acknowledging the importance of incorporating technology into mental processes, Pragmatism attributes primarily "instrumental thinking" to the mind. By making everything mental into practice, that is, something to be gauged on the means-end continuum, Pragmatism hardly leaves room for obtaining distance from technical devices, much less for encouraging disciplines dedicated to psychic freedom from the enthrallment with the devices. If word-processing technology distracts in the formulation of thoughts from integrity of mind, then Pragmatism celebrates the fruitfulness and productivity of the interface. Because contemplative formulation is recognized merely as a by-product of instrumental reasoning, Pragmatic thinking has of itself no abiding center from which distraction could occur; where no psychic private space is recognized as existing in and for itself, there is no (Pragmatic) justification for investigating any disciplines that could serve to counter the automated symbol-making of word processing. But once the psychic framework of word processing becomes manifest on its own terms, then the notion of practices takes on meaning as a counterbalance to automated writing.

Pragmatism emphasizes thinking as a practice, but practice in the Pragmatic sense is not an attentive gathering of the mind that transcends the mundane. Rather than protect certain qualities of thought, practice for the Pragmatist grounds or establishes thinking in the immediate feeling of a problematic situation. It then becomes possible for the Pragmatist to identify integrity of mind with successful achievement in manipulating mundane things through scientific and calculative modes of thought, or at least through an instrumental or coping attitude.

More recent American philosophy has become rightly suspicious of the Pragmatic notion of practice. The Pragmatic orientation has exercised such far-reaching and devastating effects on the human environment that its notion of practice has become largely discredited, though the influence of this view in education has only slightly diminished.[11] Current philosophy seeks to supplant the older emphasis on practice by redefining the notion of practices in such a way as to counter the Pragmatic understanding. Practice in the Pragmatic sense is now being converted into a more conscious, less habit-based notion, one which is more amicable to conscious discipline in the sense we are describing. Albert Borgmann, for instance, in *Technology and the Character of Contemporary Life*,[12] tries to define a new set of practices. Borgmann defines "focal practices" that counter the usual instrumental, exploitative attitude accompanying technological cultural development. Borgmann argues that the very kind of things technology produces are shallow and distracting when it comes to focusing human involvement. To be sure, the things or commodities produced by current technology are outstanding for their convenience and economy. But, the argument goes, these disposable, throwaway items are no longer things in the pretechnological sense. There is an ontological shift. Pretechnological practices once supported focal things—things that integrate human intensity with a deeply satisfying involvement on the human scale.[13] These focal things that supported the human sensory world are uprooted by technology: processed food and the Big Mac offer fast food for human convenience and efficiency but supplant the focal practices characteristic of the human culture of the common table, with its ceremonial manners and earth-based splendor (homemade bread, fresh eggs, and maybe even a local wine); the resistance of the earth itself becomes a supportive power when gathered by things belonging to the traditional culture of the table. Similarly, the automobile moves us from point A to point B but conceals the world as a dramatic background for the release of physical energies, something still preserved in the focal practice of jogging and sports. Borgmann's extensive analyses of such practices include a search for ways to support them. The search is urgent, according to Borgmann, because the logic of technological automation is relentless in its replacement of "focal things and practices" with devices and commodities.[14]

Though far more profound in conception, Borgmann's focal practices have much in common with the reversion activities mentioned earlier. The point of both is to exert a counterbalance to the one-dimensional ethos of productivity and consumption. While Toffler's concern with reversion activities is directed toward sustained mental health and personal well-being in the conventional sense, Borgmann suggests ways in which the world itself is at stake in pervasive practices and disciplines. Borgmann's ontological point of departure thereby overcomes the subjectivism of mental health. His starting point does not, however, make central the human-machine interface. Borgmann's approach is concerned with the full attentiveness of human powers and with the struggle against the distracting pull of pragmatic instrumentalism. But the earthiness of Borgmann's focal practices does not allow us to conceive practice as maintaining psychic integrity within the interface itself. Focal practices as such are not patterns of action that offset the automation of word processing, for such patterns must be exercised within the electronic element itself. To find the full import of the ontological perspective, we must look to the originating impulse of the world itself, that is, where things come to presence in language, where the psyche can attain full presence of mind.

It is the power of text-processing software as an environment for the mind which requires us to turn to the inner side of the human-machine interface. And the mind's alertness to reality, the psychic attentiveness and acuity in disclosing entities, is continuous with the quality of the new symbolic element. This is especially true for aspects of psychic life that have to do with privacy, intimacy, and the integrity of personal thought. The electric element fosters an experience of the world that is increasingly monitored, linked, and driven into productive stress. The ontological disclosure of things as sharply perceived, intimately felt identities will be blurred accordingly.

The philosophical approach in this study has not been systematic in the sense of offering an explanation for everything. Nor has the inner necessity of any starting position been proven, the only necessity being the intrusion of the phenomenon on our lives and the demands for reflection it provokes. Our speculation has striven for consistency without establishing any finally necessary grounds. The compensatory disciplines to be discussed, then, are less a set of logically deduced necessities than a loosely interconnected group of suggestions, recommendations more characteristic of counsel than of scientifically derived theorems. It should be noted, though, that without some authoritative counsel (education) it is unlikely that any of the suggestions will become disciplines in the strict sense of the term, for self-discipline can be learned only if one is first disciplined by others. Creative self-discipline is, of course, the aim of all external discipline, so no external discipline should be so harsh that it snuffs out creativity and independence rather than building self-confidence. Otherwise discipline is counterproductive.

What the consistency of our study does demand is a sketch of the kind of disciplines that might follow from the contrasts of the previous chapter, or at least a sample of some of the directions disciplines might take in the interface. When the psychic framework of word processing is set alongside the psychic framework of the book, then certain possibilities arise for human efforts to compensate for the psychic trade-offs involved in the transformation of the mind. Many of the devices developed in modern life are themselves attempts to compensate for the losses involved in the transformation and redirection of human energies that is the cultural price of industrial life. No single device can ever provide sufficient leverage to move the whole world of the psyche. But there are procedures and modes of operation which can deepen the human interaction in the interface and which do so in ways that deliberately recall the psychic frameworks that existed prior to that of word processing. Computerized processing of texts will inevitably become the prime symbolic element for human language. But the philosophical acceptance of this inevitability is not the hard, deterministic type which scoffs at all human endeavor to interact with destiny. The determinism that resigns itself to any and every kind of present, flattening it out into a caused necessity, is as much a rejection of the human spirit as is the retreat into antiquarian nostalgia or the shallow euphoria of futuristic optimism about technology. Through discipline the human being counters shifts and moves with the flow of history—not simply accepting historical change but listening and responding to it. Discipline is itself the paradoxical identification of freedom with necessity, for through discipline a person feels like doing something only after the task has been imposed as something that has to be done.

Our concrete proposals for influencing self-transformation at the interface are guided by the broad paradigm of contemplative concentration as found in the discipline called meditation.[15] This is the inner side of discipline. The paradigm is affiliated with what the Japanese call *do* (as in judo or kendo, both exploratory pathways) or what the Germans call *Übung* ("practice"). Psychologists in the United States have recently drawn on a variety of Oriental meditation techniques in the current work on stress reduction. One result of this research is the so-called clinically standardized meditation (CSM) developed by Patricia Carrington, lecturer in psychology at Princeton. This she has refined into the discipline of "releasing."[16] Meditation is not, of course, completely unknown in the West, especially in religious contexts, but its many levels and styles of conscious self-transformation have been cultivated more assiduously in the Far East than in the West. Studies now being done in the United States employ empirical methods to elucidate the effects meditation has as a personal discipline. Meditation, or releasing, is an exercise used therapeutically to suspend, for a specified period, the compulsive overpush characteristic of our times. Clinically standardized meditation was developed to counter the continuous sense of pressure pervading human life today, which transpires more and more in the human-machine interface. The discipline of releasing serves as an umbrella paradigm for disciplines that counter the effects of word processing. Several specific kinds of releasing—ways of countering automated manipulation and formulation under stress—are performable at the interface.

Releasing is Oriental meditation understood metaphorically, that is, conceived in the context of modern life in the Western hemisphere. Creative transformation, as I have stressed throughout, is an essential feature in the transmission and unfolding of all cultural phenomena, not only word processing. To counter a ubiquitous technostress, it is useful then to draw on pretechnological cultures as their teachings become increasingly available in the West. The elaborate systems of Eastern meditation, of *samadhi*, *dhyana*, or *Ch'an*, become in the West the therapeutic practice of releasing. In the East, of course, such practices are not regarded as objectively transmissible and scientifically certified; the practices are transmitted through a wisdom tradition that is manifestly oracular in style. Only in the East have philosophy and psychology cultivated a dominant concern with the *quality of attention* and with "attentiveness" (Krishnamurti); the West has for the most part turned to different forms of controlling and managing behavior. Because of the concern with living attention, the East transmits wisdom through the oracular tradition, through living speakers who directly convey a certain kind of attention. The oracular tradition locates ultimate knowledge in a state of direct awareness rather than in predictive hypotheses or verifiable propositions. The Western assimilation of these traditions will therefore alter the style in which they are legitimized.[17]

One version of the meditative practice of releasing is to adopt, deliberately and on a regular basis, an attitude that opens up moments of inner silence by letting go of the anxious push to control situations that is so much the norm in contemporary life. Releasing begins by selecting and focusing attention on any neutral object, a subvocalized sound (the Indian *mantra*), one's own breathing, or the gentle whirr of the cooling fan on a computer. As distractions arise and attention wanders, concentration must be brought back gently to the sound or object, and in this way one continues the varying focus of attention for ten to twenty minutes. Such releasing helps one let go of the unconscious automatisms accumulated in the constant drive to control and be productive.[18] The aim of releasing is an inner silence free from the continual urge to change things. So the aim is, paradoxically, to relinquish all aims—though, in its clinically standardized form, releasing is depicted as a practice useful within the teleology of the therapeutic context.

The aim of releasing, then, is to return to zero, as Zen masters put it, to regain a certain formlessness or omnidirectional potential. Eastern philosophies—whose cosmologies are imbued with the aims of psychic transformation—refer to this state as the void, not in the sense of a negative emptiness, but in the sense of what is devoid of rigid predeterminations. Oriental thought posits this formless spontaneity within the human spirit, emphasizing that it is not a state to be gained external to oneself but it is rather an abiding possibility that can still be rediscovered in the psyche even after years of conditioning. In this sense, releasing is akin to a meditative mood, which, like all moods, is something that cannot be manipulated but to which one must first be open in order to enter. True concentration and presence of mind are not tense and anxious and seeking for closure; true focus of mind allows things to come forth into focus where they attain their own form and closure. There is a false definiteness based on haste as there is a real definition for things when they come into their own.

The practice of releasing has more than psychological import for word processing in that it touches the ontological dimension as well. Things can appear to stand out and appear in full presence of mind only where there is first a vertical background world of silence or open formlessness. What Max Picard called "the world of verbal noise"[19] is a condition where one thing passes into another, where everything easily slides into everything else, where there are only horizontal connections without frontiers inside or outside the human being. Language that no longer has a relationship to silence, language as an autonomous and encoded system of symbols, loses the vertical source that refreshes and fortifies meaning. The overabundance of the electronic network of symbols is equivalent to an annihilating emptiness where restless curiosity swallows up the sharpness of truth in a sea of information overload. In this symbol pollution, everything without exception gets symbolized—which nullifies the act of symbolization as a unique event. In the general symbolic noise, and fortified by the power of the computer, the most stupid formulation reaches the same level as the most intelligent: the transfer and production of symbols goes on and on. To make things appear, language must preserve an intimacy with silence; otherwise language loses that infinity of mind, that sense of open chaos, from which spoken things take their definiteness, their definition. If it does not pause, language becomes verbal noise, an ocean of finite symbols drowning the hints of taut meaning in the loose wash of noisy chaos where meaning is swallowed up. In the world of symbol pollution, silence alone protects what is left of the integrity of things; it can minimize the damage inflicted by continual exploitation; it alleviates momentarily the insistence on human purposes. Silence brings things back from dissipation to a measure of wholeness, for, even though it remains to a great extent an undefined chaos, silence can be supportive and pregnant with wholeness.

Symbolic form is a central notion in several twentieth-century philosophies, but seldom is form brought together with its necessary correlate of silence. The notion of thought formulation I have articulated here has only a superficial resemblance to the philosophical doctrine of neo-Kantianism. Neo-Kantians such as Ernst Cassirer and Susanne Langer locate symbol formation at the heart of their philosophy, which defines the human being essentially as the *animal symbolicum*. Neo-Kantians understand all expressions of human life, political, artistic, scientific, and religious, as occasions for symbol formation. All human expressions are developing phases in an ascent that culminates, for the neo-Kantian, in logical systematics. The cognitive systematics of symbolic logic, then, becomes the pinnacle of expression where the pure forms of symbol formation are brought to full lucidity and self-evidence. The system of natural language expressions ideally yields a stable network of logical relations, universal predicates, indexical terms, and existential referents. Such a theory of meaningful forms neglects the intrinsic opacity of reality, which is to say, the theory understands form in a way that does not allow for the inherently elusive nature of formulation on which every form is based and to which it must return for intelligibility. Theories of form that do not take into account the elusive nature of formulation have no place for the silence that refreshes formulations of reality at the interface. For them, *formulation* is based on *information*, on pregiven, stable entities. The neo-Kantian philosophy of symbolic forms fails to recognize the background of ontological silence which bestows on symbols the gravity of reality apprehension.

As suggested before, any references whatsoever to inner psychic life run counter to the pragmatic automation of writing and to the construal of language as information code to be manipulated. Inner life easily becomes a mere obstacle in the world of Total Management. But in the last analysis full human presence of mind is crucial for any endeavor. Consider the experience of a professor at an American university, someone well acquainted with Eastern thought. He employs deep meditative states while writing. Seated for hours at a computer terminal, he uses word processing to write books and articles. The professor's students, already acclimated to computers and word processing, are fascinated—and somewhat troubled—by the way he regularly stops at the keyboard, looks over or away from the monitor, and sits for sometimes as long as twenty minutes in silence. The students are puzzled by his ability to abstract himself from the engaging process of computerized writing, and they ask him, "What are you doing?" His answer, "I'm thinking," further perplexes the students. Any references at all to inner psychic life run counter to the tendency of automated symbol manipulation to understand language as information code, as immediate messages holding together a vast network of dynamic production. The silence of a deeply meditative presence of mind may meet at first with incomprehension but it is the basis of any discipline that counters the shifts in thought that are characteristic of word processing. By practicing contemplative discipline we begin to take seriously our ability to achieve more complete presence and attention—both necessary for full attentiveness to things and to others. The disciplines of presence of mind and the contemplative capacity are often incorrectly associated with selfishness when in fact such presence of mind is the necessary condition for quality time spent with others and for true communication, that is, with full attention and presence of mind. Much extroverted and busy togetherness fits into productivity but ultimately undermines the ability to be together. As we saw in previous chapters, word processing threatens to make written thought mechanically repeatable but devoid of personal presence.

As in other areas, the new technologies of control bring with them a release of attention and dispense with certain aspects of steady mental focus, that is, they make possible greater distraction as they offer more power. The power of the symbol formation of word processing can be understood by analogy with Musak. The attrition of attention and the erosion of contemplative apprehension of musical forms in our time is well known. Commercially installed Musak is symptomatic of rhythmic sound on tap, musical sound that has lost the power to move as well as the power to induce musing on a level deeper than department store browsing. The debasing use of music in this fashion underscores the shift of Western music from a once sacred chant (plainsong) to classical objective complexity to emotional escape and then finally to the entertainment of the jingle and the hit song. In the Far East, musical tones are understood to be not merely emotionally moving but are even cosmic in import. In Tibetan sound art, vocal overtones are regarded as vibrations of the universe in that precise overtone humming brings the subject into harmony with the universe by expanding consciousness from egoistic subjectivity to open responsiveness. The more subjective passions of Western music become greatly reduced in the framework of electronic reproduction and then deteriorate to the point of totally destructive trivialization in the gooey acoustic backgrounds of airport terminals and department stores. An analogous transformation occurs in the symbolic elements in which linguistic symbols are stored and manipulated. Previously, in the discussion of the contemplative integrity fostered by the book (chapter 6) I suggested the musical analogue by referring to the symphonic intelligence exemplified in the psychic framework of the traditional book. The analogy with music is germane to any discussion of pure attention, and it could have been used here as the main paradigm in place of meditation.[20]

Holding Acceleration: Blockbusting and Clustering

In describing the phenomenon of word processing I noted how computer technology introduces thought augmentation and is not simply an adjunct for traditional composition. Idea processors, outliners, and other aspects of automation reveal a new basic unit for thinking in symbols. The automated unit of formulation is usually referred to as the idea, which should not be confused with the Platonic sense of idea discussed in chapter 6. The automated idea is invariably larger in size, in character count or bytes, than the sentence or even the conventional paragraph. These fragments of text can be easily manipulated and readily rearranged in different patterns and juxtapositions. The facility of creating these blocks, of moving and reusing them, contributes to increased acceleration in the pace of digital writing. An impression is created that the initial drafting of a composition and the revising of it are one and the same, that the processes of invention and of reflective criticism are identical. From the standpoint of traditional contemplative formulation, this impression is illusory.

One discipline for furthering contemplative presence of mind treats the basic units of word-processing composition as blocks to be busted. David and Virginia Noble have developed a practice called blockbusting which weds the power of automated manipulation with the reflective analysis of what is written on the word processor.[21] Blockbusting is based on a set of macros, which are user-defined keystrokes stored in computer memory and invoked to run automatically by pressing a key or two. The sophisticated macros developed by the Nobles operate on a digital text in two ways: first they disassemble the text into separate sentences and then reassemble, at a different command, the broken text. A blockbusting macro instantly reformats a written text first by seeking the punctuation marks for sentence separation, such as periods and question marks, and then inserts two carriage returns after each sentence, which leaves the text broken down into skeletal form. By instantly formatting text in smaller units of statement, these blockbusting macros present a different look at symbolized thought, enabling the writer or reader to hold onto a thought and see it within the logical context of a linear sequence of surrounding sentences. The writer can then reorder the set of statements or expand on any individual statement or add new material to create better logical connections. The separation of sentences into individual units also provides space between sentences so that transitional thoughts may be added. In this way, blockbusting macros create an automated environment for making text revision more contemplative.

Blockbusting in effect halts the accelerated pace of symbol formulation and provides a contemplative pause in writing on a computer. The technique of blockbusting does not relinquish the power of digital writing but suggests a concrete way of tempering its power. The practice employs the automated power of the computer to temper the dissipating pace of digital writing. It helps dispel the facile ease which is frequently attacked by critics of word processing. Just as the automation of spell checking has a subliminal effect on the choice of words at the interface, so too blockbusting alters in subtle ways the approach to computerized text production. The peripheral anticipation of a later analysis of logical sequence affects the immediacy of the involvement in word processing.

Blockbusting fosters a predominantly analytical approach to text and the thought process. The computer is therefore superbly suited to this exercise which turns accelerated processing back upon itself to provide a different kind of involvement. One of the aims of the Nobles' book is to show how powerful word management technology can go hand in hand with traditional prose composition. They show a tight connection between the computer programming tool and composition analysis that uses conventional patterns for organizing paragraphs and sentences. Our point here is rather a formal one—dealing with formulation itself—and does not go into the many valuable strategies for organizing and editing paragraphs that the Nobles offer as the content of blockbusting analysis. Whatever of the many traditional strategies one might use for self-critical revision, any strategy that employs blockbusting will of itself mitigate the stressful productivity inherent in computerized writing. Blockbusting is an automated instance of the paradigm of meditative releasing—or at least it can be within the psychic framework of word processing. Blockbusting introduces a silent pause through which can emerge the fertile openness of a more firm formulation, through which the forms of things can come to fuller presence.

Another practice that brings contemplative discipline into word processing comes from a more holistic direction than blockbusting. Rather than employ automated computer power to correct automation itself, this writing practice moves away from and outside the interface to supplement directly the limitations of digital writing in the interface. The technique derives from the teaching of creative writing and has been presented clearly in the book *Writing the Natural Way* by Gabriele Lusser Rico.[22] Despite its presentation in terms of "techniques for stimulating right-brain processes," the natural way of writing describes a procedure for protecting the psychic vitality of thought formulation by breaking away from the productivity flow of computer-processed texts.[23] The natural way is one which returns to pen and writing pad, but it is not for this reason that it is truly natural. It is a natural discipline because it locates the source of formulation in the writer's authentic voice.

Rico describes voice as "the authentic sound, rhythm, texture of a unique consciousness on the page.... Voice is an expression of the natural you unfettered by the stultifying injunctions about writing you have labored under."[24] Thought is patterned in a distinctive rhythm when it is a genuine expression of the intellectual-emotional complex. The pattern of expressions in which an idea recurs in rhythmically connected variants is not linear and takes its cues less from sequential logic than from felt clusters of associated words and phrases. Rico borrows something of the "lateral thinking" expounded for years by Edward de Bono, who has sought to put some system into "brainstorming" or "creative thinking."[25] Voice in writing is to be found more through exploring hidden, subconscious associations than through the linear logic that proceeds from heading to subheading to development of the main premise. Voice can be brought forth only through subtle coaxing and through looking peripherally at what we think. Creativity in one's own voice is part of the mysterious realm of expression.

Rico calls the practice clustering. Using a large sheet of paper and a pen or pencil, the writer gathers related ideas around a central notion. But this is not at all the same procedure as outlining. Clustering begins with a nucleus word which is written down and then encircled on the piece of paper. Any word connection or phrase that comes to mind is then written down rapidly somewhere outside the encircled nucleus word. A certain sense of randomness or of not being able to logically specify the connection must characterize these associations. Unlike outlining, clustering does not aim to establish an order or subordination of ideas. Each new word or phrase is connected to the preceding circle so as to create radii from the nuclear concept, the only logical provision being that something strikingly new should begin at the central nuclear word. The graphically haphazard quality of clustering is essential, for it preserves the sense of personal expression apart from any need to communicate the thoughts or present them publicly. The association process with pen or pencil should become a spontaneous doodling with lines and arrows, creating directions and subtle emphases that no typestyles could mimic. A relaxed receptivity to ideas in any form or connection leads to the generation of a new spurt of associations. At first, from a purely rational viewpoint, a cluster seems to be a tangle or maze.

But the common result is a delicate web of personal expressions held tenuously together by a subjective thread of barely conscious insight. The process brings out unexpected ideas that can then be formulated with increasing degrees of rational connection. The piece of writing built up from clusters will exhibit unique personal rhythms of thought that would be filtered out by more formal approaches to composing a text. The search for authentic formulation draws on psychic depths that are usually barred from conscious organization. And barred from digital systems. For clustering cannot properly be done in the computer interface (though some software house will surely venture forth and implement de Bono's lateral thinking). Clustering requires the unprogrammable motions of the human hand contacting psychic depths through doodling. Doodling cannot be programmed for the interface. Computers, too, have certain physical limits which clustering overcomes through the personal graphics of doodling. An open-ended wholeness is possible that is screened out by the physical limits of the computer. Clustering is like an expandable graphic or map of thought discoveries. The last five chapters of this book, for instance, were of necessity mapped out with pen and paper—on a 57-1/2 inch piece of continuous paper. No computer screen could have contained it. No software outliner could permit such a sense of wide-open creative freedom combined with such peculiarities of connection. Clustering reminds the writer and thinker of the sense of psychic wholeness in the world of increasingly fragmented texts and of automated text manipulation. Clustering also recalls the sense of private inner depths in the psyche, of whole vistas incommensurable with the encoded network of human symbols. It recovers a uniquely personal event in the face of the mechanically repeatable.

Both practices, blockbusting and clustering, develop in one a taste for transcending the interface with its special virtues and perils. They both engender a felt sense of wholeness of attention, promoting an integrity of intellect. Both might be used as disciplines for releasing, for the pause of the deep silence of formulation in the midst of the vast network of digital text. They can be done to coax out a meditative mood, not to increase productivity. By integrating such disciplines into word processing, we begin to offset the Western proclivity for instant verbalization and for obsessive rational control. We begin to learn other sides of our humanity, just as the Orient must learn its own opposite. The Western world has yet to learn silent hesitation, the depth of what cannot be said, and the limits of the responsiveness of verbal terms and of its rhetoric.

Other skills and practices could also be examined. The criticisms of chapter 7 are several, and many more criticisms will come from a variety of angles once the full scope of the transformation is grasped by thoughtful people who care about books. With these criticisms will come opportunities for the further refinement of disciplines that counter the transformations of thought and language brought about by word processing. Other paradigms besides meditation will be needed to think out the central problem of discipline for psychic integrity at the interface. The interface itself is growing in scope and scale. As our technology becomes increasingly indispensable for life enhancement and even for survival, we will need to grasp the logic of transformation as it permits of disciplined human response. Treatment of the intimate aspects of the interface, such as word processing, will have to be accompanied by further philosophical reflection on the large-scale technological enterprise upon which the human race is now embarking.

So there is no summary and conclusion here. The nature of the phenomenon under consideration simply does not permit of definitive results. To destabilize through questioning the new model of symbolic intelligence is already a result—though not in the scientific sense. For bringing the interface into question effects a gain in indeterminacy. As the phenomenon unfolds in coming years, the results of philosophical critique remain at best a question put to the phenomenon, an inquiry that seeks another dimension of the phenomenon itself at the interface. Only through sustained questioning can the psychic dimension be held open so as to create a free interplay between mind and machine. To assert an iso-morphic compatibility of mind with machine or, conversely, to assert an absolute independence of mind and machine are equally tantamount to shutting down the free interplay within which the relationship of mind and computer can be held in question and formulated anew.

Notes

Introduction

1. Jonathan Kamin, *The ThinkTank Book* (Berkeley: Sybex, 1984), p. 218. The book elaborates on the powers of a program written by Living Videotext for idea processing on the microcomputer. The program makes possible rapid manipulation of hierarchically arranged data (text) so that it creates a "database managing system" for organizing a piece of writing as it occurs in the mind-computer interface. While Kamin's statement refers specifically to outline programs, many other writers attribute positive changes to word processing as such. To cite one, at the meeting of the American Philosophical Association in 1984, Janice Moulton wrote, "What are the philosophical implications of these changes? With word processing we will be able to think more carefully and deeply."

2. Andrew Fluegelman, *Writing in the Computer Age: Word Processing Skills and Style for Every Writer* (Garden City, N.Y.: Doubleday, 1983), pp. 234–35.

3. The logic of this evolution was worked out by one of the founders of the theory and implementation of word processing, Douglas Engelbart, in his "A Conceptual Framework for the Augmentation of Man's Intellect," the opening paper of *Vistas in Information Handling, Volume I: The Augmentation of Man's Intellect by Machine*, ed. Paul W. Howerton and David C. Weeks (Washington, D.C.: Spartan Books, 1963). See chapter 4 below for a discussion of Engelbart's theory.

4. Gore Vidal, *New York Review of Books*, vol. 31, no. 5, March 1984, p. 20.

5. Erik Sandberg-Diment, "Computers Don't Always Help Writers Make Sense," in the *Louisville Courier Journal*, June 30, 1984. In his book *They All Laughed When I Sat Down at the Computer* (New York: Simon & Schuster, 1985), pp. 124–25, Sandberg-Diment, computer columnist for the *New York Times*, has a similar passage: "I wonder how much we are losing, on the whole, as we gain. No doubt the same question was raised when the typewriter was new, and even when papyrus first became an annoying novelty to Mesopotamian clay tablet inscribers. Still, I have the

impression we are heading toward a future filled with the emperor's new words, where word processing cranks out fast-food prose, becoming to writing what xerography has become to the office memo: a generator of millions of copies of contentless phrases assembled for appearance's sake—rarely read, much less reflected upon." For more instances, see Adeline Naiman, "Avoiding 'Compubabble,'" *Personal Computing* 9:3 (March 1985): 47. In pointing out the clipping cited from the *Courier*, the university press editor added a personal note as follows: "From what I've seen so far from authors using word processors, he's right!" This first reaction is a telling one, even if only in revealing our general anxieties.

6. For another thumbnail history of word processing, see Janette Martin, "New Dimensions in Word Processing," *PC World*, January 1985, pp. 42–51.

Chapter 1. Thought, Word, and Reality

1. There are some sensitive passages on the "universalizing" effort of the mind in Hannah Arendt, *The Life of the Mind*, vol. 1, *Thinking* (New York: Harcourt Brace Jovanovich, 1977), esp. "Invisibility and withdrawal," pp. 69ff. Authoritative scholarship on the way ancient philosophy severed theoretical consciousness from practical concerns can be found in Nicholas Lobkowicz, *Theory and Practice: History of a Concept from Aristotle to Marx* (Notre Dame: University of Notre Dame Press, 1967); see also Hans Jonas's brief essay "The Practical Uses of Theory," in his *The Phenomenon of Life: Toward a Philosophical Biology* (New York: Dell, 1966).

2. This approach to social psychology is dealt with in considerable detail by Sherry Turkle, *The Second Self: Computers and the Human Spirit* (New York: Simon & Schuster, 1984). See also Margaret Boden, *Artificial Intelligence and Natural Man* (New York: Basic Books, 1981), and the book that stimulated Turkle's study, Seymour Papert *Mindstorms: Children, Computers, and Powerful Ideas* (New York: Basic Books, 1980).

3. Anaximander was born in Miletus around 610 B.C. Out of the mainstream of philosophy beginning with Thales, Diogenes Laertius designates Anaximander—and not Thales—as the *archē*, or origin, of Ionian philosophy. While admitting Thales to be Anaximander's teacher, Diogenes nonetheless ascribes to Anaximander the origin of that succession which goes through Socrates and ends with Clitomachus in the New Academy. This line of philosophy Diogenes distinguishes from that which begins with Anaximander, goes through Aristotle, and ends with Theophrastus. The former line, the Anaximander-Socrates-Cli-

tomachus line, I should like to consider the philosophical lineage which most clearly preserves the origin or originating impulse of philosophy. See *Diogenes Laertius* 1. 13-14, where he states: "philosophias de duo gegonasin archai, he to apo Anaximandros kai he apo Pythagorou."

4. Even in the supposedly "closed" Olympian world of Homer we see the warrior Achilles, when he withdraws in anger to sulk over the loss of Briseis, sit down by the seashore and burst into tears while looking at the gray, "*boundless* ocean," *Iliad* 1. 350; "apeirona pontōn" is Aristarchus's reading.

5. See, for instance, Aristotle's *Posterior Analytics* 72b5-20, 81b30-82b; *Metaphysics* 1006a5-12, 1012b20-25; *De Anima* 407a22-30; *Ethics* 1094118-22, 1113a3.

6. *Physics* 187a20, 203b6, 294b21; *De Caelo* 295b11.

7. Simplicius's commentary on Aristotle's *Physics* contains the fragment "archē ton onton to apeiron." See the standard edition of *Die Fragmenta der Vorsokratiker*, 3 vols., ed. Hermann Diels and Walther Kranz (reprint, Zurich, 1964), 1:89.

8. Translations of Heraclitus are mine unless stated otherwise. Another translation of Fragment 92 is Charles H. Kahn, *The Art and Thought of Heraclitus: An Edition of the Fragments with Translation and Commentary* (Cambridge: Cambridge University Press, 1981): "We should let ourselves be guided by what is common to all. Yet, although the Logos is common to all, most men live as if each of them had a private intelligence all his own." In Greek, the fragment runs: "Dio dei hepesthai toi xynou. Tou logou d'eontos xynou, zoousi hoi polloi hōs idiēn echontes phronēsin."

9. In the brief reconstruction of Heraclitus's teaching here, I follow the general lines suggested by Albert Borgmann, *The Philosophy of Language: Historical Foundations and Contemporary Issues* (The Hague: Martinus Nijhoff, 1974), esp. pp. 4-16. A suggestive review by M. F. Burnyeat, "Message from Heraclitus," of the Heraclitus edition by Charles Kahn, appears in *New York Review of Books* (May 13, 1982), pp. 45-47. My references to Heraclitus are, obviously, guided by the task at hand, which is to understand the phenomenon of word processing.

10. "Plurisignification" is the term used by Philip Wheelwright in his study *Heraclitus* (New York: Atheneum, 1964). "Polysemy," a term frequently used today, especially in literary studies, is a variant. The

danger of invoking all these technical words is, of course, that the security of univocal terms may begin to overtake the intrinsically ambiguous subject matter, which is the whole point to be grasped by the words. It would not be the first time that a point is missed by overly determined analysis. This missing-the-point is itself, though, benign inasmuch as it demonstrates further the inextricability of ambiguity—which is another point in favor of Heraclitean reflections on language.

11. Diels and Kranz, eds., *Die Fragmenta*, fragment 1.

12. Ibid., fragments 84a, 64, 119, 89, 75, and 97. In the Wheelwright translation, fragment 64 reads: "The thunderbolt pilots all things." The bolt of lightning was, for the archaic peoples, the sign of Zeus, the overpowering Sky-God. That unexpected and unwanted changes guide history is consonant with Heraclitus's grasp on the reality of logos as a fire. Fire lives off transformation and continuously new contexts: "Fire in its advance will catch all things by surprise and judge them" (fragment 66).

13. The *logismos* in the words *hypologistē* and *mikrohypologistē* refers to "reasoning" or "discursive thought process," which is one meaning in the systematic ambiguity of the ancient logos. The word has been variously rendered in English by "language," "speech" (Latin *vox*), "conception," "intellect," "meaning," "proportion," and "reason." It is called "the underlying organizational principle of the universe" in F. E. Peters, *Greek Philosophical Terms: A Historical Lexicon* (New York: New York University Press, 1967), pp. 110ff. The term goes through the history of Western thought, through science, religion, and philosophy, as a distinguishing mark of what is fundamental to the West. See also Hermann Fränkel, *Early Greek Poetry and Philosophy*, trans. Moses Hadas and James Willis (New York: Harcourt Brace Jovanovich, 1973), esp. pp. 371ff. Further bibliography can be found in *The Encyclopedia of Philosophy*, s.v. "Logos."

14. The notion of *wu-ming*, the "nameless," is found in its most influential Chinese form in Lao-Tse, *Tao Te Ching*, chap. 37. See, for instance, the translation of the *Tao Te Ching* by Gia-Fu Feng and Jane English (New York: Vintage Books, 1972). There the phrase *Wu Ming Chih P'u* is rendered by "formless substance," clearly a contradiction in terms according to the logos tradition. The difference between Eastern and Western tradition can be held in the imagination by first reading the elusive, laconic poem by Lao-Tse and then afterward reading one of the

Dialogues by Plato. A particularly poignant contrast with the confident stillness of the Lao-Tse book is the Platonic dialogue *Phaedo*, where the mythical Socrates, on his deathbed, engages his sad friends with the "music" of his unrelenting verbal argumentation—about the logical possibility of the soul's survival after death.

15. Some early twentieth-century philosophers of religion sought to emphasize the spoken utterance—and not the alphabetized word—as the most genuine meaning of *word* in Western religions. By interpreting the history of religion as the plight of the genuine word, they sought to restore a sense of the word as speech, a sense most closely connected with the earliest phases of Hebrew religion. They did so out of an understanding of their own personal faith, as they understood it. Among these were Eugen Rosenstock-Huessy, Martin Buber, and Franz Rosenzweig. In English, see Eugen Rosenstock-Huessy, *Speech and Reality* (Norwich, Vt.: Argo Books, 1970), which considers religious issues from the viewpoint of the social implications of grammar, with grammar always conceived as articulated speech; see also his religious history of Western culture as the history of speech, *Out of Revolution: Autobiography of Western Man*, (Norwich, Vt.: Argo Books, 1969).

16. My translation. See also Johann Wolfgang von Goethe, *Faust*, trans. Walter Kaufmann (Garden City, NY: Doubleday Anchor, 1961), pt. 1, ll. 1214ff. The progressive series of Faust's translations—or transformations—of the biblical opening reads in the original, "Im Anfang war das *Wort*," "Im Anfang war der *Sinn*," "Im Anfang war die *Kraft*," "Im Anfang war die *Tat*."

17. The reference is to the lost first part of Aeschylus's trilogy on Prometheus, of which we have only the *Prometheus Bound*. The first part of the trilogy was entitled *Prometheus the Fire-Bringer*. In the former, Prometheus says,

I taught them to determine when stars rise or set—
A difficult art. Number, the primary science, I
Invented for them, and how to set down words in writing—
The all-remembering skill, mother of many arts.

(Aeschylus, *Prometheus Bound*, trans. Philip Vellacott [New York: Penguin Books, 1961], ll. 455–62) This designation of writing as an extension of the skills of memory is the key suggestion for the transformation theory treated in chap. 2.

Chapter 2. The Theory of Transformative Technologies

1. It should be mentioned, however, that while Havelock notes the accusations of historical relativism coming from several philosophical camps, he fails to respond directly to the charges on a philosophical level. He merely poses the conflict by asking whether certain philosophical premises can be reconciled with oral theory, or oralism. A typical passage occurs in the final chapter of his most recent book, *The Muse Learns to Write: Reflections on Orality and Literacy from Antiquity to the Present* (New Haven and London: Yale University Press, 1986). Here Havelock describes conflicts with logical analysis, Kantian Idealism, and with views based on religious mysticism or on the postulate of an invariant human nature. His treatment (pp. 121–22) does no more than state the antagonisms. It is easy, he points out, for philosophers to "either argue that the technology of the alphabet was not important because such capacities have always existed or else to damn and dismiss pre-alphabetic orality as a truly primitive condition of communication that we are fortunate to have left behind." This leaves mutual dismissal and antagonism at a stalemate until either oral theorists realize how problematic are the notions of time and of historical world or until philosophers learn to admire the rich and illuminating detail of concrete studies outside their field of speculation. The standoff between an anxious, reactive absolutism and a putatively uncritical historicism is sterile; such a factitious opposition results in the abstract dialectic of shadows.

2. "In non-literate cultures the task of education could be described as putting the whole community into a formulaic state of mind. The instrument for doing this was to use the tribal epics as a paradigm.... The epic poet's language would constitute a kind of culture language, a frame of reference and a standard of expression to which in varying degree all members of the community were drawn. In our own culture of writer and readers the existing body of prose literature performs this same function for the common members of the language group." Eric Havelock, *Preface to Plato* (Cambridge: Harvard University Press, 1963), p. 140. Hereafter cited as *Preface*.

3. In *Preface*, chap. 8, entitled "The Homeric State of Mind," Havelock writes of the "fundamental idiom of communication" (p. 138); of the "habit patterns of a non-literate culture" (p. 139); of the "oral state of mind" (p. 141); of "a kind of culture language, a frame of reference and a

standard of expression to which in varying degree all members of the community were drawn" (p. 140). Again, the presupposition of all these terms, and a legion of similar terms in Havelock's book, is that thinking is inherently linked to sharing thought through language or that thought and communication are not fundamentally separable.

4. *Preface*, p. 135.

5. Ibid.

6. Chapters 3 and 4 of *Preface* are entitled "Poetry as Preserved Communication" and "The Homeric Encyclopedia." The titles signal an interpretation of literature as a system of information.

7. *Preface*, p. vii.

8. For a typically frustrated attempt to apply McLuhan's categories and fanciful style to the computer revolution, see, for instance, Stan Augarten, "The Micro is the Message," *PC: The Independent Guide to IBM Personal Computers* 4:19 (September 17, 1985): 87-91. Augarten ends by throwing up his hands and concluding that McLuhan's apocalyptic statements about computers show that McLuhan "grossly misunderstands the nature of computers."

9. Chapter 4 below on the dynamics of the psyche explores the epistemological assumptions behind this claim of the transformation theory.

10. "For human thought structures are tied in with verbalization and must fit available media of communication: there is no way for persons with no experience of writing to put their minds through the continuous linear sequence of thought such as goes, for example, into an encyclopedia article. Lengthy verbal performances in oral cultures are never analytic but formulaic. Until writing, most of the kinds of thoughts we are used to thinking today simply could not be thought. Orality is a pervasive affair." Walter J. Ong, *Rhetoric, Romance, and Technology: Studies in the Interaction of Expression and Culture* (Ithaca: Cornell University Press, 1971), p. 2. The scope of this claim was first developed in Walter J. Ong, *The Presence of the Word: Some Prolegomena for Cultural and Religious History* (New Haven: Yale University Press, 1967).

11. Walter J. Ong, *Ramus, Method, and the Decay of Dialogue: From the Art of Discourse to the Art of Reason* (Cambridge: Harvard University Press, 1958).

12. The historical scholarship in this matter from which the transformation theory draws is Elizabeth L. Eisenstein, *The Printing Press as an Agent of Change: Communications and Cultural Transformations in Early-Modern Europe*, 2 vols. (Cambridge: Cambridge University Press, 1979).

13. "The thesis of these two earlier works [*Presence of the Word* and *Rhetoric, Romance, and Technology*] is sweeping, but it is not reductionist, as reviewers and commentators, so far as I know, have all generously recognized: the works do not maintain that the evolution from primary orality through writing and print to an electronic culture, which produces secondary orality, causes or explains everything in human culture and consciousness. Rather, the thesis is relationist: major developments, and very likely even all major developments, in culture and consciousness are related, often in unexpected intimacy, to the evolution of the word from primary orality to its present state. But the relationships are varied and complex, with cause and effect often difficult to distinguish." Walter J. Ong, *Interfaces of the Word: Studies in the Evolution of Consciousness and Culture* (Ithaca: Cornell University Press, 1977), pp. 9–10.

14. Ong's full-length treatment of the shift from ancient, rhetorically centered culture to modern, literary culture is *Rhetoric, Romance, and Technology*.

15. Curiously, the speculative range of Ong's theory does not attain to the impact of digital writing. One reason for this may be contingent on personal circumstances more than on theoretical limits, namely, the fact that Ong's communal life as a member of the Jesuits has not permitted convenient access to a personal computer for his writing—at least till this writing. In private conversation Ong did say that his writing procedures employ manual typists, a situation which does afford him cut-and-paste and other editing maneuvers built into electronic writing. But, if the thesis of this book is on track, then no analogous procedures can properly serve to substitute for the experience of prolonged writing on a computer.

16. It is no accident that Lucien Lévy-Bruhl, one of the main founders of modern sociology, was well grounded in the philosophy of Immanuel Kant. Developing some of the ideas of another founder of sociology, Emile Durkheim, Lévy-Bruhl wrote extensively about "mental patterns" in, for example, *Les fonctions mentales dans les sociétés inférieures*

(Paris: Alcan, 1910), and *La mentalité primitive* (Paris: Alcan, 1922). Early sociology took up the study of "collective representations"—a Kantian phrase—or the "mentality" of the social group. These are some of the early sources for the transformation theory, seeing that the sociological theory stemming from Lévy-Bruhl and Durkheim, including much American sociology, began with the juxtaposition of primitive or underdeveloped peoples and scientific or modern peoples. This contrast anticipates, of course, the oral-literate contrast in the transformation theory. See Robin Horton, "Lévy-Bruhl, Durkheim and the Scientific Revolution," in *Modes of Thought: Essays on Thinking in Western and Non-Western Societies*, ed. Robin Horton and Ruth Finnegan (London: Faber & Faber, 1973).

Chapter 3. The Finite Framework of Language

1. The German distinction between *Geschichte* and *Historie* is relevant here. Many interpreters do not fully understand this distinction and therefore fail to bring over its meaning into their reading and thinking about Heidegger in the English language. The result is very often the charge that Heidegger is a determinist or nihilist who is submissive before history. In English, our words *history* and *historical* seem to be semantically anchored to the totality of facts as the object of the study of the historian. In German, *Geschichte* is the series of ongoing events that constitute history, which then in turn become *Historie*, or the object of historical study. Heidegger's concern is not simply with *Geschichte* but with *Urgeschichte*, or the latent history of reality as the background against which everyday history takes place.

2. As is well known, Hans Georg Gadamer developed a methodology or, to be exact, a reflection on methodology derived from this aspect of Heidegger's theory of existential worlds. See *Wahrheit und Methode: Grundzüge einer philosophischen Hermeneutik* (Tübingen: Mohr, 1960), trans. Garrett Barden and John Cumming, under the title *Truth and Method* (New York: Seabury, 1976). Gadamer's reflection tends toward a formalism which does not turn self-reflectively, as does Heidegger's theory, to an apprehensive projection of the current world. In personal conversation and in his latest writings, though, Gadamer has tended to become increasingly existential in his interpretations of Western philosophy and of the contemporary world.

3. "Der Mensch spricht. Wir sprechen im Wachen und im Traum. Wir

sprechen stets; auch dann, wenn wir kein Wort verlauten lassen, sondern nur zuhören oder lesen, sogar dann, wenn wir weder eigens zuhören noch lesen, stattdessen einer Arbeit nachgehen oder in der Musse aufgehen. Wir sprechen ständig in irgendeiner Weise," from Martin Heidegger, "Die Sprache," the opening essay of *Unterwegs zur Sprache* (Pfullingen: Neske, 1959); the English translation is by Albert Hofstadter from the essay "Language" in *Poetry, Language, Thought* (New York: Harper Colophon, 1971), p. 189.

4. For a discussion of these distinctions, see Otto Pöggeler, "Heidegger's Topology of Being," and the subsequent discussions with Pöggeler in *On Heidegger and Language*, ed. and trans. Joseph J. Kockelmans (Evanston: Northwestern University Press, 1972), pp. 107–46, especially Pöggeler's answer to the remarks by James Edie, p. 140ff.

5. See n. 7 for a relevant reference to Grassi's work.

6. Both points are discussed by the writer and pathologist Lewis Thomas, the first in the chapter on "Information," in *Lives of a Cell* (Toronto: Bantam Books, 1974), and the second in "The Corner of the Eye," in *Late Night Thoughts on Listening to Mahler's Ninth Symphony* (Toronto: Bantam Books, 1984).

7. "Die Sprache ist das Haus des Seins" is found in the "Letter on 'Humanism'" ("Brief über den 'Humanismus'"), in *Wegmarken* (Frankfurt: Klostermann, 1967), p. 164; trans. Frank Capuzzi, under the title *Martin Heidegger: Basic Writings*, ed. David F. Krell (New York: Harper & Row, 1977), p. 213. The full citation runs: "Man is not only a living creature who possesses language along with other capacities. Rather, language is the house of Being in which man ek-sists by dwelling, in that he belongs to the truth of Being, guarding it." Ernesto Grassi, proceeding from Heidegger's theory of world and of truth, has criticized Heidegger's polemic against "Humanism." Grassi claims, convincingly I think, that Heidegger overlooked certain undercurrents in Italian Renaissance Humanism which, in Grassi's reading, corroborate and extend Heidegger's notion of truth by a radical retrieval of imagination and metaphor. See Ernesto Grassi, *Heidegger and the Question of Renaissance Humanism: Four Studies* (New York: State University of New York, 1983). My chapter 3 develops Heidegger's notion of existential truth in terms of metaphor and is thereby indebted to Grassi's interpretation as well as to some suggestions made by Grassi in private discussions about the place of metaphor in computer technology.

8. Martin Heidegger, *Hebel—der Hausfreund* (Pfullingen: Günther Neske, 1957); trans. Bruce Foltz and Michael Heim under the title "Hebel—Friend of the House," in *Contemporary German Philosophy*, vol. 3 (University Park: Pennsylvania State University Press, 1983), pp. 89-101.

9. See the provocative book by Henry Veatch, *Two Logics* (Evanston: Northwestern University Press, 1969).

10. *Die Metaphysische Anfangsgründe der Logik im Ausgang von Leibniz* (Frankfurt: Klostermann, 1978), originally vol. 26 of the *Gesamtausgabe*; trans. Michael Heim, under the title *The Metaphysical Foundations of Logic* (Bloomington: Indiana University Press, 1984). See also the translator's introduction to that book.

11. Martin Heidegger, *The Question Concerning Technology and Other Essays*, trans. William Lovitt (New York: Harper & Row, 1977); originally published as "Die Frage nach der Technik," in *Vorträge und Aufsätze* (Pfullingen: Günther Neske, 1954) and reprinted in *Die Technik und die Kehre* (Pfullingen: Günther Neske, 1962).

12. This is in 1985-86 termed a state-of-the-art idea processor. It was written by Forefront Software and is published by Ashton-Tate.

13. William Harrison, *Framework: An Introduction* (Culver City, Cal.: Ashton-Tate Publishing Group, 1984), p. 30.

14. The first half of the citation is from ibid., the second half from a flyer published by Ashton-Tate, Inc.

15. Ibid., p. 5.

16. Ibid. Other passages read as follows:

> Probably the most significant way FRAMEWORK's outline capabilities will improve your productivity, however, is by a subtle process of stimulating you to be more organized and systematic in your own work. Because the outlining capability is there, you are reminded to think of it. Once you use it for one task, you tend to think of it for other purposes, as well. And when you see the effort you can save with dynamic outlining, you will tend to adopt it almost without thinking into your repertoire of tricks for personal productivity. (p. 84)

> The second capability of the whole is less tangible. It is Framework's ability to induce more systematic thinking about your

work. Because Framework puts a whole series of work-saving and
productivity-raising tools at your fingertips, including the exclusive capability of dynamic outlining, it encourages you to find
ways to use them. One work-saving experience tends to lead to
others. As a result, you inevitably tend to give more careful
thought to your work and the ways you can apply Framework to
improve it. (p. 31)

17. Heidegger, "The Age of the World Picture," in *The Question
Concerning Technology,*, p. 134. Note that here the structure of the
neologism *Gebild* is modeled after *Gestell*, the kind of gathering of things
into a world that enframes.

18. For example, in ibid., p. 24, where the German *Herausgeforderte* is
translated as "challenged forth" or "provoked."

19. Harrison (*Framework: An Introduction*, p. 31) writes, "In a real
sense, the main product of Framework as a whole is an increase in
personal productivity."

20. The founder of Apple computers, Steven Jobs, for example, says in
an interview: "I'm just a guy who probably should have been a
semitalented poet on the Left Bank. I got sort of sidetracked here. The
space guys, the astronauts, were techies to start with. John Glenn didn't
read Rimbaud, you know; but you talk to some of the people in the
computer business now and they're very well grounded in the philosophical traditions of the last hundred years and the sociological
traditions of the Sixties." Cited in *Newsweek Access*, Fall 1984, p. 44.
Regarding the poetic vocation of Apple company's software writers it
might be noted, somewhat sympathetically, that the nature of software
poetry does indeed have a touch of Left Bank surrealism about it. For
instance, the process of deleting a text file on an Apple Macintosh
microcomputer can be accurately described as follows: "First you drag
the folder down to the trash can with the mouse and then you empty it."
But a new sense of technological poetry is, in fact, conferred on the
software of Apple computers through the connection of iconic visualiza-
tion with written alphabetic symbols.

21. This very threat to human creativity is the major theme of gradually
developing literature on the cultural history of Silicon Valley and the
conflict between the hackers, who build technology with earnest
playfulness and with enthusiastic responsiveness to its potential, and
the executive entrepreneurs, who seek to standardize and maintain

proprietary rights over technological breakthroughs. Examples include Paul Freiberger, *Fire in the Valley: The Making of the Personal Computer* (Berkeley: Osborne/McGraw-Hill, 1984); Charles T. Sherman, *Up and Running: Adventures of a Software Entrepreneur* (Inglewood, Cal.: Ashton-Tate, 1984); Adam Osborne and John Dvorak, *Hypergrowth* (Berkeley: Idthekkethan, 1984).

22. Chris DeVoney, *MS-DOS User's Guide* (Indianapolis: Que Corporation, 1984), pp. 17, 85.

Chapter 4. The Psychic Framework of Word Processing

1. Howard Rheingold, *Tools for Thought: The People and Ideas behind the Next Computer Revolution* (New York: Simon & Schuster, 1985), pp. 248–49. See also Rheingold's treatment of Hubert Dreyfus's challenge to artificial intelligence research, in ibid., pp. 161–62, where a computer chess match held in 1967 against critic Dreyfus is described. Dreyfus insists today that he never made the unqualified, generic claim attributed to him by Rheingold and others, namely that "a chess playing program of any significance could never be built." See Dreyfus's new book *Mind over Machine: The Power of Human Intuition and Expertise in the Era of the Computer* (New York: Macmillan Free Press, 1985), p. 112, where he tries to set straight the account. It would be, of course, an *ad hominem* fallacy to suppose that Dreyfus's defeat by a chess program diminishes the appropriateness of his criticism—though such embroglios do give philosophers pause before launching primarily negative polemics in the lively sphere of human culture.

2. Hubert Dreyfus, *What Computers Can't Do: The Limits of Artificial Intelligence*, rev. ed. (New York: Harper Colophon, 1979), pp. 164–65. See all of Dreyfus's chapter 4 for his arguments and distinctions.

3. This is the term used for the title of chapter 4 of Walter Ong, *Orality and Literacy: The Technologizing of the Word* (London: Methuen, 1982), and it occurs in the title of the first chapter of Ong, *Rhetoric, Romance, and Technology*. The term occurs frequently in Ong's writings, and its use has prompted critics like Pattison to refer to Ong as "a child of the sixties" and to conclude that his work is "indelibly stamped by its [that era's] influence"; see Robert Pattison, *On Literacy: The Politics of the Word from Homer to the Age of Rock* (New York: Oxford University Press, 1982), p. 222.

4. Ong, *Orality and Literacy*, pp. 79ff.

5. Rheingold, *Tools for Thought*, p. 243.

6. This was Douglas Engelbart's aim in thinking out and setting up the first word-processing hardware and software: "Both the language used by a culture, and the capability for effective intellectual activity, are directly affected during their evolution by the means by which individuals control the external manipulation of symbols.... We are introducing new and extremely advanced means for externally manipulating symbols. We then want to determine the useful modifications in the language and in the way of thinking that could then result." See Engelbart, "A Conceptual Framework," p. 14. The term *bootstrapping* is more than a fortuitous metaphor—"lifting yourself up by your own bootstraps." It seems intrinsic to the metaphorical structure of thinking about and with computers. Every time you "boot up" the computer, you invoke the long history of the enhancement of human thought through symbol manipulation.

7. The earliest versions of the thesis of this book, going back to January 1984, were couched in the terminology of *mental habits*, *Denkgewohnheiten*, and *habitudes mentales*. Others have since found the terms useful in the analysis of word processing. The attempt here is to develop, on a deeper and more consistent level, a terminology still more appropriate to the phenomenon.

8. For instance, Nietzsche's famous aphorism: "Every habit lends our hands more wit but makes our wit less handy." In *The Gay Science*, bk. 3, no. 247, trans. Walter Kaufmann (New York: Vintage, 1974), p. 215.

9. See the by now classic *The Concept of Mind* (London: Hutchinson & Co., 1949). What Ryle dubs "the traditional notion of mind" and finds so misleading is a notion that has been filtered through the Cartesian philosophy of the *ego cogito*, or "I think." It should not be confused with the Platonic notion of mind, especially in the postmodern sense I develop in later chapters.

10. For a brief description of how this epistemological philosophy continues to fare in the Anglo-American universe of discourse, see Charles Taylor's review of Richard Wollheim, *The Thread of Life*, in *New York Review of Books* (November 22, 1984), pp. 51–55.

11. Engelbart, "A Conceptual Framework," pp. 3, 15ff. Emphasis added. Much of Engelbart's work at that time was done at the Stanford Research

Institute under contract by the Air Force Office of Scientific Research, Directorate of Information Sciences.

12. Jacques Barzun, *The House of Intellect* (New York: Harper & Brothers, 1959), p. 6. The point here relates to the terms in which Barzun presents his thesis. What Barzun is actually trying to get at regarding the nature of what he calls "Intellect" is quite relevant to the critique of word processing, as we shall see in chapters 6 and 7.

13. In correspondence dated July 18, 1984, Walter Ong wrote, "You are quite right in aligning my thinking with phenomenology, for it is, I suspect, phenomenological at least in notable ways, though not in every way. I have never programmed myself for this alignment. My mind simply works this way, often enough, anyhow, and it worked this way before I had read any phenomenologists. Thought takes phenomenological form naturally at our present stage of consciousness, although there are of course other concurrent shapes it also takes, in my own case and that of others. Hannah Arendt once told me (we were fellow Fellows at the Center for Advanced Studies at Wesleyan University in Connecticut in 1961–62) that my mind works dialectically. I am sure that it does. Lots of 'buts' and 'howevers.' Perhaps not so many as in Kierkegaard." (Cited by permission.)

14. For an argument against connecting theoretically the physical senses with cognitive "noetics" see Jonathan Miller, *Marshall McLuhan* (New York: Viking, 1971), chap. 4. Miller argues against McLuhan's notion that the members of a culture undergo shifts in "sensory bias" with the introduction of different artificial means for enhancing sense perception, such as the telescope and microscope. Miller's counterargument seems to rely on the fact that such shifts are not quantifiable and on the putative permanence of the "natural" state of the physical sense organs.

15. Chapter 3 of *Orality and Literacy* is entitled "Some Psychodynamics of Orality" and contains some of the contrastive features mentioned here. Further references to Ong's theory of social-sexual changes can be found in the bibliography to that book.

16. Diels and Krantz eds., *Die Fragmenta*, fragment 45: "psyches peirata ion ouk an exeuroio, pasan epiporeuomenos hodon. Houto bathun logon echei."

17. I am thinking of the work of James Hillman and kindred psychologists. See, for instance, James Hillman, *Re-Visioning Psychology* (New York: Harper & Row, 1975).

18. The primary discussion of the two gods and their respective realms is found in the second book of Plato, *The Laws*, though the interpretation I give relies on many passages in other Dialogues. Chapter 6 below treats more of Plato's notion of psychic motion.

19. One instance of this kind of international philosophical exchange is the Zurich Discourses held in Europe over the last several years. The presence of Zen scholars from the Kyoto School and of Japanese psychiatrists has brought new reflections to the consideration of rational discussion. See, for some published results of the Discourses, *Das Gespräch als Ereignis: Ein semiotisches Problem*, vol. 1, ed. Ernesto Grassi and Hugo Schmale (Munich: Wilhelm Fink Verlag, 1982), pp. 35–57. An English translation is forthcoming.

20. *The Complete Tales and Poems of Edgar Allan Poe* (New York: Vintage Books, 1975), p. 350.

21. Ibid., pp. 270–71.

22. See on this point Arthur Koestler, *The Act of Creation* (New York: Dell, 1967), p. 636.

23. Engelbart, "A Conceptual Framework," p. 17f.

Chapter 5. The Phenomenon of Word Processing

1. Parallels of this sort have been made before. This one occurs in a letter to the author by Scott Fitzgerrell, currently of Channelmark Corporation, a software firm in San Mateo, California. On more than one occasion in conversation with writers I have noticed the word *God* mentioned in association with computers as centers for the organization of meaning— and this without the least prompting from philosophers or theologians.

2. In an essay on metaphor, Max Black asks parenthetically, "Would it not be unsettling to suppose that a metaphor might be self-certifying, by generating the very reality to which it seems to draw attention?" There is a slightly different point here than that of "generative metaphors," which establish new connections among existent things. It is the ontological nature of computerized symbolization, its touching the heart of experienced reality, that makes computer metaphors unsettling. The unsettling nature of a radically different reality apprehension brings us not to a judicious isomorphism between already existent realities but to groping efforts to articulate a new kind of existence in which we can still hope to

inherit something of the previous reality. Quotation from Black is contained in "More about Metaphor," in *Metaphor and Thought*, ed. Andrew Ortony (Cambridge: Cambridge University Press, 1982), p. 37.

3. *WordStar Reference Manual* for version 3.3 (San Rafael, Cal.: Micro-Pro International Corporation, 1983), pp. 3-10.

4. *Reference Guide to XyWrite III* (Bedford, Mass.: XyQuest, Inc., 1985), pp. 3-6, 3-7.

5. "User's Guide for CED: DOS Command Editor," p. 6 (a public domain program copyrighted by Christopher J. Dunford). The program is a part of the evolution of a utility program called DOSEDIT, which is widely used today on MS-DOS systems. The program supplements the primitive, inadequately implemented Disk Operating System (DOS) on personal computers. The documentation for CED is quite thorough and competent as far as documentation goes.

6. John Seely-Brown, "From Cognitive to Social Ergonomics and Beyond," May 1985, unpublished paper from the Xerox Palo Alto Research Center (PARC). The paper is to appear in *New Perspectives on Human-Computer Interaction*, ed. by D. A. Norman and S. W. Draper (Hillsdale, N. J.: Lawrence Erlbaum Associates, 1985).

7. *Reference Guide to XyWrite III*, p. 3-7.

8. For references, see Seely-Brown, "From Cognitive to Social Ergonomics and Beyond."

9. Or, for another example, consider this situation: While writing on a file the size of the present chapter, I decide to call in some notes I made in another file. After giving the command to call in the notes, and after seeing the notes come up on the screen, I try to scroll to the bottom of the notes. A drive light goes on, then goes off, and an error message comes up: "Cannot scroll—Out of memory." Now, it is possible for me to cut out some of the material in order to provide more memory for what I am currently writing. On the other hand, if I have some mental model of the flow of information in the program I am using, I will realize that the scrolling of large files takes place by continually storing a certain amount of the top or bottom of the file on one of the disk drives as I move through the text (using so-called virtual memory). With such a model in mind, I can log onto another drive (if I have one, or a RAM drive) and use it for the current default drive. In this way the program will have the space to keep the top or bottom of the document on virtual memory and so allow

me to scroll through the large file. The mechanical whirring of the drive, the light going on, and the error message are not adequate indicators to instruct me on possible solutions for removing the obstacles I encounter. It is necessary to have formed a mental model of the system.

Another obvious way in which computer usage necessitates a mental model of the system's operations is the constant need to evaluate the compatibility of different information systems and communication devices. Such knowledge is acquired only at the price of experience and—as is often the case in matters of understanding—such experience requires prior knowledge. The circle is only broken by plunging into it.

10. See *PC Magazine*, August 20, 1985, p. 59, for a brief description of the historical phase referred to here.

11. Along with *Wordix*, *Edix* is a component of *The Professional Writer's Package 2.0*. *Edlin* belongs to the MS-DOS system created by Microsoft.

12. Edward Foster, "Outliners: A New Way of Thinking," *Personal Computing* 9:5 (May 1985): 74.

13. *THINK* is a public domain program written by Larry Groebe, and *IDEA* is available on a ROM chip from Traveling Software of Seattle, Washington. Both of these are close cousins of *ThinkTank* for the IBM personal computer.

14. To say that the program is Aristotelian in inspiration, however, is not to say it is classical. There is surely a hermeneutic or highly interpretive moment in a software package which announces itself as a "tool for knowledge management," however classical its intentions. At best, this is neoclassicism. The psychic framework of Aristotelian logic differs essentially from that of an outliner in the electronic element. In the following chapter I consider the classical framework with its emphasis on the contemplative attitude, and in chapter 7 I will contrast this attitude with the psychic framework that fosters better thought management and productivity.

15. Engelbart, "A Conceptual Framework," p. 24. And on the same page:

> The means available to humans today for developing and mani-
> pulating symbol structures are both laborious and inflexible. To
> develop an initial structure of diagrams and text is difficult, but
> because the cost of frequent changes is often prohibitive, one
> settles for inflexibility. Also, the flexibility that would be truly

helpful requires added symbol structuring just to keep track of the trials, branches, and reasoning thereto that are involved in the development of the subject structure. Present symbol-manipulation means would soon bog down completely among the complexities that are involved in being more than just a little bit flexible.

16. *ThinkTank* is published by Living Videotext of Mountain View, California. Part of the description of the program comes from David Winer, who created it. Some of his notions can also be found in Kamin, *The ThinkTank Book*, chap. 10.

17. There is, for instance, the program discussed in chapter 3, *Framework* by Ashton-Tate. In the case of *Framework*, the outliner shares a similar time and movement, but the psychic framework differs in that vast amounts of text, database material, or calculational spreadsheet can be incorporated directly into the outline. As such, the very notion of outline is stretched as a metaphor and what results is an integrative symbol system of another magnitude altogether.

18. *Freestyle* is published by the Select Division of Summa Technologies in Kentfield, California. Gary Cole of Summa Technologies was helpful in discussing outliners with me.

19. In this last mentioned direction, there is, for instance, *Logic-Line* by Clarity Software in Chesterland, Ohio.

20. Gerald M. Weinberg, *The Whole Earth Software Catalog*, ed. Stewart Brand (Garden City, N.Y.: Quantum Press, 1984), p. 160.

21. This is the way the matter was put by the writer and computer journalist Jerry Pournelle. He writes (in reference to the *Valdocs* operating system on the Epson computer): "I'm not sure what 'computer literacy' is. If it means the ability to sit down at any microcomputer and within hours to days be able to do useful work with it, then I'm all for it: but you won't learn that kind of computer literacy if they've crippled your machine in order to make it 'user friendly'.... It's as if the Ford company decided to install a new set of 'user friendly' controls in their cars. Why should you have to learn about brake pedals and steering wheels? Out with them! There have to be easier ways! Of course you'll never be able to drive anything but a Ford." In Jerry Pournelle, *The Users Guide to Small Computers* (New York: Baen Books, Simon & Schuster, 1984), p. 288.

22. "Once I spent the better part of a day trying to alphabetize a list of

names using my computer's alphabetizing program. It came out scrambled. It came out backwards. It came out alphabetized by the second letter of the first name. I could have done it by hand in half an hour. But the feeling of joy when it finally did work right was so strong, so sustaining, that it gave me nourishment to survive the next dozen problems in good mental health." John Bear, *Computer Wimp* (Berkeley: Ten Speed Press, 1983), p. 20. Bear insists throughout his book that you do not need to learn programming to use computers. True enough—in the formal sense. But by his own testimony, *experto crede!*

23. Full details of this story can be found in *PC Magazine* 4:16 (August 6, 1985): 59.

24. All these programming languages appear as optional appendages to the direct interface. They nevertheless affect working on the interface. With *XyWrite*, for instance, each command to the word processor is entered on a "command line" which has both a "format" symbolization, such as "RMVSCR" for "Remove Screen," and an "ABBREV" (abbreviated) form such as "RS." To "DF," one learns, means to "dump notes" or "place the footnotes in the text." Jargon derived from programmer's mnemonics are a far cry from direct English.

25. Bruce Rodgers on the IBM Professional Special Interest Group (Sig 131) of CompuServe in January 1985.

26. Colette Daiute has conducted several research projects at the Harvard Graduate School of Education and she arrived at this conclusion. See her "Can the Computer Stimulate Writers' Inner Dialogues?" in *The Computer in Composition Instruction*, ed. William Wresch (Urbana, Ill.: National Council of Teachers of English, *NCTE*, 1984), pp. 131–39.

27. See several of the papers in Wresch, ed., *The Computer in Composition Instruction.*

28. A description and history of invisible writing, or freewriting, on computers is in Ruth Von Blum, "WANDAH: Writing Aid AND Author's Helper," in Wresch, ed., *The Computer in Composition Instruction*, pp. 154–72.

29. For example, this passage from Frank Herbert with Max Barnard, *Without Me You're Nothing: The Essential Guide to Home Computers*, (New York: Simon & Schuster, 1980):

Someday we will attach a computer directly to the human nervous system. Computer storage will flow directly into your thoughts—in graphic symbols, in words written or oral, in pictures projected onto your inner eye, and in sounds uttered for "your ears alone." High-speed computer sorting will respond to your unspoken mental demand.... On that day your personal computer will probably be a pea-size device implanted in your flesh. Mass storage and the data banks will be some place outside your body, lined to you by something like microwave.... There is no doubt that this connection between flesh and machine will occur—a kind of ultimate prosthesis. Several current developments make this apparent.... Don't imagine that this evolution can be outlawed. The first brain surgeon able to engage a tight instantaneous link with his medical library and other surgeons *while he is operating* will lead the way for all other surgeons to follow. When that surgeon demonstrates a computer-assisted ability to operate at a microscopic level, perhaps even at a cellular level, there will be a stampede of surgeons to join him.... What we have with computers is an interactive evolutionary process. It applies equally to us and to computers. It is deeply involved with our desires, some of which are instinctual and unconscious. Because of this, a tight symbiotic relationship between human and computer can be predicted with certainty. (pp. 206–07)

Herbert is the author of the *Dune* series in science fiction.

30. In the introduction to William Chamberlain, ed., *The Policeman's Beard Is Half Constructed: Computer Prose and Poetry by RACTER* (New York: Warner Books, 1984). Also: "Effective naming of files requires creative thinking. You want a name that is unique and descriptive enough to help you recall what's in the document later. A name like LETTER is OK if you've written only one. A better one might be LREAGAN 1/14 standing for 'the letter to Ronald Reagan on Jan 14.' Your other love letters could be labeled similarly. However, if you have only 8 characters to use for a file name, it will take ingenuity to make your files unique and memorable. For instance, LRR1/14." Fred Stern, *Word Processing and Beyond: The Introductory Computer Book* (Santa Fe: John Muir Publications, 1983).

31. William James, *Psychology: Briefer Course* (New York: Collier-Macmillan, 1972), p. 183.

32. Several neologisms have been used to describe what I call linkage. Terms used by others include *compunications* and *telematics*. *Compunications* was coined by Anthony Oettinger of Harvard to describe the merger of computers, telephone, and television into a new kind of digital

code, a single yet differentiated system that allows for the transmission of data or interaction between persons or computers "speaking to" computers through telephone lines, cables, microwave relays, or satellites; *telematics* is the translation of the French neologism *télématique*, which was created by Simon Nora and Alain Minc; see the introduction to Simon Nora and Alain Minc, *The Computerization of Society* (Cambridge: The MIT Press, 1981).

33. For Ted Nelson's development of the idea of hypertext and links, see Rheingold, *Tools for Thought*, pp. 303ff. Rheingold describes Nelson's scheme in this way:

> A system with backtracking, versioning, and links would create the possibility of a new way of organizing thoughts into words, a non-sequential form of writing that was never possible before computers, a literary process he [Nelson] called *hypertext*. Hypertext could apply to scholarship as well as to poetry. The rate and volume of scientific publication have overwhelmed the coping capacity of our old print-era technology.... With a hypertext system, each scientific document could have links to its intellectual antecedents and to documents regarding related problems. The entire body of relevant scientific literature could be collapsed into each individual document. The links would function in the same way as footnotes, but with immediate access to the cited material, as if each footnote was like a window or door into the cited document.

Doug Engelbart actually built a very similar feature into an early system of his called the oNLine System (NLS) at the Augmentation Research Center (ARC). For more on Engelbart's ideas, see the discussion of mind augmentation in Rheingold, *Tools for Thought*, pp. 174–204.

34. The concept of versioning capabilities was also first explored by Ted Nelson, according to the account in Rheingold, *Tools for Thought*, p. 302.

35. One sample of this kind of publishing is William Bates, *The Computer Cookbook* (Englewood Cliffs, N.J.: Prentice-Hall, 1983). On page 352, there is the following notice: "An electronic edition of this book is transmitted to NewsNet, the business information service. Users of NewsNet can search the text of the book for key words, and receive updates to the book as they are written by the author. A telephone modem is also used to transmit the text of the book via Tymnet to a translator in Japan."

36. Colette Daiute, *Writing and Computers* (New York: Addison-Wesley, 1985), pp. 22, 19, and 27.

37. Pamela McCorduck, *The Universal Machine: Confessions of a Technological Optimist* (New York: McGraw-Hill, 1985), p. 65.

38. Patricia Marks Greenfield, *Mind and Media: The Effects of Television, Video Games, and Computers* (Cambridge: Harvard University Press, 1984), p. 139.

Chapter 6. The Book and the Classic Model of Mind

1. James, *Psychology: Briefer Course*, p. 17.

2. I am thinking here of James's classic *The Varieties of Religious Experience.*

3. The original inscription reads as follows:

```
HOC HOC SEPULCRUM RESPICE
QUI CARMEN ET MUSAS AMAS
ET NOSTRA COMMUNI LEGE
LACRIMANDA TITULO NOMINA
NAM NOBIS PUERIS SIMUL
ARS VARIA PARAETA SERAT
EGO CONSONANTI FISTULA
SIDONIUS ACRISPER STREPENS
HOC CARMEN HAEC CARAECCN
PUERI SEPULCRUM EST XANTIA
QUI MORTE ACER BARAPTUSES
IAM DOCTUS IN COMPENDIA
TOLIT ERARUM E NOMNUM
NOTARE CURRENTI STILO
QUOD LINGUA CURRENS DICERE
IAM NEMO SUPERARET LEGEN
IAM VOCE ERILI COEPERAT
A DOMNE DICTATUM VOLANS
AUREM VOCARIAT PROXIMAM
HEU MORTE PROPERA CONCIDIT
ARCANA QUIS SOLUS SUI
SCIT VRVS DOMINEVIT
```

A photograph of the stone with inscription can be found in Hugo Borger, *Das Römisch-Germanische Museum Köln* (Munich: Verlag Georg D. W. Callwey, 1977), with a picture of the monument on p. 173. A German translation of the inscription is on p. 60; the English translation is mine.

4. In *Metaphysics* 1.982b20, Aristotle distinguishes sharply between those activities aimed at practical utility and those higher studies which are not pursued for the sake of the practical necessities of life. His analysis of self-sufficient activities and intrinsic causes can be found at the beginning of book 1 of the *Nicomachean Ethics*. In the *Politics* (bk. 8, chap. 2), Aristotle discusses *banausic* crafts and warns against bringing so much "mechanics" into education that the psyche is narrowed by it and becomes less capable of generalizing from experience. To be truly human, in Aristotle's philosophy, it is necessary to actualize the human power of *nous*, or contemplative reason, which is an imitation of the Unmoved Mover's activity (*Metaphysics* 1072b13, 1177a20-21f.).

5. A prime example is the semimonastic ascetic community of Egyptian gnostics who lived a frugal existence at the edge of an oasis about three-quarters of the way upstream between Cairo and Luxor. In the fourth century A.D. they created a sacred library of religious texts known today as the Nag Hammadi Library. The community supported itself largely through a strong literary business, in the production of papyrus, making skins and book covers from goatskin, and preparing books and copying documents for others. Their codices are some of the earliest book-form writings that have survived from an age that used mostly scrolls. The library was later buried by a group of unorthodox monks, shortly after the Paschal Letter of Bishop Athanasius of Alexandria in 367 A.D., which urged the expulsion of heretics and their books from the Pachomian Christian monasteries in the area. The library was unearthed in 1945. See James M. Robinson, ed., *The Nag Hammadi Library* (New York: Harper & Row, 1981), and Elaine Pagels, *The Gnostic Gospels* (New York: Vintage Books, 1981).

6. Elizabeth Eisenstein goes into a particularly detailed account of religious traditions in her study *The Printing Press as an Agent of Change: Communications and Cultural Transformations in Early-Modern Europe* (Cambridge: Cambridge University Press, 1979).

7. Jean Leclercq, O.S.B., *The Love of Learning and the Desire for God: A Study of Monastic Culture*, trans. Catharine Misrahi (New York: Fordham University Press, 1982), pp. 72-73.

8. Ibid., pp. 73-74.

9. "Scriptis enim codicibus nunquam impressi ex equo comparantur; nam orthographiam et ceteros librorum ornatus impressura plerumque negligit. Scriptura autem maioris industrie est." Johannes Trithemius, *De Laude*

Scriptorum, trans. Roland Behrendt of the Monastic Manuscript Microfilm Library at St. John's Abbey, Collegeville, Minn. (Latin-English edition Lawrence, Kan.: Coronado Press, 1974; original Latin-German edition published in Würzburg in the *Mainfränkische Hefte*, Heft 60, 1973), p. 65. In some of the brief passages quoted I retranslate in order to make the citation flow more smoothly, but differences from Behrendt's English translation are slight. Quotations in the following two paragraphs are cited from pages 61, 47, 49, 35, 63.

10. See, for instance, Nietzsche, *The Gay Science*, p. 238 (section 296). Most current critiques of self-identity and fixity of thought run in the tradition of Nietzsche, as does the so-called deconstructionist movement in literary criticism along the inscrutable lines of Jacques Derrida. To mention but two works that take up the argument: Xavier Rubert de Ventos, *Self-Defeated Man* (New York: Harper & Row, 1975), a translation of *Moral y Nueva Cultura*, and James Ogilvy, *Many Dimensional Man: Decentralizing Self, Society, and the Sacred* (New York: Oxford University Press, 1977).

11. Some Plato interpreters, such as Stanley Rosen, emphasize the public or dramatic effects of Socrates' inward turn to thought. No doubt Socrates does "place Aristodemus in an embarrassing situation" by causing him to go on ahead to the party alone and uninvited, and Socrates' silence does "prepare him for the banquet." But the point of the self-sufficiency of contemplative awareness is easily lost if we look to rhetorical effects rather than to the intrinsic act of thought itself; the danger is to reduce contemplative thought to the level of an instrument, to a kind of public statement or a manipulation of people. See Rosen, *Plato's Symposium* (New Haven: Yale University Press, 1968); for a different kind of interpretation, see *The Symposium of Plato*, ed. John Brentlinger (Amherst: University of Massachusetts Press, 1970), pp. 22–23.

12. H. D. F. Kitto (*The Greeks* [Baltimore: Penguin, 1951]) says about the ancient Greeks:

> It is not only the philosophers who have this mental habit of disregarding what is on the surface—the transitory appearances of things, their multiplicity and variety—and trying to reach the inner, the simplifying, reality. Do we not find something very similar in Greek sculpture, which, until the beginning of the fourth century at least, made not the slightest attempt at portraying the individual, but strove always to perfect its representation of The Athlete, or

The God? We certainly find something similar in Greek Tragedy. Between the Greek and our own classical drama there is the same sort of difference as there is between Greek and Gothic architecture, and the differences illustrate this habit of mind that we are discussing. As Gothic architecture delights in multiplicity of parts, in the utmost contrast of light and shade, and in ornamentation that draws upon the whole realm of nature—on birds, beasts and flowers, on figures of kings, saints and angels, and on grotesques too—so does Elizabethan tragedy, on its crowded and various stage, present the whole complexity and richness of life—kings and citizens, counsellors and soldiers, lovers, comics, children, fairies. Everything is there. It has been said that a Gothic cathedral is never finished, and conversely Shakespeare has often been cut—but who could add anything to a Greek temple that would not be an obvious excrescence, or cut a scene from a Greek play without making it unintelligible? . . . Aeschylus had no intention of writing a 'historical' play, but a play rather on the idea that Hybris (in the case of Persians, the wanton defiance of the will of Heaven shown by Xerxes) is punished by Heaven. . . . It is not the event, but its inner meaning, that Aeschylus is dramatizing; and if the historical events, in any particular, do not express the inner meaning clearly enough, Aeschylus alters them, thus illustrating in advance the dictum of Aristotle that poetry is more philosophical than history. . . . There is a difference between giving a picture of life by building up a synthesis, through significant selection, combination and contrast, and interpreting it in the Greek fashion. The one leads to variety and expansiveness, the other to simplicity and intensity. As the Greek is trying not to give a representative picture of life, but to express one conception, as forcibly and as clearly as he can, the form that he achieves is much more logical and taut. (pp. 182–84)

13. Paul Friedlander, for instance, stresses the way in which the special qualities of the dialogue in Plato's writings expand the possibilities of written symbols: "The dialogue is the only form of book that seems to suspend the book form itself. Plato also inherited the insight from Socrates that there is no ready-made knowledge simply transferable from one person to another, but only philosophy as an activity, the level of which is invariably determined by one's partner." Paul Friedlander, *Plato: An Introduction*, trans. Hans Meyerhoff (Princeton: Princeton University Press, 1969), p. 166. But Plato, as he addressed his contemporaries, could

locate transcendence, or nobility, neither in live questioning nor in glib speech and cleverness (sophistry); he could find it in the stabilizing mind of definitions and fixed intuitive looking, as fostered by the book. A similar problem for the symbolic element of nobility is posed for the modern poet by Wallace Stevens in his Harvard lecture of 1941, "The Noble Rider and the Sound of Words," published in *The Language of Poetry*, ed. Allen Tate (Princeton: Princeton University Press, 1942), pp. 91–125. Stevens points out that Plato's image of the charioteer in the *Phaedrus* does not provide the contemporary sensibility with an immediate grasp on transcendence through the sense-content of rapid movement or speed, since speed is now commonplace; whereas the stance put forth in a certain elaborate eloquence, in the sound of words, may in our time serve as the imaginative material for envisioning nobility. For Stevens, it became the elegant sound of words that offered a special loftiness and nobleness, apart from all utility and everyday self-concern: "Poetry is a peacock."

14. Today academic philosophy continues this identification of philosophic intelligence with literate thought. Keynote speeches at meetings of the American Philosophical Association, for example, are still delivered by reading from lengthy essays written so densely that they could not possibly be comprehended on one hearing by the hundreds of professionals in the audience. Such speeches carry the burden of modeling philosophic intelligence, and they do so precisely by refusing to be speeches.

15. For a clear and scholarly treatment of the Platonic understanding of the psyche's energies as they are shaped and made integral by the circular, steady order of the ideas, see Lynne Ballew, *Straight and Circular: A Study of Imagery in Greek Philosophy* (The Netherlands: Van Gorcum, 1979), pp. 79–107.

16. The Aristotelian tradition also contains most of the components of contemplative vision which I attribute to Platonism, only it is the word *nous*, or "insight," rather than "idea" which carries the content I refer to. *Nous* was also used by the pre-Socratics, as noted in chapter 1. The Greek verb *noein* prepares the way for Plato's notion of idea. The verb means "to know," but its meaning is quite specific, and even in Homer and the pre-Socratics the word has a range of meaning pertinent to what we call here the formulation of an idea. In his authoritative study "Noos and Noein in the Homeric Poems" (*Classical Philology* 38 [1943]), Kurt von Fritz treats the meaning of the word *noein*, and his results can be condensed in this

way: The sense of this verb is distinct from that of other verbs of perception. But the difference lies more in degree than in kind. It is not that *noein* involves a nonperceptual process; rather it involves one that is superior in focus, steadiness, incisiveness, and penetration. It is "a kind of mental perception...a kind of sixth sense which penetrates deeper into the nature of the object." The process of *noein* is also superior in range; it is "a mental vision" which not only penetrates deeper but also "sees further" both in space and in time than our eyes. The term "signifies a further step in the recognition of the object; the realization, for example, that this brown patch is not only a human being but an enemy lying in ambush." Other examples would be: the realization that this old woman is the goddess Aphrodite in disguise, or that what appears as a friend is actually a foe. The function of *noein* is such that "it penetrates below the visible surface to the real essence of the contemplated object." As a form of cognition *noein* in Homer is superior to both *idein*, "to see," and *gignoskein*, "to get to know." See Alexander Mourelatos, ed., *The Pre-Socratics: A Collection of Critical Essays* (New York: Anchor Press, 1974), pp. 23–85.

17. *Republic* 10.611D, Shorey translation in the Loeb Classical Library.

18. Ibid., 6.500C.

19. This is the truth contained in the following statement by Jacques Barzun, *The House of Intellect* (New York: Harper & Brothers, 1959): "The alphabet is a fundamental form to bear in mind while discussing the decay of Intellect, because intellectual work presupposes the concentration and continuity, the self-awareness and articulate precision, which can only be achieved through some firm record of fluent thought; that is, Intellect presupposes Literacy" (p. 6).

20. "In omnibus requiem quaesivi et non inveni, nisi seorsum sedans in angulo cum libello." These lines are the Latin inscription on Kempis's picture at Zwoll, Holland, where he is buried. They were supposed to have been written by him in his own copy of his *Imitation of Christ*, as vouched for by Rosweyd in his preface to the 1617 edition of the book.

21. Henry Miller, *Sexus: Book One of the Rosy Crucifixion* (New York: Grove Press, 1965), pp. 24–27.

22. This is especially emphatic in the famous passage of Plato's *Seventh Letter* (343–44), where the true and fixed being of the thing (*to on*) is contrasted with the various ways we have access to things: words, definitions, physical images, and knowledge. The latter are all in different degrees variable or unstable or arbitrary, while the best thoughts are those

which enjoy the unchanging silence of the thing pondered by thought. The thing contemplated cannot be reduced to the fleeting instruments or symbols used to grasp the thing. Thus any kind of writing, including the book, is inadequate for the full expression of truth. But, of these instruments the written book is the most instructive, since through it the mind practices the stabilizing silence of the world of ideas.

23. Marxist aesthetics attributes the book-length novel to the celebration of bourgeois sensibility. The leisure and privacy needed for reading novels gives the Marxist view a certain cogency. But as the quality of middle-class life itself becomes the subject of the novel, the content of the novel becomes an unsettling scrutiny of bourgeois sensibility and not a celebration. Think of novels such as *Madame Bovary* whose main theme is the narrow constriction of middle-class existence in the modern world. Flaubert's story would be impossible without the private life cultivated in and through books, as Emma and Léon agree in their chat at the dinner table. It would be very hard to feel sympathy for Emma Bovary if she nourished her fantasy life by reading a computer terminal. Personal romance through the romantic book goes back to Paolo and Francesca in Dante's *Divine Comedy*. It is simply not the same thing to experience a taped book on audiocassette in a moving automobile—much less on the interactive screen of the cathode ray tube.

24. This seems to be, and may actually be, the insight of Roland Barthes: "Now the subject ... is an anachronic subject, for he simultaneously and contradictorily participates in the profound hedonism of all culture (which permeates him quickly under cover of an art de vivre shared by the old books) and in the destruction of that culture: he enjoys the consistency of his selfhood (that is his pleasure) and seeks its loss (that is his bliss). He is a subject split twice over, doubly perverse." Also: "Not to devour, to gobble, but to graze, to browse scrupulously, to rediscover—in order to read today's writers—the leisure of bygone readings: to be aristocratic readers." From Roland Barthes, *Pleasure of the Text*, trans. Richard Howard (New York: Hill & Wang, 1977), pp. 13, 14.

25. Ray Bradbury, *Fahrenheit 451* (New York: Ballantine, 1953), p. 55.

Chapter 7. Critique of the Word in Process

1. McCorduck, *The Universal Machine* (New York: McGraw-Hill, 1985), p. 54.

2. W. H. Auden, *The Dyer's Hand and Other Essays* (New York: Vintage, 1968), p. 17.

3. Colette Daiute writes, "A fiction writer noted that he does not type his daily journals because the impersonal look of type distances him from his material. He writes these journals to discover his deep feelings and ideas, so he tries to maintain a personal quality in his writing, including the way it looks. He finds that handwriting, much more than typewriting, highlights connections in the self." In *Writing and Computers*, p. 42.

4. Alain is the pen name of Emile-Auguste Chartier (1868–1952).

5. Alain, *Système des Beaux-Arts* (1917), as cited by Richard Pevear in the foreword to his translation of Alain, *The Gods* (New York: New Directions, 1974).

6. Martin Heidegger, *Parmenides* (Frankfurt: Klostermann, 1982), pp. 118–19; originally lectures given in the winter of 1942–43, vol. 54 of the *Gesamtausgabe*. My translation. In this passage, Heidegger is commenting on the ancient Greek notion of "action" (*pragma*).

7. Peter Lyman, "The Book and the Computer in an Age of 'Computer Literacy,'" *Newsletter of the American Council of Learned Societies* (Winter-Spring 1984): 22.

8. From a letter to the author on October 25, 1985, from David M. Levin, author of *The Body's Recollection of Being: Phenomenological Psychology and the Deconstruction of Nihilism* (Boston: Routledge & Kegan Paul, 1985) and of other philosophical works. In his letter, Levin goes on to say: "Mainly, I think, this is because I give so much of myself to philosophical writing: books and shorter papers. After an average of 5 hours of writing per day, strenuous, exhausting, often a terrible struggle, I'm hardly in a mood to pour my heart out, or anyway pour myself into, a personal letter. No energy for that."

9. Daniel Tanner, professor of education at Rutgers University, in a letter to the *New York Times* (August 10, 1983). In a similar vein, Erik Sandberg-Diment writes: "Maybe I'm so visually oriented that I need to see physical scribblings in front of me on my yellow pads before I can feel that I have brought order to my thoughts. Whatever the case, I certainly don't like collapsing them to some nebulous world behind the screen where I have to shuffle them electronically instead of physically. Besides, there's a great deal to be said for the pleasures of crumpling up a poorly penned page and propelling it with rather more force than necessary in the

general direction of the wastepaper basket." Sandberg-Diment, *They All Laughed When I Sat Down at the Computer*, p. 117.

10. See, for instance, the interview with Gary Kildall, *PC Magazine*, November 12, 1985, pp. 95f. Kildall designed the CP/M operating system, which was the first widely used system for personal computers; he also founded Digital Research Incorporated.

11. In 1984, technical documentation alone in the United States amounted to over 2.5 trillion pages. Reported by Xerox Systems Group in El Segundo, California. See the report and comparison in *High Technology* (April 1986), p. 18.

12. Alvin Toffler, *Previews and Premises* (New York: William Morrow, 1983), p. 112.

13. David A. Hoekema, "Microcomputer Use for Learned Societies and Scholars," in *Proceedings and Addresses of the American Philosophical Association* 58:5 (June 1985): 741–46.

14. Craig Brod, *Technostress: The Human Cost of the Computer Revolution* (Reading, Mass.: Addison-Wesley, 1984).

15. Ibid., p. xii.

16. Brod divides the subjects of contemporary psychotherapy into two categories: the technoanxious and technocentered individuals. He maintains that industrial-era methods of treating clients are no longer adequate because of the psyche's context-dependency in the computer interface. Brod's criticism of what he calls "communication-oriented psychotherapy" is as follows:

> One wonders what happened to the richness of the therapeutic encounter. Psychotherapists now talk in terms of "functions," "messages," "codification," and "systems of communication." It is all too reminiscent of the "effective procedures" of electronic space. Fright and anxiety are downplayed; concern for messages replaces concern for emotions. Gone are the existential questions, the painful confrontation with the self. The objective of psychotherapy becomes correct thinking, "appropriate messages" based on "accurate perception."
>
> When therapists take this approach with technocentered patients, they exacerbate the situation. The patients, without much anxiety, can join the therapist in an exchange of information—perhaps even a perfectly honest exchange. The cure is taken to be clarity of think-

ing. Many therapists refer to patients as "handling the process well," "doing good process work," or "improving their interpersonal processes." The patients can learn to improve their ability to communicate without fundamentally changing at all; in fact, their underlying condition can become even more obscured than before. When patients switch to therapists who do not take a communication-theory approach, the problems often persist. Patients have learned to take all the potentially profound experiences of therapy sessions and turn them into statements explaining why they "process experience" the way they do.

Communication-oriented psychotherapists feel most comfortable with technology-oriented patients. Herein lies the problem. Nothing is gained by partially altering a pathological condition, only to reinforce it at the roots; psychotherapy of this kind is an obstacle to change. At issue in a psychotherapy session is what it means to be fully alive. The struggle to obtain a sense of wholeness, a grasp of one's identity, and a development of rounded passions must grow into new experiences for the patient.

What is curative is not better communication, although this is undeniably important, but an encounter that leads to discovery of needs and a confrontation with the experiential truth of one's existence. Anything less than this will only limit the human potential of patient and therapist alike.

Ibid., pp. 219–20.

17. Ibid., pp. 6–7.

18. Ibid., p. 16.

19. Ibid., p. 17.

20. Cogent here is the language used by Dennis Longley and Michael Shain, *The Microcomputer User's Handbook* (New York: John Wiley & Sons, 1984): "Word processing systems and applications represent the vanguard of the technological assault on the office. Wherever introduced they are likely over time to produce no less dramatic changes in working practices, individual responsibilities and interpersonnel [sic] relationships than the advent of automation did on the factory floor" (p. 99). Also pertinent is the motto of the shareware program *PC OUTLINE*: "Organization at your Fingertips." In this kind of documentation, management is defined as "skill in handling."

21. See Joseph Weizenbaum, *Computer Power and Human Reason: From Judgment to Calculation* (San Francisco: W. H. Freeman, 1976), pp. 115f., which analyzes the appeal of hacking, or obsessive programming, as a pathological attachment to the role of "lawgiver and creator of one's own universe." In brief, Weizenbaum maintains that computer manipulation holds the allure of power, and, like all power roles, is addictive. The special feature of power in the computer environment is that, within the completely stipulative and nonmaterial environment of the computer program, power is absolute and therefore corrupts more easily and more quickly. Compulsive pathology, according to Weizenbaum's analysis, is even more likely to arrest computer users than is mere distraction.

22. Eric Maloney, *80 Micro* (August 1985): 8.

23. Copyright Spite Software of Portland, Oregon.

24. Again, regarding the subtle changes introduced by using a program, see chap. 3, n. 16.

25. One writer says, for instance:

> I've noticed a change in my own writing over the last several years. Once upon a time, when all I used was a typewriter or notebook, I would spend days writing a piece in my head before I committed it to paper. When I finally sat down at my desk, I knew exactly what I wanted to say and how I wanted to say it. The result was usually quick, simple prose set down in a single draft.
>
> As I've come to use a word processor almost exclusively, the discipline of that pattern has slowly dissipated. I find myself approaching a writing task with hardly an idea of what I'm going to say, and not much concern about it. Why should I worry? If I don't like how these little pixels are arranged, I can just turn them off and light up another string, until I find a combination that suits me.
>
> The result is often a partly conceived or vaguely expressed idea, an idea that I might have discarded if I'd first exercised it in my mind.

Maloney, *80 Micro*, p. 8. Also, in a message to the author on CompuServe (January 1985), Maloney writes, "Personally, word processing has hurt more than helped my writing. I've always been a one-draft writer, and will sometimes spend days shaping a piece in my mind before I put something down on paper. A word processor makes me lazy, because it's so easy to hack around on the keyboard. I also tend to over-write with a word processor, smoothing out the rough edges until all of the original energy is gone."

26. "When writing with a word processor or text editor, as I'm doing now, I find that my writing is much more 'stream of consciousness' than it is when I'm writing something out by hand or (God forbid!) using a typewriter. Much more like when I'm dictating." Paul Graf on the IBM Sig (Special Interest Group) of CompuServe.

27. The program was Turbo Lightning, a memory-resident spelling program from Borland International, and the comments were made on the IBM Special Interest Group of the CompuServe information service.

28. Fluegelman, *Writing in the Computer Age*, p. 152.

29. From a letter dated August 17, 1985 to the author by Edward Giese, president of Acroatix Incorporated (the company's name being derived from *Acroatics* or *Acroamatics*, ancient words describing those teachings of Aristotle too subtle to commit to writing). The Acroatix software firm publishes a program called *TMPC* (Time—The Most Precious Commodity) for the portable Model 100 laptop computer. Based on the time management book by Stephanie Winston, *The Organized Executive*, this program is more than a complex calendar and appointment program. It channels the user into setting priorities of tasks and planning personal time in general. As a subliminal interface, *TMPC* should be compared with my discussion of the psychic framework of time at the end of chapter 4. *TMPC* manifests another element of felt time besides the traditional calendar or clock or appointment pad. It is certainly more than a planning utility or tool. There is no question of merely using the program as surrogate calendar or handy appointment notebook. The program takes over scheduling and planning in the sense that, if you use it over a period of time, it alters the way you interface with the plans and items of business in your life. The main metaphor operative in *The Most Precious Commodity* is that of the stick man "running" or "flying" to the "warehouse" of planned projects in order to set priorities for commodities of time. The user comes to identify with the hectic stick man and a certain experience of time is fostered. The awareness of time comes to be defined as a set of commodities to be parceled out and distributed.

30. An experimental study at the Massachusetts Institute of Technology led by Steven R. Lerman was cited in *The Chronicle of Higher Education* 31:5 (October 2, 1985): 32.

31. See *Literary Essays of Ezra Pound*, ed. T. S. Eliot (New York: New Directions, 1968), p. 26: "The language of prose is much less highly charged, that is perhaps the only availing distinction between prose and poesy. Prose permits greater factual presentation, explicitness, but a much greater amount of language is needed."

32. This is precisely the analogy used by the semiotician Gyula Decsy:

> The most expensive (and emotionally most impressive) sign is the tacteme: we travel by jet thousands of miles in order to touch (kiss) a relative or a person we love, or just to see (from a very close distance) a beautiful architectural monument in Italy, France or Egypt. The close natural view (optical sign, direct visualization) is almost as expensive as the tacteme. The *televiseme* (photo or TV picture) is less expensive, but never so fascinating, as the *direct-viseme*. Least expensive (and completely indifferent emotionally) are the *ectremes*—the unordered imprints on the tape of the computer.

Gyula Decsy, ed., *Global Linguistic Connections* (Bloomington, Ind.: Eurolingua, 1983), p. 45. This fascinating little book is very clearly itself a semiotreme.

33. As described in Howard Rheingold's account of Ted Nelson's vision in *Tools for Thought*, p. 303.

34. See Veatch, *Two Logics*. Veatch at the time cast the philosophical duality into the terms of the now dated split in academic philosophy between the so-called traditional and analytic philosophies then prevalent.

35. One such type of criticism of word processing may be seen to come from the general direction of "Existential" philosophy. Following Martin Buber's work on *I and Thou*, such criticism considers personal encounter (not to be confused with communication) to be the prime source of authentic language. Buber, for instance, claims the logically first words were neither nouns nor verbs but sentences. That is, language has essentially to do with statements made by people actually present to one another, responsive to one another, and exploring and describing a shared situation. From this conception of language comes the general characterization of language as situation words. From this philosophy, word processing presents another aspect of the increasing detachment of language from interactive immediacy. See Heinrich Ott, "Hermeneutic and Personal Structure of Language," in *On Heidegger and Language*, ed. Joseph Kockelmans (Evanston: Northwestern University Press, 1972), p. 179.

36. Read about, for instance, Steven Levy's experiences with his own writing in "Send Me No Abstract," *Popular Computing* 5:2 (December 1985): 32–37. At the time of this writing, data programmers and publishers are beginning to work together on possible "auto-paraphrase" programs and on licensing requirements needed for the promising new laser-storage technology, which will bring about a quantum jump in information (text) for the personal computer. See, for instance, *CD ROM: The New Papyrus* (Microsoft Press, 1986), and "CD-ROM Conference: Lured by 600 Megabytes on Disk," Craig Stark, *PC Magazine* 5:8 (April 29, 1985): 42.

37. Oliver Taplin discussing Homeric scholarship after Milman Parry's death (December 5, 1935): "From 'Homer Comes Home,'" *New York Review of Books*, vol. 33, no. 4 (March 13, 1986), p. 42.

38. Rheingold describing Ted Nelson's vision in *Tools for Thought*, p. 304.

39. Read about the important pioneering work in Roy Amara, John Smit, Murray Turoff, and Jacques Vallee, "Computerized Conferencing, a New Medium," *Mosaic* (January-February 1976). The authors suggest:

> The computer as a device to allow a human group to exhibit collective intelligence is a rather new concept. In principle, a group, if successful, would exhibit an intelligence higher than any member. Over the next decades, attempts to design computerized conferencing structures that allow a group to treat a particular complex problem with a single collective brain may well promise more benefit for mankind than all the artificial intelligence work to date.

Comparing the potential of "teleconferencing in the micro revolution," here are some remarks by the science fiction writer Jerry Pournelle:

> Actually, the original symposium in which everyone sat around a bowl of wine after dinner had very real limitations. If conducted by a master like Socrates or C. S. Lewis, it could be amazingly productive; but all too often—even without the bowl of wine—such sessions degenerate into a babble of half-baked and unrelated notions. One participant contributes a potentially good idea. Another comments on it. A third hasn't been paying attention and bursts forth with a brand-new subject. A fourth thinks the two subjects are related, even when they aren't, and in trying to puzzle out how misses the next ten minutes of talk. A fifth tries to get the conversation back to the original point. And so forth.
>
> Computer nets—in technical parlance, "computer mediated communications" or CMC—have the power to change all that.

From "The Real Electronic Village," *Popular Computing* (October 1985): 45. Colette Daiute also notes in *Writing and Computers* that in schoolroom computer use "the collective work emerges with no handwriting differences to identify individual writers. The children even change one another's sentences slightly, so that few sentences remain that were written by an individual author. The voice is not as unified as if it were written by one author, but all of the children have learned something about collecting details for a piece, using text for arguing, and anticipating a reader" (p. 27).

40. *Laws* 664a, Pangle translation, p. 45.

41. Milan Kundera, *New York Review of Books*, June 13, 1985, pp. 11–12. Another way to put this is to say that computerized writing empowers every Monsieur Homais in the world to set up his own Emma Bovary on par with Flaubert's text. This is the other side of the thrill of self-publishing discussed in chapter 5.

42. For a criticism of the traditional publishing industry, see Jacques Barzun's criticism of the procedures of copy editors in *The American Scholar* 54:3 (Summer 1985).

43. Anthony Smith, *Goodbye Gutenberg: The Newspaper Revolution of the 1980s* (New York: Oxford University Press, 1980), pp. 300–17.

44. As stated by Brian Aveney ("Post-Industrial Publishing," *Electronic Publishing and Bookselling* 1 [January 1984]: 21), the distribution of publications will undergo a transformation:

Distribution will become largely obsolete as a separate function in publishing with the eventual disappearance of the edition-printed products of industrial model publishing. Distribution will become a computer-controlled process of downloading text or video signals to the user's personal computer memory or directly to a printer or viewer. In a reversal of current realities distribution will occur before manufacturing in the on-demand environment.

45. Cited in Raymond Cogniat, *Georges Braque*, trans. Mark Paris (New York: Harry N. Abrams, 1976), p. 60. Originally in the *Cahier de Georges Braque: 1917–1947* (Paris: Maeght, 1948), p. 16: "Ceux qui vont de l'avant tournent le dos aux suiveurs. C'est tout ce que les suiveurs méritent."

46. George Orwell, *1984* (New York: Mentor, 1983), p. 6.

47. See John J. Fialka, "Study Sheds Light on Vulnerability of Computers to Electronic Spying," *The Wall Street Journal*, October 18, 1985, p. 27.

Fialka gives a brief overview of studies done in Holland and of the Tempest system of protection developed and recommended by U.S. government spy agencies.

48. The Data Encryption Standard was developed by IBM and adopted and approved by the National Bureau of Standards in 1977 after the NBS formally solicited encryption algorithms from the public. The one that NBS chose was called the Data Encryption Algorithm (DEA) and was developed by IBM, under the code name Lucifer. DEA is now in the public domain, and it can be used without cost. Many U.S. and international banks have converted to DES for coding their payment instructions. In August 1985, the U.S. Treasury Department announced that all instructions for moving funds in or out of it would have to be coded with DES.

49. See the comments of Dr. Harold Highland, editor of the journal *Computers and Security*, in *PC Magazine* 5:1 (January 14, 1986): 180.

Chapter 8. Compensatory Disciplines

1. Toffler, *Previews and Premises*, p. 113.

2. Rilke's sonnet, in translation by Robert Bly, is from the *Sonnets to Orpheus* (part 1, no. 21), and runs:

Spring is here, has come! The earth
Is like a child who has learned her poems—
So many poems!... Her study, long,
Strenuous, earns it ... the prize comes to her.

Her teacher was stern. We loved the white
Showing in the beard of the old man.
What is blue and what is green have distinct names—
What are they? Earth knows all that by heart!

Earth, free now of school, lucky one, come,
Play with the children. We want to tag you,
Wholly glad earth. The most whole catches you.

Earth's teacher, how much he taught her!
So much! And what lies printed inside roots,
Inside long, involved stalks: earth carries that and sings it!

Published in *Kenyon Review* 4:2 (Spring 1982) in the essay "The Eight Stages of Translation."

3. Craig Brod, for instance, points out:

> The United States has made fewer studies on the societal impact of the computer than have western European countries. In these countries, particularly West Germany and Sweden, government, industry, and universities cooperate to assess the effects of the technology in detailed and well-controlled studies. In the business world, the assumption in the United States, as always, is that the invisible hand of the marketplace rewards companies that implement the new technology correctly and punishes those that do not. We assume that the former will have happy, well-adjusted, and therefore productive employees, while the latter will be plagued with work stoppages. Faith in the "bottom line" as the measuring stick of all things is misplaced, however. It cannot take into account the cultural mutation that occurs as maladaptation to computers grows. Checks and balances no longer work when technostress is the rule.

Brod, *Technostress*, p. 223.

4. John Dewey, *How We Think: A Restatement of the Relation of Reflective Thinking to the Educative Process* (Boston: D. C. Heath, 1933), p. 72. By referring American philosophical attitudes back to the Pragmatism of John Dewey, I am concerned not so much with the current academic study of philosophy in America, where Dewey is in fact neglected, but with the world of involvements which, historically and theoretically, John Dewey expressed and still, to a great extent, expresses.

5. Ibid., p. 73.

6. Ibid., p. 72. For a quite different and more artistic sense of making oneself as an American, see the fascinating book by Stephen Donadio, *Nietzsche, Henry James, and the Artistic Will* (New York: Oxford University Press, 1978).

7. Dewey, *How We Think*, p. 49.

8. Dewey writes, "But while we cannot learn or be taught to think, we do have to learn how to think well, especially *how* to acquire the general *habit* of reflecting" (ibid., p. 35). And: "It is highly questionable whether the practice of thinking in accordance with some logical formula results in creation of a general habit of thinking, namely one applicable over a wide range of subjects" (p. 29). Skill or habit becomes a formal quality without content, a quality of the subject who learns. It is as if the psyche has of itself no independent health or needs of its own.

9. Ibid., p. 35.

10. Dewey's review of Ernest Dimnet, *The Art of Thinking*, appeared in *Saturday Review of Literature* (December 1, 1928, p. 423), under the title "The Way to Think."

11. There are some signs of change. There is, for instance, a new emphasis in art education, an area which has for decades depended on the Pragmatic emphasis on doing and on unreflective creativity. Studies are now calling for a shift toward discipline-based art education, by which is meant undergirding the creation of art works with substantial contemplative studies, such as reasoning about aesthetic theories, seeing art in the context of cultural history, sharpening the focus on ideas as they are made visual or aural. See *Beyond Creating: The Place for Art in America's Schools*, a report published by the J. Paul Getty Center for Education in the Arts (1985); also the three-volume empirical analysis on the same topic by the Publications Department of the Rand Corporation (1700 Main Street, Box 2138, Santa Monica, CA 90406). Such an aesthetic education also provides a paradigmatic discipline for regaining a sense of contemplative wholes, especially where memory work is involved and where images are learned on the deepest levels of identification. Memorizing the integrity of beautiful forms has always been a hallmark of the Platonic tradition in education. Traditional music, as opposed to modern music, is characterized by the dominance of a temporally unifying oneness to which all variants are subordinated. Hence felt time is brought to a static fullness of presence through harmony and repetitive pattern. Without the prior buildup of recollective presence there could be no appreciation of the modernist's pure tones and minimal sound concepts.

12. Albert Borgmann, *Technology and the Character of Contemporary Life: A Philosophical Inquiry* (Chicago: University of Chicago Press, 1984).

13. "Focal practices," Borgmann suggests, can "restore a depth and integrity to our lives that are in principle excluded within the paradigm of technology." He maintains that focal practices can protect "the concrete things and events that finally matter" (ibid., pp. 208–09).

14. "Technology is itself a sort of practice, and it procures its own kind of order and security. Its history contains great moments of innovation, but it did not arise out of a founding event that would have focal character; nor has it produced focal things. It rather has a debilitating tendency to scatter our attention and to clutter our surroundings.... The more strongly we sense and the more clearly we understand the coherence and the character

of technology, the more evident it becomes to us that technology must be countered by an equally patterned and social commitment, i.e., by a practice" (ibid.).

15. Another paradigm that could equally well have been chosen is that of the aesthetic forms experienced in visual art works. Such a paradigm goes in a different direction but could also be used to underscore the central importance of contemplative thought. It would have to be shown, for instance, how the fixed format of the fleeting moment in the works of Impressionist painters was necessarily prior to, in a stronger sense than that of historical chronology, the development of photography. The training of the contemplative eye provides a psychic framework within which realistic uses of light can be applied to the everyday uses of more mundane visual information. One can, of course, think of Impressionism as influenced by early photography. But the aesthetic sense is shaped more truly by deliberate concentration on an intensely rich static image. The bright radiance of photographs (once called sunprints) required the prior contemplative sinking in of light in Impressionism. So too digital text would have been impossible without the book.

16. Patricia Carrington, *Releasing: The New Behavioral Science Method for Dealing with Pressure Situations* (New York: William Morrow, 1984).

17. In the matter of the mutual assimilation of East and West, a remark by Bin Kimura, the Japanese psychiatrist at the University of Nagoya, is illuminating. When asked in conversation about the effects of computerization on the Japanese psyche, Dr. Kimura said, "Working with the logic of computers is operative only at the outermost layer of the Japanese psyche and a recently added one at that. Underneath are deep wellsprings of emotions and intuitive feelings which remain completely unaffected by the logic and organization of computers. From these emotional resources the Japanese live out the real substance of their daily lives." It should also be mentioned here that one of the most striking differences in the psychiatric practice in Japan is its relatively sparse use of verbal communication and its heavy reliance on silent presence.

18. For Carrington's more complete descriptions, see *Releasing* as well as her earlier book *Freedom in Meditation* (New York: Doubleday, 1977; repr. Kendall Park, N.J.: Pace Educational Systems, 1984). In the former, she says, "There is a subtle relationship between releasing and meditation. Each of these practices helps us to feel less urgent, more open, and more responsive to our own needs and those of others. Your releasing program

can therefore be even more productive if combined with the regular practice of meditation" (pp. 245–46). To see the extent of the metaphor that takes up alien traditions of Eastern meditation, note the use of "productive" here. Also note that in the introduction to *Freedom in Meditation* she describes her efforts as directed at "*managing* meditation" (p. xvii) and of producing a "Clinically Standardized Meditation." Clearly, the transposition of cultural forms is a delicate and creative affair, something like the balancing act of translating from one language to another. There is no way to render an uncontaminated creation if the outcome is to be a living thing.

19. Max Picard, *The World of Silence*, trans. Stanley Godman (South Bend, Ind.: Regnery/Gateway, 1952), pp. 172–97.

20. Indeed, some critics describe the current situation of serious music in terms that raise close analogies with the problems of text linkage raised earlier with regard to word processing. Samuel Lippman, for instance, sees a major problem in the trivialization and degradation of mentality required to produce musical art works today. The contemplative whole is torn into shreds in the name of education and democratic access. The intimacy of mind essential to appreciating the classical tradition becomes rare due to the very institutionalization that aims to perpetuate the tradition. See Samuel Lippman, *The House of Music: Art in an Era of Institutions* (Boston: David R. Godine, 1984), esp. the epilogue.

21. David Noble and Virginia Noble, *Improve Your Writing with Word Processing* (Indianapolis: Que Corporation, 1984). The many sample macros presented in this book are worked out in detail for several word processing programs that run on the IBM PC and compatibles. These ready-made macros serve as samples to suggest how most programs can be customized to do blockbusting, if not with built-in macros then at least with the use of separate keyboard enhancers such as Prokey or Superkey.

22. Gabriele Lusser Rico, *Writing the Natural Way: Using Right-Brain Techniques to Release Your Expressive Powers* (Los Angeles: J. P. Tarcher, 1983).

23. For comments on hemispheric specialization with regard to psychic frameworks, see chapter 4 on what was called "the crude phrenology of our time."

24. Rico, *Writing the Natural Way*, p. 136.

25. See Edward de Bono, *Lateral Thinking: Creativity Step by Step* (New

York: Harper & Row, 1970). De Bono's concern has centered not so much on creative writing as on fashioning alternatives to the deductive Aristotelian logic to which our most conspicuous cultural institutions are predisposed. He attempts to systematize ("step by step") the power of innovative insight.

Bibliography

Abramson, Jeffrey B., F. Christopher Arterton, and Gary R. Orren. *The Electronic Commonwealth: The Impact of New Media Technologies on Democratic Politics.* New York: Basic, 1988.

Aeschylus. *Prometheus Bound.* Translated by Philip Vellacott. New York: Penguin, 1961.

Alain [Emile-Auguste Chartier]. *The Gods.* Translated with foreword by Richard Pevear. New York: New Directions, 1974.

Alexander, Frederick Matthias. *The Resurrection of the Body: The Writings of F. M. Alexander.* With a preface by John Dewey. Edited by Edward Maisel. New York: University Books, 1969.

Arendt, Hannah. *The Life of the Mind.* Vol. 1: *Thinking.* New York: Harcourt Brace Jovanovich, 1977.

Aristotle. *De Anima.* Loeb Classical Library, 1968.

———. *De Caelo.* Loeb Classical Library, 1960.

———. *Ethics.* Loeb Classical Library, 1968.

———. *Metaphysics.* Loeb Classical Library, 1961.

———. *Physics.* Loeb Classical Library, 1970.

———. *Posterior Analytics.* Loeb Classical Library, 1966.

Auden, W. H. *The Dyer's Hand and Other Essays.* New York: Vintage, 1968.

Ballew, Lynne. *Straight and Circular: A Study of Imagery in Greek Philosophy.* The Netherlands: Van Gorcum, 1979.

Barrett, Edward, ed. *The Society of Text: Hypertext, Hypermedia, and the Social Construction of Information.* Cambridge: MIT Press, 1989.

———. *Text, Context, and Hypertext: Writing with and for the Computer.* Cambridge: MIT Press, 1988.

Barthes, Roland. *Pleasure of the Text.* Translated by Richard Miller. New York: Hill & Wang, 1977.

Barzun, Jacques. *The House of Intellect.* New York: Harper Brothers, 1959.

Bates, William. *The Computer Cookbook.* Englewood Cliffs, N.J.: Prentice-Hall, 1983.

Bear, John. *Computer Wimp.* Berkeley: Ten Speed, 1983.

Benedikt, Michael, ed. *Cyberspace: First Steps.* Cambridge: MIT Press, 1991.

Benjamin, Walter. "The Work of Art in the Age of Mechanical Reproduction." In *Illumi Nations,* edited by Hannah Arendt. New York: Schocken, 1969.

Berk, Emily, and Joseph Devlin, eds. *The Hypertext/Hypermedia Handbook.* New York: McGraw-Hill, 1991.

Berry, Wendell. *A Continuous Harmony: Essays Cultural and Agricultural.* New York: Harcourt Brace Jovanovich, 1970.

Birkerts, Sven. *The Gutenberg Elegies.* Boston: Faber & Faber, 1994.

Boden, Margaret. *Artificial Intelligence and Natural Man.* New York: Basic, 1981.

Bolter, Jay David. *Writing Space: The Computer, Hypertext, and the History of Writing.* Fairlawn, N.J.: Erlbaum, 1990.

Borgmann, Albert. *Crossing the Postmodern Divide.* Chicago: University of Chicago Press, 1992.

―――. *The Philosophy of Language: Historical Foundations and Contemporary Issues.* The Hague: Martinus Nijhoff, 1974.

―――. *Technology and the Character of Contemporary Life: A Philosophical Inquiry.* Chicago: University of Chicago Press, 1984.

Bradbury, Ray. *Fahrenheit 451.* New York: Ballantine, 1953.

Brand, Stewart, ed. *The Whole Earth Software Catalog.* Garden City, N.Y.: Quantum, 1984.

Brahm, Gabriel, and Mark Driscoll. *Prosthetic Territories: Politics and Hypertechnologies.* Boulder: Westview, 1995.

Braque, Georges. *Cahier de Georges Braque, 1917–1947.* Paris: Maeght, 1948. Partially reproduced in Raymond Cogniat, *Georges Braque,* translated by Mark Paris. New York: Harry N. Abrams, 1976.

Brod, Craig. *Technostress: The Human Cost of the Computer Revolution.* Reading, Mass.: Addison-Wesley, 1984.

Brook, James, and Iain Boal. *Resisting the Virtual Life.* San Francisco: City Lights, 1995.

Bush, Vannevar. "As We May Think." *Atlantic Monthly,* July 1945: 106–7.

―――. *Science Is Not Enough.* New York: Morrow, 1967.

Carrington, Patricia. *Freedom in Meditation.* New York: Doubleday, 1977. Reprint. Kendall Park, N.J.: Pace Educational Systems, 1984.

————. *Releasing: The New Behavioral Science Method for Dealing with Pressure Situations.* New York: William Morrow, 1984.

Chamberlain, William, ed. *The Policeman's Beard Is Half Constructed: Computer Prose and Poetry by RACTER.* New York: Warner, 1984.

Colford, Ian. *Writing in the Electronic Environment: Electronic Text and the Future of Creativity and Knowledge.* Halifax, N.S.: Dalhousie University, School of Library and Information Studies, 1996.

Daiute, Colette. *Writing and Computers.* New York: Addison-Wesley, 1985.

de Bono, Edward. *Lateral Thinking: Creativity Step by Step.* New York: Harper & Row, 1975.

Decsy, Gyula, ed. *Global Linguistic Connections.* Bloomington, Ind.: Eurolingua, 1983.

De Kerckhove, Derrick. *The Skin of Culture: Investigating the New Electronic Reality.* Toronto: Somerville House, 1995.

————. "A Volcanic Theory of Art." In *Press Enter: Between Seduction and Disbelief,* edited by Louise Dompierre, 87–99. Toronto: Power Plant Contemporary Art Gallery, 1995.

Delany, Paul, and George Landow, eds. *Hypermedia and Literary Studies.* Cambridge: MIT Press.

de Ventos, Xavier Rubert. *Self-Defeated Man.* New York: Harper & Row, 1975.

DeVoney, Chris. *MS-DOS User's Guide.* Indianapolis: Que Corporation, 1984.

Dewey, John. *How We Think: A Restatement of the Relation of Reflective Thinking to the Educative Process.* Boston: D. C. Heath, 1933.

Diels, Hermann, and Walther Kranz, eds. *Die Fragmenta der Vorsokratiker.* 3 vols. Reprint. Zurich, 1964.

Diment, Ernest. *The Art of Thinking.* New York: Simon & Schuster, 1928. Reprint. Greenwich, Conn.: Fawcett, 1956.

Ditlea, Steve, ed. *Digital Deli.* New York: Workman, 1984.

Donadio, Stephen. *Nietzsche, Henry James, and the Artistic Will.* New York: Oxford University Press, 1978.

Dreyfus, Hubert. *Mind over Machine: The Power of Human Intuition and Expertise in the Era of the Computer.* New York: Macmillan Free Press, 1985.

————. *What Computers Can't Do: The Limits of Artificial Intelligence.* New York: Harper Colophon, 1979.

Dunlop, Charles, and Rob Kling, eds. *Computerization & Controversy.* San Diego: Academic, 1991.

Edwards, Deborah M., and Lynda Hardman. "Lost in Hyperspace: Cognitive Mapping and Navigation in a Hypertext Environment." In *Hypertext: Theory Into Practice,* edited by Ray McAleese. Norwood, N.J.: Ablex, 1989.

Eisenstein, Elizabeth L. *The Printing Press as an Agent of Change: Communications and Cultural Transformations in Early-Modern Europe.* 2 vols. Cambridge: Cambridge University Press, 1979.

Eliot, T. S., ed. *Literary Essays of Ezra Pound.* New York: New Directions, 1968.

Engelbart, Douglas. "A Conceptual Framework for the Augmentation of Man's Intellect." In *Vistas in Information Handling,* Vol. 1, *The Augmentation of Man's Intellect by Machine,* edited by Paul W. Howerton and David Weeks. Washington, D.C.: Spartan Books, 1963.

Flim, Leona. "Bookish Versus Electronic Text: Ivan Illich and Michael Heim." Ph.D. diss., University of Calgary, 1991.

Fluegelman, Andrew, and Jeremy J. Hewes. *Writing in the Computer Age: Word Processing Skills and Style for Every Writer.* Garden City, N.Y.: Doubleday, 1983.

Fränkel, Hermann, *Early Greek Poetry and Philosophy.* Translated by Moses Hadas and James Willis. New York: Harcourt Brace Jovanovich, 1973.

Freiberger, Paul. *Fire in the Valley: The Making of the Personal Computer.* Berkeley: Osborne/McGraw-Hill, 1984.

Friedlander, Paul. *Plato: An Introduction.* Translated by Hans Meyerhoff. Princeton: Princeton University Press, 1969.

Gadamer, Hans-Georg. *Wahrheit und Methode: Grundzüge einer philosophischen Hermeneutik.* Tübingen: Mohr, 1960. Translated by Garrett Barden and John Cumming under the title *Truth and Method.* New York: Seabury, 1976.

Goethe, Johann Wolfgang von. *Faust.* Translated by Walter Kaufmann. Garden City, N.Y.: Doubleday Anchor, 1961.

Grassi, Ernesto. *Heidegger and the Question of Renaissance Humanism: Four Studies.* New York: State University of New York Press, 1983.

Grassi, Ernesto, and Hugo Schmale, eds. *Das Gespräch als Ereignis: Ein semiotisches Problem.* Munich: Wilhelm Fink, 1982.

Gray, Susan H. *Hypertext and the Technology of Conversation: Orderly Situational Choice.* Westport, Conn.: Greenwood, 1993.

Greenfield, Patricia Marks. *Mind and Media: The Effects of Television, Video Games, and Computers.* Cambridge: Harvard University Press, 1984.

Hanna, Thomas. *Somatics: Reawakening the Mind's Control of Movement, Flexibility, and Health.* Reading, Mass.: Addison-Wesley, 1988.

Hardison, O. B. *Disappearing Through the Skylight: Culture and Technology in the Twentieth Century.* New York: Viking, 1989.

Harrison, Bill. *Framework: An Introduction.* Culver City, Calif.: Ashton-Tate, 1984.

Havelock, Eric. *Preface to Plato.* Cambridge: Harvard University Press, 1963.

Heidegger, Martin. *Basic Writings.* Edited by David Krell. New York: Harper & Row, 1977.

———. "Hebel: Friend of the House." Translated by Bruce Folz and Michael Heim. In *Contemporary German Philosophy.* Vol. 3. University Park: Pennsylvania State University Press, 1983.

———. *The Metaphysical Foundations of Logic.* Translated by Michael Heim. Bloomington: Indiana University Press, 1984.

———. *Parmenides.* Frankfurt: Vittorio Klostermann, 1982.

———. *Poetry, Language, Thought.* Translated by Albert Hofstadter. New York: Harper Colophon, 1971.

———. *The Question Concerning Technology and Other Essays.* Translated by William Lovitt. New York: Harper & Row, 1977.

———. *Wegmarken.* Frankfurt: Vittorio Klostermann, 1967.

Heim, Michael. "The Art of Virtual Reality." *Virtual Reality* Special Report 1, no. 4 (Winter 1994): 9–22.

———. "The Computer as Component: Heidegger and McLuhan." *Philosophy and Literature,* October 1992, 33–44.

———. "Cybersage Does Tai Chi." In *Falling in Love with Wisdom: American Philosophers Talk About Their Calling,* edited by David Darnos and Robert Shoemaker. New York: Oxford University Press, 1993. 205–9.

―――. "The Design of Virtual Reality." In *Cyberspace Cyberbodies Cyberpunk: Cultures of Technological Embodiment.* Edited by Mike Featherstone and Roger Burrows. London: Sage, 1995. 65–77.

―――. "The Erotic Ontology of Cyberspace." In *Cyberspace: First Steps.* Edited by Michael Benedikt. Cambridge: MIT Press, 1991. 59–80.

―――. "Infomania." In *The State of the Language.* Edited by Christopher Ricks and Leonard Michaels. Berkeley: University of California Press, 1990. 300–306.

―――. *The Metaphysics of Virtual Reality.* New York: Oxford University Press, 1993.

―――. "Nature & Cyberspace." In *Bodyscapes: Body and Discourse.* Edited by Svend Larsen, Mette Bryld, Jacques Caron, Nina Lykke, and Niels Nielsen. Odense, Denmark: Odense University Press, 1995. 183–203.

―――. "Remembering the Body Temple." *Healing Tao Journal* 1, no. 4 (1991): 10–12.

―――. "Searching for the Essence of Tai Chi." *Healing Tao Journal* 1, no. 2 (1989): 10–12.

―――. "The Sound of Being's Body." *Man and World: An International Philosophical Review* 21, no. 1 (1988): 48–59.

―――. *Virtual Realism.* New York: Oxford University Press, 1997.

Herbert, Frank, with Max Barnard. *Without Me You're Nothing: The Essential Guide to Home Computers.* New York: Simon & Schuster, 1980.

Hillman, James. *Re-Visioning Psychology.* New York: Harper & Row, 1975.

Hoekema, David A. "Microcomputer Use for Learned Societies and Scholars." In *Proceedings and Addresses of the American Philosophical Association.* Vol. 58, no. 5.

Horton, Robin, and Ruth Finnegan, eds. *Modes of Thought: Essays on Thinking in Western and Non-Western Societies.* London: Faber & Faber, 1973.

Illich, Ivan, and Barry Sanders. *ABC: The Alphabetization of the Popular Mind.* San Francisco: North Point, 1988.

James, William. *Psychology, Briefer Course.* New York: Collier-Macmillan, 1972.

Johnson, Willard. *Riding the Ox Home: A History of Meditation from Shamanism to Science.* Boston: Beacon, 1982.

Jonas, Hans. *The Phenomenon of Life: Toward a Philosophical Biology.* New York: Dell, 1966.

Joyce, Michael. *Of Two Minds: Hypertext Pedagogy and Poetics.* Ann Arbor: University of Michigan Press, 1995.

―――. "Selfish Interaction: Subversive Texts and the Multiple Novel." In *The Hypertext Hypermedia Handbook.* Edited by Emily Berk and Joseph Devlin. New York: McGraw-Hill, 1991.

Kahn, Charles H. *The Art and Thought of Heraclitus: An Edition of the Fragments with Translation and Commentary.* Cambridge: Cambridge University Press, 1981.

Kamin, Jonathan. *The ThinkTank Book.* Berkeley: Sybex, 1984.

Kitto, H. D. F. *The Greeks.* Baltimore: Penguin, 1951.

Kockelmans, Joseph, ed. and trans. *On Heidegger and Language.* Evanston: Northwestern University Press, 1972.

Koestler, Arthur. *The Act of Creation.* New York: Dell, 1967.

Landow, George P., ed. *Hyper Text Theory.* Baltimore: Johns Hopkins University Press, 1994.

Landow, George P., and Paul Delany, eds. *The Digital Word: Text-Based Computing in the Humanities.* Cambridge: MIT Press, 1993.

―――. *Hypertext: The Convergence of Contemporary Critical Theory and Technology.* Baltimore: Johns Hopkins University Press, 1992.

Lao-Tse. *Tao Te Ching.* Translated by Gia-Fu Feng and Jane English. New York: Vintage, 1972.

Leclercq, Jean, O.S.B. *The Love of Learning and the Desire for God: A Study of Monastic Culture.* Translated by Catharine Misrahi. New York: Fordham University Press, 1982.

Levinson, Paul. *Mind at Large: Knowing in the Technological Age.* Greenwich, Conn.: JAI, 1988.

Levy-Bruhl, Lucien. *Les Fonctions mentales dans les sociétés inférieures.* Paris: Alcan, 910.

―――. *La Mentalité primitive.* Paris: Alcan, 1922.

Lewis, Thomas. *Late Night Thoughts on Listening to Mahler's Ninth Symphony.* Toronto: Bantam, 1984.

―――. *Lives of a Cell.* Toronto: Bantam, 1974.

Lippman, Samuel. *The House of Music: Art in an Era of Institutions.* Boston: David R. Godine, 1984.

Lobkowicz, Nicholas. *Theory and Practice: History of a Concept from Aristotle to Marx.* Notre Dame: University of Notre Dame Press, 1967.

Longley, Dennis, and Michael Shain. *The Microcomputer User's Handbook.* New York: John Wiley & Sons, 1984.

McCorduck, Pamela. *The Universal Machine: Confessions of a Technological Optimist.* New York: McGraw-Hill, 1985.

McKnight, C., A. Dillon, and J. Richardson, eds. *Hypertext: A Psychological Perspective.* New York: E. Horwood, 1993.

McLuhan, H. Marshall. *The Gutenberg Galaxy: The Making of Typographic Man.* Toronto: University of Toronto Press, 1962.

———. *Understanding Media: The Extensions of Man.* New York: McGraw-Hill, 1964.

Miller, Henry. *Sexus, Book One of the Rosy Crucifixion.* New York: Grove Press, 1965.

Miller, Jonathan. *Marshall McLuhan.* New York: Viking, 1971.

Milton, John. *Areopagitica.* In *Complete Poems and Major Prose.* Edited by Merritt Hughes. New York: Bobbs-Merrill, 1957.

Mourelatos, Alexander, ed. *The Pre-Socratics: A Collection of Critical Essays.* New York: Anchor, 1974.

Nelson, Theodor Holm. *Computer Lib Dream Machines.* Redmond, Wash.: Tempus, 1987.

———. "Computopia Now!" In *Digital Deli.* Edited by Steve Ditlea. San Francisco: Workman, 1984.

———. *Literary Machines.* Sausalito, Calif.: Mindful, 1990.

Nielsen, Jakob. *Hypertext and Hypermedia.* San Diego: Academic Press, 1990.

Nietzsche Friedrich. *The Gay Science.* Translated by Walter Kaufmann. New York: Vintage, 1974.

Noble, David, and Virginia Noble. *Improve Your Writing with Word Processing.* Indianapolis: Que, 1984.

Nora, Simon, and Alain Minc. *The Computerization of Society.* Cambridge: MIT Press, 1981.

Ogilvy, James. *Many Dimensional Man: Decentralizing Self, Society, and the Sacred.* New York: Oxford University Press, 1977.

Ong, Walter J. *Interfaces of the Word: Studies in the Evolution of Consciousness and Culture.* Ithaca: Cornell University Press, 1977.

———. *Orality and Literacy: The Technologizing of the Word.* London: Methuen, 1982.

———. *The Presence of the Word: Some Prolegomena for Cultural and Religious History.* New Haven: Yale University Press, 1967.

———. *Ramus, Method, and the Decay of Dialogue: From the Art of Discourse to the Art of Reason*. Cambridge: Harvard University Press, 1958.

———. *Rhetoric, Romance, and Technology: Studies in the Interaction of Expression and Culture*. Ithaca: Cornell University Press, 1971.

Ortony, Andrew, ed. *Metaphor and Thought*. Cambridge: Cambridge University Press, 1982.

Orwell, George. *1984*. New York: Mentor, 1983.

Osborne, Adam, and John Dvorak. *Hypergrowth*. Berkeley: Idthekkethan, 1984.

Pagels, Elaine. *The Gnostic Gospels*. New York: Vintage, 1981.

Papert, Seymour. *Mindstorms: Children, Computers, and Powerful Ideas*. New York: Basic, 1980.

Pattison, Robert. *On Literacy: The Politics of the Word from Homer to the Age of Rock*. New York: Oxford University Press, 1982.

Peters, F. E. *Greek Philosophical Terms: A Historical Lexicon*. New York: New York University Press, 1967.

Picard, Max. *The World of Silence*. Translated by Stanley Godman. South Bend, Ind.: Regnery/Gateway, 1952.

Plato. *Laws*. Translated by Thomas Pangle. New York: Basic, 1980.

———. *Phaedrus*. Translated by R. Hackforth. Indianapolis: Bobbs-Merrill, 1952.

———. "Seventh Letter." In *Epistles*. Translated by Glenn Morrow. Indianapolis: Bobbs-Merrill, 1962.

Poe, Edgar Allan. *The Complete Tales and Poems of Edgar Allan Poe*. New York: Vintage, 1975.

Poster, Mark. *The Second Media Age*. Cambridge: Blackwell, 1995.

Rheingold, Howard. *Tools for Thought: The People and Ideas behind the Next Computer Revolution*. New York: Simon & Schuster, 1985.

Rico, Gabriele Lusser. *Writing the Natural Way: Using Right-Brain Techniques to Release Your Expressive Powers*. Los Angeles: J. P. Tarcher, 1983.

Robinson, James M., ed. *The Nag Hammadi Library*. New York: Harper & Row, 1981.

Romanyshyn, Robert. *Technology as Symptom and Dream*. New York: Routledge & Kegan Paul, 1989.

Rorty, Richard. *Philosophy and the Mirror of Nature*. Princeton, N.J.: Princeton University Press, 1980.

Rosenstock-Huessy, Eugen. *Out of Revolution: Autobiography of Western Man.* Norwich, Vt.: Argo, 1969.

———. *Speech and Reality.* Norwich, Vt.: Argo, 1970.

Rouet, Jean-Francois, et al., eds. *Hypertext and Cognition.* Mahwah, N.J.: Lawrence Erlbaum, 1996.

Rushkoff, Douglas. *Media Virus.* New York: Ballantine, 1994.

Ryle, Gilbert. *The Concept of Mind.* London: Hutchinson, 1949.

Sale, Kirkpatrick. *Rebels Against the Future: The Luddites and Their War on the Industrial Revolution.* Reading, Mass.: Addison-Wesley, 1995.

Sandberg-Diment, Erik. *They All Laughed When I Sat Down at the Computer.* New York: Simon & Schuster, 1985.

Seely-Brown, John. "From Cognitive to Social Ergonomics and Beyond." In *New Perspectives on Human-Computer Interaction,* edited by D. A. Norman and S. W. Draper. Hillsdale, N.J.: Lawrence Erlbaum, 1985.

Sherman, Charles T. *Up and Running: Adventures of a Software Entrepreneur.* Inglewood, Calif.: Ashton-Tate, 1984.

Smith, Anthony. *Goodbye Gutenberg: The Newspaper Revolution of the 1980s.* New York: Oxford University Press, 1980.

Stern, Fred. *Word Processing and Beyond: The Introductory Computer Book.* Santa Fe: John Muir, 1983.

Streitz, N., A. Rizk, and J. André, eds. *Hypertext: Concepts, Systems, and Applications: Proceedings of the First European Conference on Hypertext.* Cambridge Series on Electronic Publishing. New York: Cambridge University Press, 1990.

Talbott, Stephen L. *The Future Does Not Compute: Transcending the Machines in our Midst.* Sebastopol, Calif.: O'Reilly, 1995.

Tate, Allen, ed. *The Language of Poetry.* Princeton University Press, 1942.

Toffler, Alvin. *Previews and Premises.* New York: William Morrow, 1983.

Trithemius, John. *De Laude Scriptorum.* Translated by Roland Behrendt, St. John's Abbey, Collegeville, Minn.; Latin-English edition printed Lawrence, Kan.: Coronado, 1974; original Latin-German edition published in Würzburg in the Mainfränkische Hefte, Heft 60, 1973.

Turkle, Sherry. *The Second Self: Computers and the Human Spirit.* New York: Simon & Schuster, 1984.

Veatch, Henry. *Two Logics*. Evanston: Northwestern University Press, 1969.

Weizenbaum, Joseph. *Computer Power and Human Reason: From Judgment to Calculation*. San Francisco: W. H. Freeman, 1976.

Wheelwright, Philip. *Heraclitus*. New York: Atheneum, 1964.

Williams, Robin. *The Non-Designer's Design Book: Design and Typographic Principles for the Visual Novice*. Berkeley: Peachpit, 1994.

Wresch, William, ed. *The Computer in Composition Instruction*. Urbana, Ill.: National Council of Teachers of English, 1984.

Wurman, Richard Saul. *Information Anxiety*. New York: Bantam, 1989.

Index

abundance, and language, 210
Adler, Mortimer, 141
aesthetics: of software, 159–60; of book, 198
AI (artificial intelligence): assumptions of, 26; not fundamental, 31
Alain, 194
algorithms, 147–49
Anaximander, 27ff; originator of philosophy, 28
anxiety: about computer writing, 3; writer's block, 207. *See also* stress
Apollonian, 115
archē, (Greek, "principle"), as "leading impulse," 26
Aristotle, 7, 29, 104; on Muses, 174
Auden, Wystan Hugh, 193
automation, and inscription, 136

Barzun, Jacques, 108
Bible: world created by book, 41
biology, 115
Borgmann, Albert, 231–33
Bradbury, Ray, 189f
Braque, Georges, 222
Brod, Craig, 201
Buber, Martin, 58

Carrington, Patricia, 235
Cassirer, Ernst, 234
Chargaff, Erwin, 115
chirographic: definition of, 62
Christianity: and logos tradition, 40; and transformation theory, 67; inventing the book, 174; monastic cult of book, 175–79
Cicero, 102
cinema: psychic framework of, 118
composition: teaching computerized formulation, 153–60
computer literacy. *See* literacy

conceptualization: contrast with psychic framework, 125
consciousness, as term, 101–02
cybernetics, 115

dabar or *davar* (Hebrew, "word"), 40
Daiute, Colette, 163
data handling: historical origin of word processing, 82
de Bono, Edward, 237
Delphi, 14, 40
Descartes, René, 105
Dewey, John: on thinking, 227ff
digital codification, 84
Dimnet, Ernest, 230
Dionysian, 115
discipline, 226f
distance: and historical past, 6; philosophical remove from culture, 14; of written symbols, 22; as abstract thinking, 55; through the visual sense, 62; Socrates' contemplative, 181; of word from idea, 188; and formulation, 193; disciplines of, 228; from interface, 225
Dreyfus, Hubert, 99; in chess match, 261n1
Dubos, René, 115

education: through Homeric epic, 56; learning on computers, 153–60; banausic narrowing, 174, 272n4; and handwriting, 178; through automated writing, 280f; in America, 226; and Pragmatism, 227; self-discipline in, 234; and creative writing, 241ff
element: as horizon of concrete significance, 23; current import of, 47; and consciousness, 102;